St. John

LIFE IN FIVE QUARTERS

*Selected readings from the archives
of the St. John Historical Society*

St. John

Life in Five Quarters

Selected readings from the archives of the St. John Historical Society

Edited and Compiled by:

Eleanor Gibney, David W. Knight, Bruce Schoonover & Robin Swank

For the St. John Historical Society, Inc.

ISBN: 978-0-9842740-0-0

LCCN: 2009938727

First Printing 2010

St. John Historical Society
PO Box 1256
St. John, Virgin Islands 00831

www.StJohnHistoricalSociety.org

You will note throughout this book variations in both writing styles and the spellings of familiar names and places. The different styles are the result of numerous authors from different eras being included in the book. Variations in spelling are the reality of the history of St. John—whether they are the result of early transcription errors or the influence of various cultures and nationalities over the years.

Cruz Bay, St John, Virgin Isles, Westindies. 1852 taken on the place. 64

"Cruz Bay, St. John, Virgin Isles, West Indies, 1852, taken on the place by Antone"

While the identity of the artist remains unsubstantiated, this may be the work of Anton Melbye, older brother and teacher of Fritz Melbye, who created some of the best-known images of St. John in the Danish Colonial Period.

Introduction

A HISTORY OF THE ST. JOHN HISTORICAL SOCIETY

Compiled from member interviews and documents in the SJHS archives

Jane Bowry, Margaret Labrenz, and Robin Swank

In February 1974, the first organizational meeting of the tentatively named "St. John Historical Society" was held at National Park Headquarters at The Creek in Cruz Bay. At that meeting the goals and objectives of the new Society were laid out and they have remained basically unchanged to the present day. The founding group proposed to take field trips to, and encourage the preservation of, historical sites, sponsor publications of historical materials, compile local family records and tape oral histories, document St. John burial sites, encourage the preservation of artifacts, and assist with the new island museum being established at the Battery. "The early days of the Society were like many organizations," remembers founding-member Jane Bowry. "We evolved without a plan. There were many of us who were anxious to know more about this paradise we were privileged to call home. The whole concept really came together when a little boy presented a Danish coin to Doris Jadan, and the need for a historical museum became evident." By April 1974 there was a slate of officers, a first membership meeting had been held, and annual dues of $2 had been collected.

By March 15, 1976, Articles of Incorporation were filed with the Territory; the application was notarized by Elaine I. Sprauve. A National Park

St. John Historical Society members and guests at a Three Kings' Day Celebration, January 8, 2006.

(Photo courtesy Bruce Schoonover)

ranger, Don Adams, was elected as the Society's first President, while Janet Boyte, Andromeada Childs, and Clarice Thomas were listed as Incorporators. "Miss Thomas was a much loved and respected teacher on the island," recalls Jane Bowry, "for so many years, we were lucky to have such a respected member of the community for advice and counsel." Walter and Florence Lewisohn were also notable early members.

The Lewisohns had recently moved to St. John from St. Croix, where they had been involved in the formation of the St. Croix Landmarks Society and were instrumental in the purchase and restoration of the Whim Greathouse Museum. Florence Lewisohn, an independent thinker and author, contributed untold hours to the Society's success. Other early members included Steve and Nancy Edwards, who came to St. John on their honeymoon in 1949; ten years later they returned to live on the island with their infant daughter Kiki. Steve formed a close friendship with John Anderson, who along with his wife, Adrienne, wrote *Night of the Silent Drums*. It was Anderson who introduced Steve to St. John history. Later, Steve became a V.I. National Park employee, and following an off-island stint working for the NPS, he returned to St. John to become a founding member of both the St. John Historical Society and the Friends of the V.I. National Park.

Throughout the 1970s the tradition of site and trail clearing and visits to historic St. John sites was established. Fortsberg and the English Battery, with National Park architectural historian Fred Gjessing; a field trip to the Bethany church grounds, with Herbert Samuels; and, Beverhoudtsberg, with Shailer Bass and John Anderson, were among the early hikes. "Mr. Herbert Samuels, the Samuels family patriarch," remembers Jane, "was a constant source of lore about island life—stories always told with love and humor." Noble Samuel was likewise fondly remembered by Jane, who states that Noble "represented the true St. Johnian, as with great dignity and humor he described the 'good ole days.'"

The early Society immediately made an impact. "In our early years," reported Jane, "the Annaberg Country School was one of the first major projects undertaken by the Society." Ruth Low's 1982 identification of the school ruins while doing research for her book *St. John Backtime*, and Steve Edward's confirmation that the remains near Mary's Creek were, in fact, the Annaberg Country School, were followed by the launch of the Society's volunteer effort to clear and stabilize the site. Jane noted that the project was a "natural" for a group of energetic retirees who came from a tradition of volunteering and saw merit in memorializing the goal of compulsory education for all children. The effort, Jane told us, brought together Society volunteers, Park personnel, well-wishers and on-lookers, in a project that remains "a cherished

memory." Reggie Callwood and Mario Benjamin of the National Park Service provided the technical expertise as restoration experts, and many St. Johnians gave advice, encouragement, and hours of labor to match the 1700 hours (over 3 years) logged by SJHS volunteers. Jane recalled that the St. Johnians, now gone, who supported the Society in its early years were respected personages such as Elaine I. Sprauve, Herman Prince, Noble Samuel, and the St. John Administrator, George Simmons. When the Annaberg School ruins were first worked on, the only access was with the aid of a rope up a steep bank along the road leading to Francis Bay. As this was too difficult to use to do any worthwhile stabilization, a path was cut from the original Danish road so that work could begin—the trail still accesses the site to the present day. Don Bowry recalls that it wasn't only about cutting bush and hacking trees out of the ruined walls. The "welcoming arms" balustrades were found in the bush pretty much intact, and were repositioned with a come-a-long and lots of manual labor. Restoration also involved a search-and-delivery mission for sand, lime (for mortar), stone, coral, and bricks, accessed both locally and from other islands, to properly restore the walls and stairways.

For many years the Society was instrumental in the volunteer staffing of the Museum at the Cruz Bay Battery, and later, at the Elaine I. Sprauve Library, under the knowledgeable guidance of Andromeada Childs. The effort to clean up the Battery for a museum must have been monumental. The Museum, reported Andro Childs and Ruth Low, had 366 visitors in one February alone; much work was done on exhibits, including a working windmill that was always the children's favorite.

Many speakers at the Society's membership meetings of yesteryear were luminaries in St. John's past. During the 1970s and early 1980s, Enid Baa, former V. I. Director of Libraries, Archives and Museums, spoke on "Preserving our Heritage and the importance of submitting historic buildings for inclusion in the National Register"; Dr. George Knight, an early guest at Caneel Bay in 1936, showed his pictures of St. John from that period; Karen Olwig presented her doctorate research on the "Impact of emancipation on family and cultural life"; and a dig at Enighed Greathouse was hosted by archaeologist Dr. Vescelius. Ethel McCully, author of *Grandma Raised the Roof*, entertained one meeting; Aimory Caron's experiences on researching historical French documents from the 1733 slave revolt were shared, and John Anderson presented recitations from his historical novel, *Night of the Silent Drums*. Jean Knight and Dr. Salvador Tabacco talked about health care on St. John, James Kean gave "An Anecdotal History of the Marsh Family," while Bernie Kemp presented "The St. John Market Basket—the Historical Basis." There was also dinner at Miss Meada's, and presentations about the "Coral Bay of Yesteryear" by Gerda Marsh and Herman Prince, "Bush Medicine" by Eulita Jacobs and her aunt Rose Carty; Senator Noble Samuel described "Growing up on St. John." Presentations were also made on island traditions and customs by Maline Sprauve, Ubaldina Simmons, Ethlyn Hall and Herbert Samuels.

Over the years field trips continued to be a popular activity, interrupted only briefly by Hurricane Hugo's devastation. Destinations included Mary's Point, Pasquero, Hope, Cathrineberg, Brownsbay, and Hawksnest, all led by Steve Edwards. In 1985 events also included snorkels over the 200-year-old Santa Monica shipwreck and another wreck off of Annaberg. A cleanup of the Enighed cemetery and the planting of inkberry trees, oleander and ground orchids at the Sprauve Library was accomplished, and a sundial with an engraved plaque was presented to the Emmaus Moravian Church. Cannon mounts at the Battery were stabilized, and, in 1987, an illegible red-stone plaque commemorating the construction of the Cruz Bay Battery was replaced with a new bronze one.

In the 1990s, the Society visited many additional St. John sites, among them Denis Bay (which seemed to have suffered an unfortunate bulldozing, destroying part of the slave quarters and strewing artifacts), Reef Bay, Rustenberg, Leinster Bay, Mt. Pleasant and Retreat, Annaberg, Vessup, Fortsberg, L'Esperance, and the deNully plantation at Chocolate Hole. The group also branched out to explore St. Thomas, Hassel Island, and St. Croix. Unfortunately, field trips were suspended for all of 1996 due to the devastation wrought by Hurricane Marilyn, and there soon came more sad times for the Society, as the deaths of Walter Lewisohn and Steve Edwards were mourned. Florence Lewisohn and Ruth Low too soon followed. The Museum at the library was closed by the V. I. Government under Governor Turnbull's administration. However, the Society's projects and community involvement continued on: stabilizing the Annaberg slave village, maintaining the Annaberg School site, installing signs at the Library, and attempting to locate a new "adopt a ruin" site. The Society gave a donation to Queen Louise Home in memory of Fred Gjessing.

At the turn of the 21st century, a monthly SJHS newsletter began publication for the 1999-2000 season. The Society was granted Tax Exempt 501(c) (3) corporation status by the IRS on June 12, 2001, and by the BIR in October of that year. The Society renewed its dedication to education by investing in our children. Andro Childs spoke with 5th graders at Sprauve School, a history project/contest for 6th grade classes at the School was conducted, and the Society co-sponsored, with the VI Audubon Society, a trip for all Guy Benjamin School students to Annaberg, as well as a seashore nature walk and an outing on the Cinnamon Bay loop trail.

The new millennium saw other projects come to fruition: mounts for the cannons at the Cruz Bay Battery were replaced through the efforts of Don Bowry and Bob Pullen. The oldest marked grave in the Cruz Bay Cemetery (Lucretia Virginia Howard Minor) was restored with the help of Vernon Sprauve, and the SJHS web site was launched in November of 2005.

Throughout the last decade, the Society has continued to sponsor dozens of speakers discussing the theme of cultural identity and has aired presentations of local and visiting historians as they recounted the island's specific history. We also endeavored to collect the memories of our St. Johnian culture bearers, recognizing that today is tomorrow's history. Elroy Sprauve presented "Growing up on St. John in the 40s and 50s," "English Creole; A History of the Spoken Word on St. John," and "St. John Place Names and Their Origins." Gilbert Sprauve spoke on "The Development of Inter-Island Transportation in the VI." Gaylord Sprauve spoke of his "Childhood Memories of Summers on St. John." Volunteers at "Christmas Then and Now," held in Cruz Bay Park by the Virgin Islands Tourist Office, demonstrated how to make traditional Christmas tree ornaments, and served tons of old-fashioned molasses cookies.

Lately it has been time to revisit many historical sites on the island with a new generation of knowledgeable St. Johnians and our energetic membership. We now document and share the information we learn on our hikes, lectures and field trips through our Newsletter and on our

Bob & Velma Pullen and Don & Jane Bowry are pictured with a new 'permanent' sign commemorating the restoration of the Annaberg Country School. These four long-time Society members were among those who originally cleared the site and stabilized the ruins of the Annaberg School. The sign at the site was dedicated on December 11, 2008, honoring SJHS members Florence and Walter Lewisohn and Steve Edwards, who funded the sign by bequest.

(Photo by Robin Swank)

website, bringing St. John history to an ever-widening audience. The Society continues to embrace its commitment to be a strong advocate for preservation and the recording and dissemination of the history of this unique and wonderful place. Looking forward, it seems a certainty that the SJHS will be there to provide many more years of dedicated service to the St. John community.

On behalf of the Society's Board of Directors we thank all of our members and friends, both past and present, for their support and contributions to our efforts. It is to all of you, that this volume is respectfully dedicated.

October, 2009

Contents

Chapter 4: The Image Makers
Historic images of St. John

Chapter 5: At Work an' Rest
Culture, Trades and Industry

Chapter 6: The Nature of Things
Science and Natural History

Chapter 7: Donkey Years to Modern Day
Recollections and Firsthand Accounts

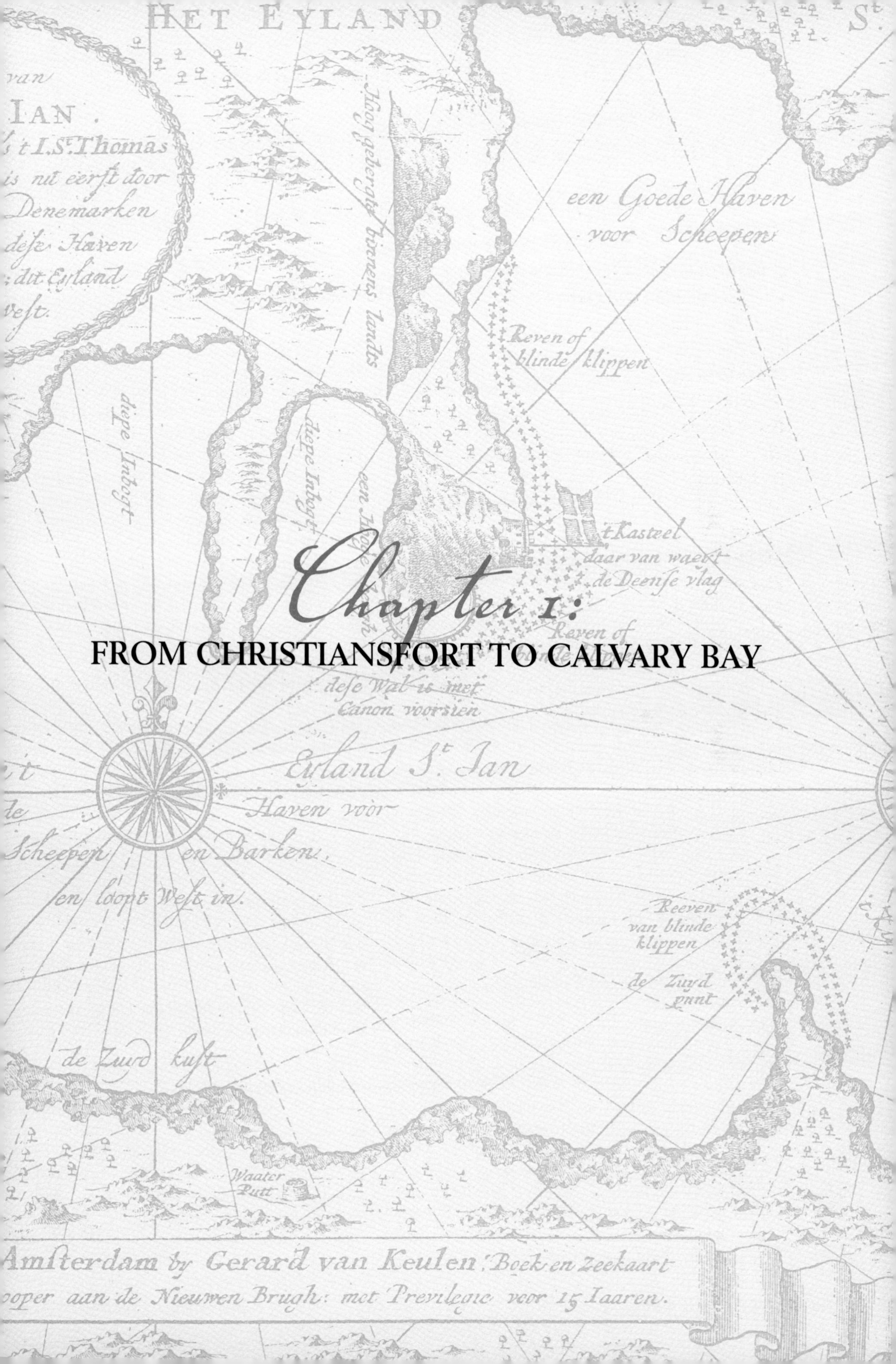

Chapter 1:
FROM CHRISTIANSFORT TO CALVARY BAY

The Danish Struggle to Colonize St. John

Presentation by Leif C. Larsen; Summarized by Jan Frey

Leif Calundann Larsen is the author of The Danish Colonization of St. John, 1718–1733 (A Publication of The Virgin Islands Resource Management Cooperative, St. Thomas, VI, 1986).

Pope Alexander VI gave sovereignty of all America to Spain, and the 1494 Tordesillas Treaty deeded the West Indies to Spain. However, the reality of the situation was that as other European powers appeared in the Caribbean by the early 1600s, Spain reluctantly accepted their presence, primarily because it was not in any position to stop them. That is not to say that relationships in the West Indies in this period were harmonious, they weren't.

Denmark was the last colonial power to establish itself in the West Indies in the late 1600s and was challenged by both the English and the Spanish. However, when the Danish King protested to His British Majesty, he responded by dismissing the governor of the Leeward Islands and replacing him with William Stapleton, with instructions to extend friendship to the Danish colonists on St. Thomas. Nevertheless, the first attempt by the Danish to settle St. John in 1675 was rejected by the British. Thus began the initial struggle for St. John, a struggle that would last for almost four decades.

In the 1680s, there was trouble between England and Denmark caused by Danish rule of St. Thomas under the regimes of the Esmit brothers and Gabriel Milan, the former of whom openly traded with pirates… something the British were trying to stop. There was also trouble over Crab Island (Vieques), which both countries claimed. The Danes established a military post there, but soon gave it up after a Scottish expedition landed. Despite strong foreign protest, Denmark maintained her claims on both St. John and Crab Island.

In 1715, the Danish Governor Mikhel Crone informed Copenhagen that he was going to inspect St. John (and Crab Island) before he retired, because soil conditions on St. Thomas were deteriorating due to nutrient depletion, and the planters were looking for alternative planting grounds. Also, a drought increased the cost of provisions, and the cane failed and had to be replanted. The Danish Company, however, did not address the issue. The next year a new governor, Governor Bredal, reported that many planters from St. Thomas wanted to move to St. John, but feared British reprisals.

In 1717, the British Governor Hamilton arrived on St. Thomas on a man-of-war during a tour of all of the Virgin Islands. He warned the Danes that he would not tolerate their cutting of timber on St. John. Unaware of this tour, the Danish Company, after remaining silent for two years, ordered Governor Bredal to colonize St. John. It is felt that the Danes were compelled to act because they had learned that the British had themselves inspected both St. John and Crab Island in the spring of 1716, and the Danes feared that they would soon settle both. Bredal and company failed to take any action in 1717 because of the fear of the English threat related to the cutting of timber, and the fact that the British had indeed occupied Crab Island beginning in September of 1717.

1718 was a critical year for the Danish government to regain control of St. John. In the spring, Governor Hamilton was being pressured by planters from Anguilla, Tortola and Spanish Town to get permission to settle St. Croix, since they too were experiencing the worst drought in memory. Fortunately, St. John was described as a "small barren mountainous island" by these planters. Therefore, the British gave the island a low priority, even though they knew an

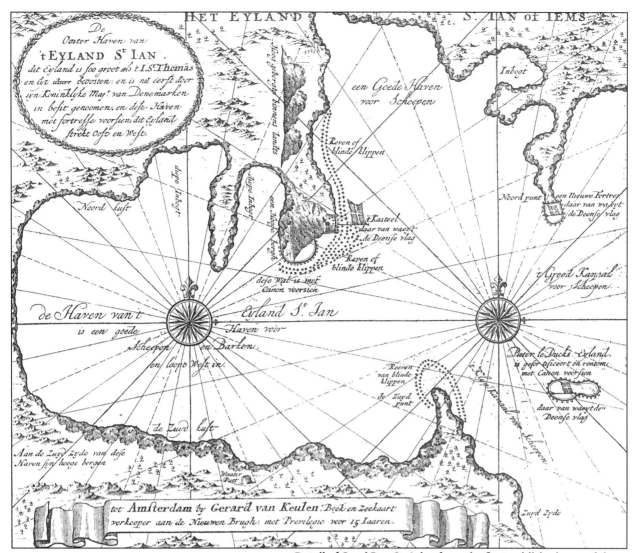

Detail of Coral Bay, St. John, from the first published map of the Danish West Indies by Gerard van Keulen, c1719

(Rigsarkivet, Copenhagen, Denmark)

occupation of St. Croix might cause trouble with the French.

At the same time, and while the Spanish had accepted the Danes on St. Thomas, their relations were not the most harmonious. The Danes were fishing and catching turtles off Puerto Rico, conducting illegal trade with Puerto Rico, and the Danish Governor Crone was himself illegally trading with the governor of Puerto Rico.

Clearly, the Danes' relationship with its neighbors in the West Indies was strained. Nevertheless, with some reluctance, Governor Bredal, on behalf of Denmark, took possession of St. John on March 25, 1718. The British responded quickly by sending a man-of-war to St. Thomas, with a demand for the return of St. John, which Governor Bredal rejected. The British Governor was ordered to "obstruct and hinder the Danes from proceeding" but was restricted from using force; therefore no action

was taken. London further rejected pleas to expel the Danes in 1722 and 1724, as it deemed St. John not worth the conflict.

Interestingly, the English failed to take control of St. John due to the unwillingness of England to support the British colonists' desires to do so; and Spain failed to gain control of St. John due to its colonists' refusal to take action, even after the Spanish Government had ordered them to proceed. Consequently, aside from two brief periods of British occupation during the early nineteenth century, St. John remained a Danish possession until it was purchased by the United States from Denmark in 1917.

St. John's Historic Christiansfort

David W. Knight; Translation by Gary T. Horlacher

The fort and associated structures that St. John residents today refer to as the "Cruz Bay Battery," were originally constructed under the administration of Governor-General Peter von Scholten in 1825 and named Christiansfort. According to a copy of the construction contract housed in U.S. National Archives, John Wright, a St. John-born free man of color, was to undertake the project, and Capt. Ingjald Mourier (later of Estate Lameshur) was to act as "inspector." The job would result in the erection of nearly all of the structures that still stand on Battery Point to the present day—

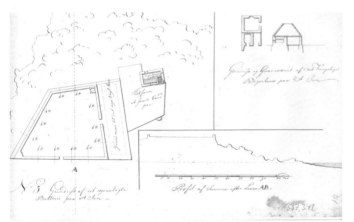

Ground plan of the Cruz Bay Battery drawn by Peter L. Oxholm, c1780

(Rigsarkivet, Copenhagen, Denmark)

including "walls, gates, jail house, slave quarters, kitchen, horse stall and privy." It was further noted that Wright would be allowed to utilize any materials he could salvage "from the ruins of the old public buildings" on the site.

This, of course, brings up the questions of what structures stood on Battery Point before 1825, and when was the first fortification erected on the site. Luckily, Danish economist Christian Martfeldt provides a brief history of the Cruz Bay Battery in his journal penned between 1765 and 1768:

> "Shortly after Governor Moth took over [c1736], he went to St. John where the inhabitants displayed the value of having a place of refuge to defend themselves against rebellion like the inhabitants of Coral Bay had. They recommended he purchase the flat and the point in Little Cruz Bay, belonging to Mulatto Franc Spanier, to build houses and on the point to establish a battery for the benefit of Cruz Bay. Also the Governor would have a secure place to stay while on St. Jan…
>
> One year later the flat was purchased for the Company, but nothing was done any further… When the land came under the crown in 1756, the Governor General went to St. John and the matter was again discussed. A couple of years later he put his intentions to build a battery in writing and 2000 barrels of lime were offered to the inhabitants if they would use their slaves for the labor. Also, the flat was to be measured out into lots for houses [later to become the town of Cruz Bay]. The Battery was to be constructed as soon as possible.
>
> It was not until July of 1764 that a commission was set up of Major Krause and Capt. Cronenberg. They recommended that Cruz Bay should become the main town and fort

Detail of "Christian's Bay" and "Little Cruitz Bay" from a map by Peter L. Oxholm, 1780

(Rigsarkivet, Copenhagen, Denmark)

for St. John. The commission also discussed where to place the battery (on the outer points or on the middle point). In September 1764, they began clearing the site they had chosen and cutting wood. Twenty eight capable slaves were provided by inhabitants each week. Work continued to mid December. By January, 7 or 8 baskets of ammunition were brought from the fort in Coral Bay—in the meantime work on the barracks and garrison continued. Master mason Brown was brought over from St. Croix, and in March–April (1765) a house for the commanding officer, a kitchen with bake-oven, and a brick building divided in five rooms were all finished."

April, 2000

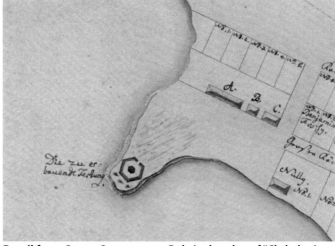

Detail from Crown Surveyor vonRohr's plot plan of "Christian's Bay" (Cruz Bay) showing a small fortification on Battery Point and three buildings noted as a barracks (A), a church (B), and a house for the commanding officer (C), c1765.

(Rigsarkivet, Copenhagen, Denmark)

July 4th, Emancipation Day on St. John

David W. Knight

Under considerable pressure from both home and abroad, in 1847 King Christian VIII of Denmark took the first cautious steps toward emancipation on the Danish West Indies islands of St. Thomas, St. John and St. Croix. On July 28th he proclaimed that all children born into slavery would from that day on be considered free, and that all unfree in the colony would become emancipated after a twelve-year preparatory period.

While perceived as a sound humanitarian design by insulated bureaucrats in Copenhagen, back in Denmark's distant West Indies colony the King's decree served little else than to elevate an already volatile climate. Tensions had run high ever since emancipation had been declared in the neighboring British West Indies thirteen years earlier. For nearly a year the colony simmered, slave owner and enslaved alike quietly considering their options. Despite words of caution and whispers of insurrection, in the end there was little else to do but let history run its course. A recounting of the earth-shaking events that were soon to unfold on the island of St. Croix is best left to the contemporary chronicler, Dutch Reformed Minister John P. Knox:

...July 2d ushered in the Sabbath morning, with its usual quietness and peace. As the day advanced, tranquil enjoyment and religious feeling seemed to reign throughout the island. Towards evening a commotion was visible; still, but few felt any uneasiness. About eight o'clock, however, there was suddenly a too fearful evidence given that the slaves had risen in rebellion. Simultaneously alarms rang out from many estates as the given signal; and as these alarms rolled on throughout every part of the island, consternation and terror, tumult and uproar, spread on all sides. Fear

in its most bitter forms now seized upon the minds of the inhabitants of Frederiksted and the estates contiguous, and many rushed immediately on board the shipping lying in the harbor. Several inhabitants applied to the authorities for orders to resist with the militia force, but they were refused. The night was one of horror, especially to those who were unable to escape from their estates...

At eight o'clock on the morning of the 3d, about two thousand Negroes from the north-side estates marched into town, armed with various weapons. They went directly to the fort, and demanded their freedom. In the absence of the Governor-General, they were told by the officer of the fort, that there was no one who had the authority to grant their request. Their numbers increasing by a band of 3,000 from the south and middle parts of the island and their passions becoming more inflamed from their associated influence, they proceeded to the destruction of property. The police-office and judge's house were completely sacked... The house of the judge's assistant shared a like fate. The whipping post met with little mercy; it was uprooted, carried in triumph to the wharf, and thrown into the sea.

At length the Governor-General arrived in his carriage from Christiansted, and entered the fort. A great crowd of Negroes had in the meantime gathered around the walls. There was an intense anxiety on the part of all to know what would be the course of the Governor-General. The commander of the fort repeatedly asked for orders. The Danish man-of-war had sailed from Bassin, and was momentarily expected. At length, to the amazement of the officers and citizens, freedom was proclaimed from the ramparts, by the Governor-General, to all the slaves in

"All unfree in the danish westindia Islands are from today emancipated"

Early on Tuesday morning, July 4th, the schooner Vigilant sailed into St. Thomas harbor bringing news of the uprising and subsequent pronouncement of emancipation on St. Croix. Again, we turn to Pastor Knox for his first-hand observations:

…Great excitement at once prevailed, and this was increased by the proclamation of freedom at the drum-head in the public streets. A crowd of women and boys followed the drum, and shouted and danced merrily; otherwise order prevailed in the town. In the country the proclamation was received by the slaves in the most quiet manner, and all continued at their work…
[Knox, 1852]

It was not until Tuesday evening that the owner of Estate Lameshur, Captain Ingjald Mourier, arrived on St. John from St. Thomas bringing the news of Governor-General von Scholten's decree. After informing Police Master Carl Hanschell of the news, Hanschell and Mourier immediately began circulating the Emancipation Proclamation throughout the island. Not long after sunset on July 4th, the slaves on estates Adrian and Rustenberg were the first to receive word of their newly-achieved freedom.

The following extract from the Carl Hanschell's Police Journal describes the situation on St. John as word spread throughout the island on the following day:

Hans Kongelige Majestæts

til Danmark, de Venders og Gothers, Hertug til Slesvig, Holsteen, Stormarn, Ditmarsken
Lauenborg og Oldenborg

Bestalter

Excellence, Generalmajor, Kammerherre, Storkors af Dannebroge og Dannebrogsmand, Storkors af Isabella den Catholskes Orden, Storofficeer af Æreslegionen, Commandeur af Guelphe Ordenen, Ridder af Ordenen du merite militaire, General Gouverneur over de danske vestindiske Öer,

JEG

Peter Carl Frederik v. Scholten

Giör vitterligt :   *Maketh known :*

1.	**1.**
Alle Ufrie paa de danske vestindiske Öer ere fra Dags Dato frigivne.	All Unfree in the danish westindia Islands are from to-day emancipated.
2.	**2.**
Negerne paa Plantagerne beholde i 3 Maaneder fra Dato Brugen af de Huse og Provisionsgrunde, hvoraf de nu ere i Besiddelse.	The Estate Negroes retain for three months from date the use of the houses and provisiongrounds, of which they have hitherto been possessed.
3.	**3.**
Arbeide betales for Fremtiden efter Overeenskomst, hvorimod Allowance ophörer.	Labour is in future to be paid for by agreement, but allowance is to cease.
4.	**4.**
Underholdningen af Gamle og Svage, som ere ude af Stand til at arbeide, afholdes indtil nærmere Bestemmelse af deres forrige Eiere.	The maintainance of old and infirm, who are not able to work, is until farther determination to be furnished by the late owners.

Givet under General Gouvernementets Segl og min Haand,
General Gouvernementet over de danske vestindiske Öer, St. Croix den 3die Juli 1848.

[L. S.]   P. v. Scholten.

Bilingual handbill of Peter von Scholten's Emancipation Proclamation
(Rigsarkivet, Copenhagen, Denmark)

5 July, 1848 – The chief constable together with Captain Mourier has continued today proclaiming the emancipation of the unfree at the other plantations on the island. Everywhere the enthusiasm was great and the feelings of the people toward their late owners were generally favorable, chiefly at plantations Leinster Bay and Annaberg, but at a couple of other plantations, namely Klein Caneel Bay, the contrary is the case. [Low & Valls, 1985]

On St. Thomas and St. John Emancipation seems to have been greeted with an almost eerie blend of jubilation and passive discontent, while the situation on St. Croix was far different. In the days following Governor-General von Scholten's decree, mayhem prevailed.

As the billowing smoke from burning cane fields carried colonial fortunes into the tradewinds, a profound transition was in process. For the people of the Danish West Indies, if there had ever been a point in time when the heirs to the hardships and miseries of the West Indiamens' legacy were to prevail over the wealth and prestige of European colonialism, this was that instant; a moment in the history of the Virgin Islands that will forever be celebrated with pride and deep reflection.

June, 2006

References:

John P. Knox, *A Historical Account of St. Thomas in the Danish West Indies* (New York, Charles Scribner, 1852).

Ruth Hull Low & Rafael Valls, *St. John Backtime, Eyewitness Accounts from 1718 to 1956* (St. John, U.S. Virgin Islands, Eden Hill Press, 1985).

From Christiansfort to Calvary Bay

The Annaberg School at Mary's Creek

David W. Knight

The ruins of the Annaberg School at Mary's Creek are among the most significant historic sites on St. John. Not only are they a wonderful example of uniquely Danish-colonial architecture in the neoclassical style, but they are also a physical representation of the first effort to institute compulsory education throughout the Danish West Indies in 1839. Consequently, that makes the remains of the Territories' schools from this period among the oldest public school buildings under the U. S. Flag, and perhaps the oldest in the Western Hemisphere dedicated solely to the compulsory education of African-Americans.

Commonly referred to as "vonScholten Schools" for Governor-General of the Danish West Indies, Peter vonScholten, who ordered their construction, the schools were to be built to a plan by Danish architect, Albert Lovmand. In all, seventeen schools were originally proposed throughout the colony: eight on

Albert Lovmand's original plan for all the vonScholten schools. The Annaberg School was a modification of this design.

(Image from the book, Vore Gamle Tropekolonier, *[Fremand, Denmark, 1966])*

St. Croix; five on St. Thomas; and four on St. John. The Annaberg School, however, was the only facility built on St. John to Lovmand's general design. Scaled down and modified to suit St. John's smaller population and hilly terrain, the Annaberg School was to provide free, compulsory education to the children of the enslaved laborers on six estates within the Maho Bay Quarter: Cinnamon Bay, Vaniniberg, Munsbery, Annaberg, Mary's Point, and Leinster Bay.

While another school was built mid-island on the Beverhoudtsberg plantation a few years prior to the Annaberg School, that structure was constructed of wood on a masonry foundation and seems never to have been utilized for its intended purpose. Two other schools were operated on St. John at the Moravian mission stations of Bethany and Emmaus, although, as in the case of the Beverhoudtsberg School, the Lovmand design was not utilized. A fifth smaller school was also erected in this period on St. John's south side, but details as to the location and duration of its operation remain uncertain. In all cases, Moravian missionaries served as teachers in the schools.

Although construction was well underway on the Annaberg School by 1847, the building was not fully completed at that time. It was not until August 12, 1856, that Brother J. Gardin penned a report for the Moravian Church periodical announcing the opening of the school:

> *"In St. Jan we have, this year, opened a school at Annaberg, on the north side of the island. The school-house, which is a very fine one, and is in a charming situation, by the sea, was built many years ago, but never used. There are now twenty-five children in attendance."*

But, while the future of the Annaberg School may have seemed promising in the summer of 1856, staffing the rather remote facility soon proved problematic. Sometime prior to October, 1861, the school was closed after Augustus Knevels was dismissed as schoolmaster on grounds of "gross immorality." From that date onward, students from Annaberg were sent to attend school at the Emmaus Mission Station in Coral Bay, and the Annaberg school building saw only brief, intermittent usage. By the concluding years of the 19th century, neglect and the scavenging of brick and other building materials had left the structure in ruins.

It has been suggested that the Annaberg School was damaged beyond use in the disastrous hurricane and earthquakes that occurred in the fall of 1867. While this might indeed have occurred, no documentation was found to support this conclusion. It may just be that researchers have long presumed that the school was damaged in order to find a logical explanation as to why it was never reopened or utilized for some other purpose at a later date. The truth, however, may not be so simple.

On consideration, it might be that the Annaberg School had simply outlived its usefulness. And, over time, the local population had come to view the site as a relic of their painful past: a reminder of slavery and the harsh constraints of the plantation system. It must be kept in mind that the purpose behind the establishment of the rural schools was to provide limited education for the children of enslaved workers, in a situation that kept those children on, or close to, the estates to which they were bound. With emancipation in 1848, came greater freedom of movement and increased opportunities for open congregation. The dwindling number of workers who remained on St. John's rural estates quickly embraced self-determination, and they naturally turned to places beyond the boundaries of the plantations to fulfill their spiritual, social, and educational needs. The busy Moravian mission stations of Emmaus and Bethany became more than church settlements, they became the very centers of community life on St. John: school, church, shelter, clinic, meeting house. The movement away from the idea that the plantation was the nucleus of one's existence was simply too strong to resist. As the missions thrived, the Annaberg School retreated into bush, a failed experiment in amelioration; too little, offered much too late.

February, 2006

Danish-Colonial Education on St. John

David W. Knight

In 1856 the Annaberg Country School opened to provide free, compulsory education to the children of St. John's rural Maho Bay Quarter. But, while the opening of the Annaberg facility is indeed a notable milestone in the history of St. John, the school was not the first of the "Country Schools" to be established on the island; in fact, it may well have been the last.

The Moravian, Dutch, and Lutheran Churches had long provided educational opportunities for free children of the privileged class in the Danish West Indies (DWI). As for the enslaved population, from their arrival in 1732 it had been a primary goal of the Moravian missionaries to provide reading instruction to slaves. It was felt that only through personal interpretation of the scripture could one find true salvation. Initially no one was to be baptized until they could read the Bible, but after confronting many communications difficulties in the multilingual colony, it became clear that it would first be necessary to transcribe religious materials into the Creole dialect.

A school ordinance issued on December 21, 1787, marks the first attempt by government to institute public education for the DWI's enslaved population. Under this ordinance, the Lutheran (State) Church was to select 4 schoolmasters from the "most well-beloved and capable Free Negroes," who were also to act as church clerks and funeral masters for the "Creole Congregation." No child of the Lutheran congregation (free or enslaved) could be denied attendance in school, and free children of all denominations could attend for a monthly fee. The ordinance also stated that "wealthy" slave parents could volunteer to pay if they were able.

Schoolchildren in Cruz Bay, 1896

(Photo by F. Borgesen [Det Kongelige Bibliotek, Copenhagen, Denmark])

It was, however, not until 52 years later that a proposal was put forward by Governor-General Peter von Scholten to establish an organized system of free, compulsory education for all unfree children throughout the Danish colony. Between 1839 and 1842, 8 "Landskole," or Country Schools, were built on St. Croix. The first school to be completed was on Estate La Grand Princess, which opened for class in 1841.

Unfortunately, all available funding to establish the Country Schools throughout the colony went into the building of the St. Croix schools, leaving no resources to build the proposed schools on St. Thomas and St. John—a situation that did not bother the planters on those islands, who still opposed education of the enslaved.

To comply, at least in part, with von Scholten's directive to provide compulsory education throughout the colony, an agreement was reached between the Moravian Church and the Royal Council of St. Thomas and St. John for the Moravians to provide compulsory education for all free-colored children, and by 1841 classes were being held at both the Emmaus and Bethany Mission Stations on St. John. By 1842 there were 28 children attending classes at Bethany, and 40 attending classes at Emmaus. Classes were held from 9am to 1pm, and focused on "the three R's," as well as Bible study, geography and singing. Throughout this period the schools proved hard to staff and at least one teacher at Bethany had to be relieved due to "mental suffering."

In February of 1843, in an effort to bring broader educational opportunities to the rural areas of the colony, funding of 1500 Rigsdallers (Rd) was allocated to build the first Country Schools on St. John. On September 9 of that year, Governor von Scholten attended a meeting at the Susannaberg plantation to launch the Country School project. In attendance at the meeting were Hans H. Berg, Stadshouptsman Knevels, Landfoged Brahde, Agent Hjardemaal, Alexander Fraiser Esq., Reverend Tolderlund, and Moravian missionaries Houser, Gardin, Blatt and Kramer, as well as one Brother Wolter.

It was decided at this meeting that:

· *4 Country Schools were to be built on St. John at Beverhoudtsberg, Annaberg (near the Munsbury line), Emmaus and Par Force.*

· *The Country School plan by architect Albert Lovmand was to be used, but would be modified for each site. The school at Par Force was to include a dwelling for the teacher.*

· *Once completed, the schools for free children were to be annexed to the Country Schools.*

· *School hours were to be 8 - 11am for all children 4 - 8 years old; older children, 8 - 16, were to attend Sunday school. Free children attended for an additional 2 hours per day.*

The school at Beverhoudtsberg was the first to be completed in 1845; Annaberg was completed by December of 1847. However, construction of the two schools had cost 3,592 Rd, more than double the amount allocated for all four planned schools, leaving no funds for operational expenses or further construction. Therefore, the Annaberg school was left vacant, while the Beverhoudtsberg school was given over to the Lutheran congregation to hold monthly services (hence, the area where it once stood is still known to this day as "Danish Church Hill").

In the end it was not Royal decree, but Emancipation, that finally forced von Scholten's plan for free, compulsory education for all children in the colony to occur. Since the Moravian Missions had long been mandated to provide education to all free children, when Emancipation from slavery was achieved in 1848, all children in the colony gained the immediate right to attend the Mission Schools.

At first, Mission Schools took on the de-facto role of the Country Schools, and so many children rushed to attend that the planters complained there was hardly anyone left on the estates to do the work. This situation soon forced a reassessment of the earlier ordinances governing the Country Schools. On November 25, 1849 a circular outlining new regulations for the Country Schools on St. John made the rounds to all estates. These regulations stated that:

· *Only children 5 - 9 years old were to attend "day school"*

· *The school day was 8am - 11am, Monday through Friday*

· *Children 9 - 12 years old were to attend Sunday school; older children could be kept an additional 2 hours as teachers' assistants, but no more than one child from each estate.*

· *Vacations were a fortnight from December 24, a fortnight in June, and a sennight from the Wednesday before Easter.*

· *Children were to be moved from day school to Sunday school at vacation breaks.*

· *Estate managers were to be notified of any child leaving school.*

· *Parents were responsible for their children's school attendance under penalty of a fine.*

· *Any owner or manager of an estate who prevented a child from attending school would be fined.*

Concern over lingering problems with the schools led Landfoged Carl Hanschell to pen a long and detailed report to the DWI School Commission regarding St. John. In this February 6, 1851, correspondence, Judge Hanschell noted that the Mission Schools had never been formally acknowledged as part of the Country School system, and that they received almost no funding or support. He also suggested that the Annaberg schoolhouse, which had remained unused since its construction in 1847, be put to use. At this point some 228 students were overcrowding the schools at Emmaus and Bethany on a daily basis. Despite the evident need, no significant changes were forthcoming; the Commission pled lack of funds.

On August 3, 1852, the Moravians took it upon themselves to open a third school to service the growing community on St. John's East End. At the new school, 30-some students were instructed in singing, prayer and bible history by Mary Dorothy Sewer, and it was stated that basic arithmetic, spelling and writing would be added to the curriculum, "…as soon as Mary Sewer mastered the topics a little better."

Finally, in August of 1856 it was reported by brother Gardin in a Moravian Periodical account that: "In St. Jan we have, this year, opened a school at Annaberg, on the north side of the island."

In the end, operating the remote Annaberg School proved problematic. Outbreaks of cholera and a lack of staffing forced intermittent closings and, after schoolmaster Augustus Knevels was dismissed, the school closed its doors after only five years of service. Although some sporadic use of the structure is documented through the 1860s, the building was eventually dismantled for reuse of its building materials and its foundations left forgotten, only to be overtaken by bush.

February, 2008

A Country School and children on St. Thomas, c1900

(Postcard by Edward Fraas [D. Knight Collection])

References

Brother J. Gardin, Account 22, August 12, 1856, *Periodical Accounts Relating To The Missions Of The Church Of The United Brethren, Established Among the Heathen*, (London, England, Walter m'Dowall, 1856).

Birgit Julie Fryd Johansen, *Slave Schools in the Danish West Indies, 1839 – 1853* (Copenhagen, Denmark, The University of Copenhagen Historical Institute, 1988).

David W. Knight, *Understanding Annaberg, A Brief History of Estate Annaberg on St. John, U. S. Virgin Islands* (St. Thomas, USVI, Little Nordside Press, 2002).

Eva Lawaetz, *Black Education in the Danish West Indies from 1732 to 1853* (St. Croix, USVI, St. Croix Friends of Denmark, 1980).

A Visit to the Bethany Moravian and the Nazareth Lutheran Churches

Summarized by Robin Swank

The St. John Historical Society joined Rudolph "Pimpy" Thomas, Reggie Callwood, and Elroy Sprauve, for on-site history lessons about two of our spiritual and architectural gems on St. John, the Bethany Moravian Church and the Nazareth Lutheran Church.

The Bethany Moravian Church and Mission House

According to an article in The St. John Drum (a local newspaper published in Cruz Bay in the 1970s) Vernon J. Nelson, Archivist at the Moravian Church Archives in Bethlehem, Pennsylvania, states that the first Moravian Mission anywhere in the world was in the Danish West Indies (now the U. S. Virgin Islands). It was a German nobleman and devout Lutheran, Count Nicolai Louis von Zinzendorf, who persuaded the Moravian Brethren to

The Bethany Moravian Mission Settlement on St. John, c1767

(C. G. A. Oldendorp, Geschichte der Mission der evangelischen Brueder auf den caraibischen Inseln S. Thomas, S. Croix und S. Jan [Published in Germany, 1777])

extend their Christian influence to the West Indies. Through the quaint Moravian practice of drawing lots, a Lutheran layman and potter, Leonard Dober, and a Moravian carpenter, David Nitschmann, were sent to the West Indies with the blessing of Danish princess Charlotte Amalie. Early Moravian missionaries were tradesmen; they were expected to support themselves in addition to ministering to the enslaved.

The early Moravian brethren had a horrific time of it in the Danish West Indies (DWI). The history of the early years of the Moravian Church in the DWI, as documented by C. G. A. Oldendorp and published in Germany in 1777, gives a grueling and detailed account of the Moravians' struggles. Bishop G. G. Oliver Maynard, who wrote about the history of the Moravian Church in the West Indies in the 1980s, equates the planting of the Moravian faith in the 18th-century Virgin Islands—with its hurricanes, famines, political and social travails, and wars and illnesses—to "Acts of the Apostles."[1] Mr. Rudolph Thomas, who is a local member of the Bethany church, read briefly from the Moravian Church's 200th Anniversary Booklet (published Sunday June 27, 1982), which also recounts some of those travails.

On St. John the Moravians did not prosper at first, in part due to the 1733 slave uprising. Moravian work truly began on St. John in 1741 at the initiation of Jens Rasmus, the pious overseer of the L'Esperance plantation, who, before being granted his freedom, had been a slave on the island of St. Thomas. The first baptisms on St. John took place in 1745; a small cotton plantation, named by the Moravians

Bethania, was purchased in 1749. Also in 1749 Brother Cornelius, a slave owned by the Danish West Indies & Guinea Company (and later by the Danish Crown—he purchased his freedom c1766), was baptized a Moravian. He was a master mason, missionary, and accomplished linguist. It was he who laid the foundations of six churches and mission houses in the DWI, including those at Bethany. The first full-time pastor Johann Schur arrived in late 1749, but died of fever on January 5, 1750. The first resident missionary Bro. Johann Brucker, was stationed here in 1754.[2]

In the 1840s unconditional baptism of infants was practiced; only one of the parents had to belong to the Brethren's church. This coincided with the introduction of compulsory education for slaves, on the presumption that education would make possible a Christian upbringing of the slave children.[2] In the 1840s the Moravians were selected to run the schools at Emmaus, Bethany and elsewhere, enlarging the Moravian opportunity. Moravians lent encouragement to the slaves to prepare themselves for the assumption of responsible positions within the church hierarchy and community.[3]

In 1860 a restriction of baptizing only "legitimate" children was introduced, causing parents to go to other churches for baptism. This stricture caused the loss of nearly half the Brethren's membership over 20 years, and eventually the more liberal 1848 regulation was restored.[2]

It was admittedly hard to focus on the difficult history of the Moravian and Lutheran missions while in the company of such engaging and good-humored story-tellers, who recounted more-recent life events in their churches. For example, when Mr. Thomas was school age there was a two-room school held in the Bethany Hall on the ground floor. (There was also an upper floor then). As Pimpy remembers, the teachers were strict and dedicated to all students' learning "one way or another, regardless of their scholarly interests... Clarice Thomas could tell you who sneezed, and you NEVER crossed her on days she wore her hair plaited." Apparently a single glance from Ms. Thomas could remind you to pump the church organ faster.

On really rainy days, school might be let out early, Pimpy reports, "so we learned to brush up against the trees 'accidentally' to wet our clothes on the way to school." The Moravian

Congregants in front of the Bethany Moravian Church on St. John, c1904

(Det Kongelige Bibliotek, Copenhagen, Denmark)

Estate L'Esperance: The Cradle of Moravian Faith on St. John

Located in the Cruz Bay Quarter of St. John, the L'Esperance estate is notable for its role in the conversion of enslaved Africans to Christianity by missionaries of the Moravian faith.

One of the earliest Moravian converts was an enslaved craftsman on J. L. Carstens' plantation on St. Thomas, Jens Rasmus. Rasmus had been one of two slaves taken to Europe as personal servants by the Moravian mission's founder, Count von Zinzendorf, when he returned from a visit to the West Indies in 1739—the other was a slave from St. John by the name of Andreas. Upon meeting Jens Rasmus, Nicolas Tonis of Amsterdam was so impressed that he appointed Rasmus overseer of his L'Esperance plantation on St. John. Tonis urged Rasmus to convert the slaves on the property to Christianity, and allowed him great liberty to spread the word of the Gospel. Soon, slaves from neighboring plantations were eagerly coming to meetings at L'Esperance, giving rise to the first Moravian congregation on St. John. It was reported that by 1745 over 136 persons would attend the religious meetings at L'Esperance, and on February 14, 1745, an enslaved man named Clas and an enslaved woman named Nora were the first of many generations of Moravians to be baptized on St. John.

It was not until 1755 that construction began on the island's first Moravian Church on a property acquired by The Mission in the Cruz Bay Quarter. The project was overseen by Jens Rasmus, who also supplied the timbers from his own property. The new church, known as Bethany, was completed in 1759 and consecrated by Brother Nathanial Seidel on April 29 of that year. Although destroyed many times, the church has been rebuilt and is still in use to the present day.

tradition of learning life skills accompanied by classwork prevailed. Learning to fish accompanied learning to swim, learning to read and memorize accompanied performing skits and making decorative flowers out of century plant tips for holiday presentations. Reggie Callwood (who was born on Tortola in the British Virgin Islands) recalls wanting to join a church that was closest to the English Methodist Church. The Methodists and Moravians often shared ministers, and his wonderful tenor voice was in demand by many churches.

Portions of the Bethany buildings have been rebuilt several times. In 1793 and in 1819, various structures were rebuilt after they were carried away by hurricanes. Maintenance of the church has remained a priority of its members, and the grounds have not been abandoned since establishment. In 1904, at the 150th anniversary of the St. John Moravian mission, a new belfry and bell were dedicated (St. John Drum, September 19, 1975); in 1919, the belfry was replaced after being damaged in the 1916 hurricane; and, in the 1960s Reggie Callwood replaced the wooden floor.

On January 31, 1975, The Drum reported that the Old Bethany Church had a new roof and was being painted and redecorated while parishioners awaited the arrival of new pews. The

The mahogany Baptismal Font in Cruz Bay's Nazareth Lutheran Church is over 100 years old.

(Photo by Robin Swank)

Drum says, "Undaunted by winds and showers, some 30 visitors joined Mr. Herbert Samuels and Miss Clarice Thomas for a walking tour of the Bethany Church buildings and grounds. The visit was sponsored by the St. John Historical Society and visitors were much interested in the solid old walls now surmounted by a new roof of the historic church, and in the rubble masonry of the mission house which formerly served as a school. They followed the path down to the graveyard, and read inscriptions on many of the gravestones, some more than 200 years old." The Drum also reported that Reverend Willard Prout, and Pastor and Bishop Hastings, dedicated the renovated church.

Because of the rain this year (Are we less hardy souls in 2008?), we did not descend to visit the two cemeteries on the grounds. The older cemetery is primarily the resting place of members of the early mission families, as in those days it was customary to bury laborers on the estates where they resided—missionaries seemed to pass on as fast as they came to the West Indies. The more recent burials are closer to the Church.

The Nazareth Lutheran Church and Hall

Mr. Elroy Sprauve began our tour by telling us that the Nazareth Lutheran Church in Cruz Bay was not built in 1720, the date over the door, although that is the date of the establishment of the Nazareth Lutheran Congregation. Lutheran work on St. John began in 1718, when the island was annexed to Denmark and joined with St. Thomas as one unit for government administrative purposes (the Lutheran Church, being the State Church of Denmark). The Lutheran parish of St. Thomas was then extended to that Island.[2] The first Lutheran Church building on St. John was built in Cruz Bay near the site of the Morris De Castro Clinic in or about 1765. The Nazareth Lutheran congregation is the second-oldest congregation in the USVI; the Frederick Lutheran on St. Thomas is the oldest.

The local Lutheran history is as tortuous as that of the Moravian brethren: many came, converted a few, and quickly died. On June 26, 1721, Pastor Jacob Tamdrup arrived on St. Thomas from Denmark bringing a silver chalice and paten for the Lutheran Congregation on St. John. These communion vessels, bearing the inscription 1721, have been in continuous use since 1723—Mr. Elroy Sprauve passed them to us to gently inspect. A lip was added to the common cup in the 1960s, to accommodate pouring wine into smaller vessels. All are shiny and elegant. The baptismal font is made of St. Thomas mahogany and is over 100 years old.

The Lutherans' cumbersome and impractical daily requirement of preparing each convert for baptism in Danish (a language unknown to the majority of the population of the DWI) or in Dutch Creole (which was unknown to the Danish missionaries) initially led to fewer converts than to the Moravian faith. As English replaced Dutch Creole as the language of the colony after the British occupations of the DWI in the early nineteenth century, the Moravians found it easier to use English in local teachings—partly because some of their missionaries at the time came from England. In 1839 the Moravians formally adopted English instead of Dutch Creole. The Lutheran Church, however, was slower to change, and it was not until 1841 that Denmark gave permission to substitute English for Creole. In his book, *Virgin Islands Story*, Jens Larsen surmises from his references that the Lutherans often sang from Creole hymnals and heard a minister chant and preach in English.[2]

On St. John, despite the great decrease in population in the early 20th century (in 1901 the inhabitants numbered 925), the Lutheran work took on new life: "A Sunday school was organized at Cruz Bay on September 2, 1904. The congregation had been 'homeless' since the 1867 hurricane destroyed its church near Susannaberg."[4] (Note: The church referred to here had originally been built as the first Country School on St. John in 1845; the site, where the ruined foundations still stand, is known locally as "Danish Church Hill"). On October 1, 1910, a building was purchased by the Sunday School from Mrs. Olivia Lucas, and, after a thorough renovation, was consecrated on April 9, 1911. As reported by Archdeacon Johannes Petersen, "We now have a cozy little church room with alter, baptismal font and pulpit, plus benches, with seating for about 140... which is all that is needed. The consecration was made by me Palm Sunday, the 9th of April in the presence of the Danish official (doctor and police assistant), the Moravian minister and many members of both the Lutheran and Moravian churches. It was given the name Nazareth Chapel."[4]

On March 9, 1915, an adjoining empty lot was purchased from Mrs. Martha Bastian, and on March 12 another lot was donated to the Sunday School.[2] The present church was built in 1958 on those lots. Between visits from ministers from St. Thomas, "laymen" conducted

Lutheran Chapel on the site of the present Church Hall, c1917
(Photo by W.Y. Ryan)

services until the first resident pastor was appointed to St. John in 1966. The lay readers, or "clerks" as they were known in Danish times, were J. E. Lindquist, who served until 1915, Carl E. Frances, who served until his death at 1936, and Mr. Henry Samuel who served from 1936 to 1966. The Rev. Ivar O. Iverson became the first resident pastor in 1966. Construction of the Church hall and parsonage began in April of 1967 on the site of the old Sunday School Chapel.[4] The new building was dedicated as "Memorial Hall" on March 10, 1968.

Later in the 20th century, along with Americanization, Lutheran Churches encountered another interesting problem. Under Danish rule the Lutheran Church, as the State Church, was the property of the Crown. The 1917 Treaty of Secession between Denmark and the United States (Transfer) gave assurance that Lutheran congregations in the former Danish West Indies would have undisturbed use of their buildings, but the ownership of church property was somehow overlooked. Legal research and diplomatic conversations later established that the churches belonged to the US Government. Eventually Congress enacted legislation, signed by President Eisenhower, conveying title of the properties to the congregations.[2] Whether the Church in Cruz Bay endured this legal snarl is unclear, as the Sunday School, not the Church, owned the building and property in which services were conducted.

During Mr. Elroy Sprauve's childhood, the Sunday school dominated holidays and every Sunday. The bell rang at 10AM, and again at 11AM, alerting people en route to hurry along. At noon it was time for Services to begin. Then there was a break between 1 and 2PM, when families would visit and lunch. At 2 in the afternoon Sunday School began. This strict schedule and the "village" approach to monitoring children's behavior is a backdrop for one of Mr. Elroy's youthful adventures. To wit, he met a family wharf-side early one Sunday morning who invited him for a sail. Thinking no-one would miss him he hid below decks until the boat was out of the harbor, and then enjoyed his day sail. "The entire Sunday school was on the dock to greet me as we sailed in," he said. "I never thought of doing that again."

These somber and stern church ladies from Cruz Bay and Lovango oversaw the genip-picking fund-raisers, and all rites of passage—baptisms, confirmations, and weddings—which made the church a center of social activity. No doubt they also monitored the membership's tithing: as one said "Present," one was expected to recite the amount of pennies donated and placed in the plate—25 cents was a lot of money. "These were somber women," Mr. Elroy says, with the same respectful look in his eyes as was in Pimpy Thomas' eyes when speaking of Bethany's teachers.

February, 2009

Sources:

[1]Bishop G. G. Oliver Maynard, *The Moravian Historical Account, Public Education via the Moravian Missionaries in St. Thomas, St. Croix, and St. John- Danish West Indies 1732-1917* [Education Review, Vol. 1, No. 4, November 1982: Special Issue: Moravian Anniversary Celebration 1732-1882].

[2]Jens Larsen, *Virgin Islands Story* [Fortress Press, Philadelphia PA, 1950, updated 1967].

[3]"Moravian Educators," by Patricia G Murphy, pp. 14-18 of [1], above.

[4]Ruth Low and Rafael Valls, *St. John Backtime-Eyewitness Accounts from 1718 to 1956* [Eden Hill Press, St. John, USVI , 1985].

The Nazareth Lutheran Church in Cruz Bay soon after construction in 1958 (Note the old Sunday School Chapel building at the left side of the photo and the unpaved streets of what is today one of Cruz Bay's busiest intersections.)

[Photo by Dr. George H. H. Knight]

Mr. Amos Benjamin in the Lutheran Chapel, c1940

[Image courtesy Elroy Sprauve]

A Brief Background of Estate Lindholm

David W. Knight

In or about 1754, Salomon Zeegers acquired a one-half share of a modest Cruz Bay Quarter cotton plantation previously deeded to Johannes and Isaac Salomons in 1727.

Salomon Zeegers was born on the island of St. Eustatius in 1729, the son of Jan Zeegers and Anna Maria Hassell. About 1753, Salomon married Anna deWindt, the daughter of Johannes deWindt of St. Thomas and Maria Battri of St. Eustatius—a prestigious union that speaks volumes for the high standing of both parties in the rigid and exclusionary plantocracy of the era.

By 1756, considerable investment had been put forth to convert the Zeegers' small Cruz Bay cotton piece into a well developed livestock and provisioning plantation. Not only was the amount of land under cultivation increased, but the property's labor force was also expanded to sixty enslaved workers, an all time high for the property. It is likely that it was during this period of activity that a new estate house befitting the social and economic standing of the owners was constructed on the site. After 1758, when Zeeger extended his St. John land holdings by the purchase of a large sugar plantation on the island's North Shore (later named Annaberg to honor his wife) the house on his Cruz Bay property became the primary residence for both estates.

The Zeegers produced four children during the course of their union: Anna, Elizabeth, Maria, and Adriana. After Salomon Zeegers' death in about 1762, his widow and daughters moved to St. Thomas and cultivation all but ceased on the Cruz Bay property. By 1764, five enslaved workers were the only remaining inhabitants on the site.

On June 6, 1765, the widowed Anna deWindt Zeegers remarried to Burger Captain Jacob Hendrick Schmaltz in the Danish Lutheran Church on St. Thomas. As husband and guardian for his wife's estate, Capt. Schmaltz became the recorded owner of Anna's properties, which included substantial holdings on both St. John and St. Thomas.

Capt. Schmaltz was a man of high prominence and considerable authority. During the late 1760s and early 1770s, all of the properties on St. John that were controlled by Schmaltz were recorded together in yearly tax rolls, hindering our ability to analyze the activities on any individual parcel during that period. It is apparent, however, that Jacob and Anna did not choose to reside on their Cruz Bay property. By 1776, when the parcel was again recorded independently in tax records, it was noted as uncultivated and totally vacant. Yet, in 1778, the tax rolls indicate that the Schmaltz property was occupied by Benjamin Lind, the widowed husband of Salomon and Anna Zeegers' daughter, Elizabeth, along with their children, Anna, Sarah, and Jacob.

Elizabeth Mooy Zeegers had married Benjamin Lind in the St. Thomas Dutch Reform Church on March 14, 1771. Lind, an employee of the Danish Crown, held the position of "Provisions Manager" for St. John. Along with his responsibility for purchasing and distributing supplies and ammunition for the island's military garrison, Benjamin also served as St. John's postmaster and customs agent.

Benjamin Lind appears to have been brought to the West Indies as a child by his father, Salomon Lind, who was a West Indies and Guinea Company employee. Upon being named to the position of "Provisions Manager" Benjamin

Lind was posted to St. John, where he lived continuously from just prior to his marriage to Elizabeth until his death on December 7, 1794. As a government agent, Lind would have been provided with lodging on St. John, but the estate house on the Schmaltz property, with its prominent location and broad vistas of town and surrounding waters, was most likely the Lind family's residence of choice. It is also probable that during this period the house served as a retreat or part-time residence for all of the extended Lind, Schmaltz, and Zeegers families while on visits to St. John.

Throughout the 1770s and 1780s, tax records show only occasional occupation on the Schmaltz's Cruz Bay property, and no cultivation whatsoever. Yet, Peter Oxholm's map, rendered in 1780 and published in 1800, clearly depicts two structures on the site enclosed by a rectangular system of stone walls. The walling in of the property's residence and associated structure may be an indication that, while the property was not being actively cultivated, it may well have been being grazed, necessitating a barrier to keep livestock away from the living area. Pasturing was not an activity that was reported in the tax records of this era, therefore no indication of such land usage is evident from those sources. The grazing of livestock, which did not require a large work force, could explain the absence of any enslaved laborers attached to the property during this time period. It might be speculated that being charged with the provisioning and supply of the St. John garrison, Benjamin Lind had made a deal with his stepfather-in-law to utilize the Schmaltz plantation for the pasturing of government purchased livestock, a premise supported by the fact that while no laborers were reported in the tax rolls on the Schmaltz parcel, Benjamin Lind, who did not own any land during this time period, was in possession of nine slaves.

In 1790, Benjamin Lind, by then a widower for some fifteen years, was recorded in the St. John tax rolls as a partner in the Schmaltz property above Cruz Bay. After the death of Capt. Schmaltz one year later, Benjamin formally acquired the plantation and set about the task of bringing its grounds back under cultivation. On April 7, 1792, Lind's mortgage, in the sum of 3,000 Rigsdalers (Danish West Indian currency), was recorded in the colony's "Register." It is from this document that we first

Susan Morse Lind holding her son, Charles Walker Lind, the great-grandson of Benjamin Lind of Lindholm on St. John

(Photocopy from the Family History Library, Salt Lake City, Utah)

learn that Lind had named his newly-purchased plantation, Lindholm.

Benjamin Lind and his children were now well established and a promising future seems to have lain ahead. By 1792, Lind had acquired nineteen enslaved laborers, who were reported to be living on and working the Lindholm plantation. It is quite likely that at least some of these slaves were craftsmen, engaged in either reconstructing or upgrading the property's estate house. The process of restoration appears to have been completed by 1793, when Lind and his three children, a white overseer, and fourteen slaves, were recorded in the tax rolls as in residence on the property. This, however, was a rather fleeting situation. By 1794 Benjamin Lind was dead, and the Lindholm property once more fell into total abandonment.

From 1795 through 1797, the uninhabited and uncultivated Lindholm was reported in the land records as the possession of a Dr. Brody; in 1798, it was recorded in the names Masman and Dierisen; and, in 1799 and 1800, it was listed solely in the name of Masman. In 1801, the fifty-acre Lindholm estate, which had formally been separated from the Johannes Salomons plantation sometime in or about 1754, was reunited with its neighboring parcel under the common ownership of William Ruan. After his purchase of Lindholm, Ruan, who already owned the Salomons parcel, merged both properties with his prospering Little Caneel Bay sugar plantation: a situation which would remain in place for the better part of the nineteenth century.

While the Lindholm estate appears to have fallen into abandonment after Benjamin Lind's death, his heirs still went on to achieve considerable stature in the Danish West Indies colony. Benjamin and Elizabeth Lind's surviving son and daughter, Anna Maria and Jacob Henrik Schmaltz Lind, both married into the same prominent merchant family on St. Thomas. Jacob married Helena Bodil Mörch, and Anna married Jens Christensen Mörch. Jacob H. S. Lind went on to hold many powerful positions in the colony, amongst them, King's Attorney, Dealings Master, Judge, Chief of Police, and Commissioner. The stately home that Jacob built in the town of Charlotte Amalie (#6 Norregaade) still stands just west of the Frederick Lutheran Church and is today used as the Lutheran Sunday School.

In 1839 Jacob and Helena Lind's youngest son, Bent Christian Edward Lind (Benjamin Lind's grandson), married Susan Walker Morse, the daughter of Samuel Finley Morse, inventor of the Morse telegraph. After leaving St. Thomas the couple moved onto their inherited sugar plantation, the Henrietta, near Ponce in Puerto Rico. Both died in the 1880s.

March, 2002

Estate Cathrineberg & Jochumsdahl

David W. Knight

The Cathrineberg & Jochumsdahl plantation is one the oldest colonial era land holdings on St. John. It is also where the first privately-owned sugar works on the island was established.

Three of the original Danish land patents that would later be merged to form the Cathrineberg & Jochumsdahl plantation were granted to Cornelius Delicat and his sons, Jochum and Jacob in 1718. By 1722 the Delicats were already producing sugar on the site. Although the history of this estate has not been extensively researched, there is a wealth of documentary information available concerning the property. Production and occupation on Cathrineberg & Jochumsdahl can be tracked by following the progressive changes shown on the many appraisals and inventories prepared for the estate over two centuries (see accompanying inventories).

Cathrineberg's impressive windmill tower dates from between 1797 and 1803. The "gangway" style of construction of this structure is fairly typical of the era, with spaces underneath the access ramps used as storerooms, detention cells and stables. What is not as common is the curious vaulted-ceilinged room directly beneath the windmill platform. It has been speculated by one prominent Danish historian that this room was intended as a chapel, as it is almost identical in design and motif to round churches found on the Danish island of Bornholm in the Baltic Sea.

Another unique (for St. John) feature at Cathrineberg is the cockpit-style animal mill located directly across the road from the windmill. Although this structure was converted to a water reservoir sometime in the late 19th or early 20th century, the underground tunnels that once provided access to the cane-crushing

Detail from a painting by Frederik von Scholten showing *Estate Cathrineberg & Jochumsdahl* (left) and *Adrian* (right), 1833

(From a print in the St. John Historical Society Archives)

machinery at the interior of the mill are still distinguishable today.

Despite the fact that Cathrineberg & Jochumsdahl was a large plantation with land well suited for sugar cane cultivation, it would appear that it was never an extremely profitable enterprise. While at one point in its history the estate controlled the additional shoreline plantations of Maria Bluff, Chocolate Hole, and Great Cruz Bay, as well as having a warehouse and landing at Cruz Bay, it did not have the kind of convenient sea access that its neighboring plantation, Adrian, enjoyed by virtue of its merger with the adjoining Trunk Bay estate.

For much of its history the owner's residence for Cathrineberg & Jochumsdahl was located at estate Chocolate Hole, where Madame Cathrine DeNully lived, for whom the Cathrineberg portion of the plantation was named. After the deNully ownership ended the name of the estate was changed to Herman's Farm, but the new name was not widely embraced, and to this day both Cathrineberg and Herman's Farm

The overgrown ruins of the windmill at *Estate Cathrineberg & Jochumsdahl, c1960*

(Library of Congress, HABS Collection, Washington, DC)

(AKA: Mermansfarm or Hammerfarm) are used to refer to the site—the name Jochumsdahl has now largely slipped from collective local memory.

Although the sugar works at Cathrineberg were rebuilt and upgraded by the Heyliger family during the great sugar boom at the turn of the 19th century, by 1847 the estate had already fallen into disrepair. When the sugar factory on the nearby Adrian plantation was upgraded and converted to steam power in 1854 Cathrineberg's buildings were mined for construction materials.

As evidenced by the accompanying photograph, by the time the National Park Service evaluated the site in the 1960s the ruins of estate Cathrineberg had become completely overgrown and were in an advanced state of deterioration—a far cry from the beautifully stabilized structure encountered on the site today.

February, 2004

1786

Inventory for Cathrineberg and Jochumsdahl Cruz Bay Quarter, St. John

Owner: The widow and heirs of Johannes deNully

Consists of, more or less:
150 acres in bush
120 acres in sugar cane
20 acres in provisions

Buildings:
1 - Bricked boiling house and curing house with 6 copper kettles
1 - Still house
1 - Animal mill, not operative
1 - ditto, much worse
1 - Rum cellar
1 - Dwelling house
1 - Overseer's house
1 - Storehouse
1 - Kitchen
1 - Horse stable
1 - Bell
1 - Mule shed
22 - Negro House

1822

Inventory for Cathrineberg and Jochumsdahl, "which are now called together Hermansfarm."

Cruz Bay Quarter, St. John

Owner: J. Heyliger heirs

Land:
70 acres of land in canes
300 acres in woods, bush or pasture at Hermansfarm
230 acres in bush or pasture on the estate Gt. Cruz Bay
A lot of land with Store and Dwelling house in Cruz Bay

Buildings:
A boiling house, still house and curing house, with loft,
A set of coppers, 4 receivers, 2 coolers, 3 ladles, 3 shovels, 3 lamps and 16 liquor casks.
2 - Stills with worm and cistern
2 - New furnaces and one old furnace at Cruz Bay
A frame of a sick house / erected
A kitchen and 2 adjoining rooms / flat roofed
A necessary
A horse stable
A stone wall of a dwelling house
A windmill / out of repair
A cattle mill with round
2 - Cattle pens
A bell
25 - Negro houses
[Note: there are 85 enslaved laborers on the plantation]

Equipment:
A new cart
A new saddle and bridle

Livestock:
18 mules, 9 cows, 8 draw-cattle or bulls, 6 bulls (2 years old), 3 bulls (1 year old), 6 heifers (2 years old), 4 heifers (1 year old), 1 heifer calf (newly calfed) and 1 red horse.

1847

Inventory for Hermanfarm

Cruz Bay Quarter, St. John

Colonial Treasury to John Elliott

Negro houses:
24 shingled houses, most of them very much lacking, 11 thatched houses, out of repair
And the walls erected for 1 shingled house (incomplete).

Works:
The walls of a former windmill and ditto cockpit cattle mill, all partly broken down.
A boiling house with 4 furnace coppers and a curing house, both entirely out of repair.
The walls of a former worm cistern and still-room

Other Buildings:
A manager's house with kitchen and servants' room, and an overseer's lodging above the curing house, both not in repair.
An old cooper-shop
3 - Animal pens
A storehouse at Cruz Bay

The Establishment of the East End Community on St. John

David W. Knight

The first documentation of a plantation having been taken up on the East End of St. John is found in the earliest Danish-colonial tax rolls compiled in 1728. From this account it is learned that on March 11, 1725, "Joh. Jac. Creutzer" received a formal deed to a tract of land that was described as "a point that stretches east of *Keybayen*, and begins at the narrowest part of the point...." As was the case with all of the new settlers on St. John, Creutzer received a tax amnesty to aid in the development of a plantation. This exemption was noted as expiring in 1732. Further, the Creutzer parcel was reported to be a "provision" plantation, on which there were no whites or other free persons in residence. Living on the property were thirteen slaves: 6 capable men, 3 capable woman, 2 male and 1 female manqueron (old persons or individuals incapable of heavy labor), and 1 boy over six years of age [SJLL, 1728].

John Jacob Creutzer was an employee of the Danish West Indies and Guinea Company who held the position of provision manager for Company ships. No major changes on the Creutzer property were noted in the tax rolls through 1733, when a slave revolt on St. John disrupted plantation development and caused a lapse in the recording of taxes until 1736 [SJLL, 1728 - 1733]. During the uprising it appears that the Creutzer plantation was abandoned, but there is no mention of any damage to the property in reports compiled after the event [LD, 1734]. It is noted in a later reference, however, that Newfound Bay, which was situated in the northeastern section of the Creutzer plantation, was "known for the rebels who during the revolt were found killed there" [Martfeldt, c1767]. Adding to our knowledge of conditions on East End during this time period is a reference by Peter L. Oxholm, who mapped

the island of St. John in 1780. In his survey report Oxholm states: "[on the East End] ...there were many animals, fruits and other products, enough to supply neighboring islands; but after the rebellion of 1733 all was deserted and there is not the slightest trace of them any more" [Low & Valls, 1985].

Contradictory to Oxholm's observation, when tax records for St. John resume in 1736 they record that the Creutzer plantation was once again occupied and worked by fifteen enslaved laborers. But, as was the case throughout the entire term of the Creutzer family's ownership, no "Whites" or free persons were living on the property [SJLL, 1728 - 1733 & 1736 - 1739; SJA, 1755].

Only minor changes on the Creutzer plantation are noted in the West Indies and Guinea Company tax rolls for the duration of the period these records are available. In 1737 the property was recorded in the name of Creutzer's son, John Jacob Creutzer Jr.; one year later, the enslaved population on the plantation reached a peak of nineteen individuals (4 capable men, 5 capable woman, 4 male and 1 female manqueron, and 5 children under 16 years of age). By 1739, the last year in which these records were compiled for St. John before transfer of the colony to the Danish Crown in 1754, ownership the East End plantation was recorded in the name of "John Jacob Creutzer's widow" [SJLL, 1736 - 1739].

Little can be gleaned from the available record concerning land use or occupation on St. John's East End between the years 1740 and 1755. In 1742, ownership of the Creutzer plantation passed to the West Indies and Guinea Company's interim governor, Jens Hansen, by virtue of his marriage to John Jacob Creutzer's widow in June of that year [LCB, 1742]. Hansen, who in 1747 became the Governor-General of the Danish West Indies, lived on St. Croix, and it is unlikely that he ever spent any appreciable time on his East End plantation [Larson, 1940]. Despite his limited association with the property, Hansen's short term of ownership (1747 - 1755) remains memorialized to the present day in the name, Hansen Bay.

It is at this juncture that the history of land use and development on East End diverges from the standard pattern of colonial-period estate structuring and monoculture production. Abandoned, remote, and desolate, with little or no established infrastructure, the Hansen Bay plantation had become a poor and neglected stepchild amidst a growing number of developing plantation estates with established field systems and active industrial compounds. The inability of the Hansen heirs to profitably liquidate their holding opened a rare window of opportunity for a small band of struggling Creole families from the British island of Spanishtown (today known as Virgin Gorda), who left their drought-plagued properties and relocated to St. John's East End in the mid-eighteenth century.

In or about 1757, Philip Sewer, Peter Sewer, William George, and Charles George, arrived from Spanishtown and established themselves at Hansen Bay [SJLL, 1756 - 1758]. With them, the men brought an "old cotton gin," but apparently no slaves [Martfeldt, c1767; SJLL, 1756 - 1758]. Family members soon followed bringing their meager household belongings and what few enslaved laborers they possessed. By 1759, the Hansen Bay property was recorded as a cotton plantation, on which there were nine free persons (4 men, 1 woman, and 4 children) and six enslaved laborers (1 capable adult, 1 manqueron boy, and 4 children) [SJLL, 1759].

In 1764, the closely-knit Sewer and George families were joined on East End by Peter Sewer's brother-in-law, Michael Ladler, who came over from Spanishtown with his wife, Maria George [SJLL, 1764; SJLP, 1774]. Peter Sewer's wife, Isabelle Ladler, had died in 1755, so Maria and Michaels' presence must have brought welcome domesticity and much needed helping hands to the Sewer household, as well as to the growing East End community [SJLRA, 1755]. By 1769 the efforts of the Sewer, George, and Ladler clan had begun to show some reward. In that year, it was recorded in the tax rolls that there were now sixty-one enslaved laborers on the Hansen Bay plantation,

thirty-one of whom were capable adults, while eight were manqueron, and twenty-two were children [SJLL, 1769].

It is unclear what the primary economic focus of the East End community was during this period, but it is evident that agriculture was not their sole source of support. While some small-scale cotton and provision farming did indeed take place, cottage industries and maritime trades were likewise engaged in. East End men have traditionally been known as seafarers, and it would appear that their activities were often of a questionable nature. In the words of Danish economist Christian Martfeldt, who compiled many volumes of observations during a prolonged visit to the West Indies between 1763 and 1768: "On the East End there are no cays, but from there to Tortola is open passage, navigable for large ships as well as for small vessels that carry on a trade which not everyone is anxious to make known" [Martfeldt, c1767].

Although the George and Sewer families had taken up their land on East End in partnership, and worked together to develop their plantation

A community picnic on East End, St. John, c1900

(Postcard by Johannes Lightbourn [Det Kongelige Bibliotek, Copenhagen, Denmark])

into a viable enterprise, from the outset they seem to have established individual households within the property boundaries. These parcels first become apparent in land records in 1774, when the tax burden on the Hansen Bay estate was divided amongst five owners: Charles George Sr., holding the largest parcel, measuring 2000 X 500 (Danish) feet; and, Nancy George, Johannes Sewer, Michael Ladler, and Philip Sewer, all having equal parcels of 2000 X 250 feet [SJA, 1774 - 1915].

After a formal division of the property the former Hansen Bay plantation began to slowly take on the character of a community. This transition occurred as members of the extended George and Sewer families, their heirs, descendants, former slaves and their descendants, began to spread out over the landscape and establish satellite in-holdings on, and around, what had previously been five, modest single-household properties. The further fragmentation of these properties begins to become evident in 1826, as one- to eight-acre parcels broken off from the earlier divisions, or established on common lands surrounding them, start to appear in tax rolls. Prior to emancipation, all of these holdings were taken up by free persons of color, many of whom were former enslaved laborers manumitted by the East End landowners, or their free-born offspring from mixed-race unions. Contributing to the growth of this community were numerous "Free-colored" immigrants from neighboring islands (both British and Danish), who gradually melded into East End society through marriage or family associations. Throughout historical documentation for East End the records reflect a labyrinth of family interconnections displayed in the proliferation of George and Sewer surnames. In short, by the latter half of the nineteenth century, the East End community could casually be regarded as one extended family.

June, 2003

References

[SJLL, 1728] West Indies and Guinea Company Archives, St. John Land Lists, 1728 - 1733 & 1736 - 1739 (Rigsarkivet, Denmark).

[SJLL, 1728 - 1733] West Indies and Guinea Company Archives, St. John Land Lists, 1728 - 1733 & 1736 - 1739 (Rigsarkivet, Denmark).

[LD, 1734] West Indies and Guinea Company Archives, Letters and Documents, 1674 - 1754 (Rigsarkivet, Denmark).

[Martfeldt, c1767] Christian Martfeldt, *Samlinger om de Danske Vestindiske Öer St. Croix, St. Thomas, St. Jan*, Vol. III. (Denmark, Manuscript in the Rigsarkivet, c1765).

[Low & Valls, 1985] Ruth Hull Low & Rafael Valls, *St. John Backtime, Eyewitness Accounts from 1718 to 1956* (St. John, U.S. Virgin Islands, Eden Hill Press, 1985).

[SJLL, 1728 - 1733 & 1736 - 1739; SJA, 1755] West Indies and Guinea Company Archives, St. John Land Lists, 1728 - 1733 & 1736 - 1739 (Rigsarkivet, Denmark).

[SJLL, 1736 - 1739] West Indies and Guinea Company Archives, Letters and Documents, 1674 - 1754 (Rigsarkivet, Denmark).

[LCB, 1742] [LCB] Church Book for the [Lutheran] Evangelical Mission on St. Thomas, 1691 - 1795 (Landsarkivet, Denmark).

[Larson, 1940] Kay Larsen, *Guvernører Residenter, Kommandanter og Chefer* (Copenhagen, Denmark, Arthur Jensen Forlag, 1940).

[SJLL, 1756 - 1758] West Indies and Guinea Company Archives, Letters and Documents, 1674 - 1754 (Rigsarkivet, Denmark).

[SJLL, 1759] West Indies and Guinea Company Archives, Letters and Documents, 1674 - 1754 (Rigsarkivet, Denmark).

[SJLL, 1764] West Indies and Guinea Company Archives, Letters and Documents, 1674 - 1754 (Rigsarkivet, Denmark).

[SJLP, 1774] West Indies Local Archives, St. John Landfoged, Probate Sessions Protocol, 1758 - 1775 (Rigsarkivet, Denmark).

[SJLRA, 1755] West Indies Local Archives, St. John Landfoged, Probate Registrations and Appraisements, 1763 - 1775 (Rigsarkivet, Denmark).

[SJLL, 1769] West Indies and Guinea Company Archives, Letters and Documents, 1674 - 1754 (Rigsarkivet, Denmark).

[SJA, 1774 - 1915] Central Management Archives, West Indies Audit Registers for St. John, 1755 - 1915 (Rigsarkivet, Denmark).

Estate Concordia

David W. Knight

Among the last properties to be formally granted during the era of the Danish settlement of St. John, were four parcels that lay in the arid and windswept southeast corner of the island, just west of the "Company's Salt Pond." By 1739, these four holdings had been merged to form a vast 475-acre cotton and livestock plantation, which would come to be known as Estate Concordia.

The property known as Estate Concordia was created when four early Danish land holdings were merged to form a single estate in about 1739. Three of these properties were initially granted to members of the Coop family in 1724: Cornelius Coop; his brother, Jochim Coop; and Jochim's son, Cornelius Coop de Jonger [Jr.]. The fourth property was taken up by Andreas Hammer in the same year.

According to the 1728 St. John tax rolls, none of the four original property owners lived on their plantations, and, during this time period, the Hammer parcel was reported as vacant. The Coop properties, however, were already being operated as a unified cotton, livestock and provisions plantation, on which one free overseer directed the labors of thirty-six enslaved workers.

By the year of the St. John slave rebellion, which began in Coral Bay on November 23, 1733, all three of the Coop properties had come under the ownership of the younger Cornelius Coop. It was in that year that the population of the Concordia estate reached its all time high of forty-seven individuals (forty-six enslaved laborers, and one free overseer).

It was not until 1739, that the undeveloped Hammer property was purchased and merged

A typical eighteenth-century cotton plantation in the West Indies

(Denis Diderot [D. Knight Collection])

with the neighboring Coop holdings to form a single 475-acre estate.

It appears evident that the Coop family's attempt to create a large and lucrative plantation ultimately ended in failure. By the mid eighteenth century, Concordia had come under the ownership of a St. Martin-born Creole by the name of William Barry, who had previously worked as an overseer on the Carolina estate in Coral Bay. When Barry died in about 1756, his son, William Barry Jr., inherited the Concordia estate. At the time, the property was reported to have only one enslaved laborer.

William Barry Jr. was married to Johanne Hazzel, and it was through this union that the Hazzel family began their long association with the Concordia estate. The Hazzels hailed from the small, rugged island of Saba, which lies roughly one hundred miles east of St. John. Already well proliferated by the mid-eighteenth century, the Hazzel men were well known for their prowess as seafarers, fishermen, and stone masons. Despite their long heritage in the West

Detail of Concordia (noted as "Hazzel") from a map by Peter L. Oxholm, 1780

(Rigsarkivet, Copenhagen, Denmark)

Mortgage inventory of Estate Concordia, 1788

(Rigsarkivet, Copenhagen, Denmark)

Indies, members of the Hazzel clan were not generally members of the elite plantocracy, but rather hard working and industrious tradesmen and mariners.

When the Danish cartographer Peter L. Oxholm visited Estate Concordia while surveying the Salt Pond area in 1780, he reported that a Peter Hazzel was living on the estate and operating a "small store," where he sold salt that was harvested from the nearby salt pond, and quicklime which was being produced on the property. There were nine enslaved laborers reported on the property in that year.

Although Peter Hazzel was living on and working the Concordia estate by 1780, the property was technically under administration by the probate court during that time. It was not until 1788 that brothers James and Peter Hazzel took on a mortgage for the purchase of Concordia for 9000 Riksdalers, Danish West Indies Currency.

The occasion of the Hazzels' mortgage provides us with the first documentary description of the Concordia property. An inventory of the estate's buildings, compiled at the time of the sale, noted that there stood on the site:

> *"A good dwelling house of hard timber and shingled, 32 feet by 16 feet, [with] a platform of lime and stone in front. [and a] magazine built of lime and stone 26 feet by 15 feet, shingled roof, [and] an excellent cistern."*

It must be noted, that the Danish word *kalk*, translated in the inventory as "lime," was the term for *coral*. Therefore, the "lime and stone" construction referred to in the 1788 inventory, describes the mixed stone and coral-block materials evident in the ruins of the building which still stands on the property to this day; the measurements (26 X 15) correspond within inches when converted from Danish measurement.

In 1809, the Hazzels sold Concordia to Jacob Eno, who soon after moved onto the estate with his wife Sarah and their two children, Sarah Susanna and Jacob Jr. (members of the Eno family also owned the neighboring *John's Folly* property). Jacob Eno utilized an average of thirteen enslaved laborers to cultivate provisions and raise livestock on the five acres of cleared land at Concordia. Fishing and salt harvesting continued to be activities carried out on the estate throughout this era.

From Christiansfort to Calvary Bay

After the death of Jacob Eno Sr. in about 1828, his son and daughter inherited equal shares in Estate Concordia. Together, the Eno siblings and their heirs continued to reside on, and work the Concordia estate; but, after Emancipation was achieved in 1848, the family found it increasingly hard to make a living from the land. Jacob Eno Jr., the last of the Eno clan to live at Concordia, died bankrupt and impoverished on the estate in 1863.

After Jacob Eno's death the stone and coral house at Estate Concordia appears to have been abandoned. However, it was re-occupied by Carl Alexander Penn and his family sometime near the turn of the twentieth century. According to an oral interview conducted by archaeologist Emily Lundberg with Carl Penn's daughter in 1986, with the exception of the house which still stands there today, all of the structures associated with the Concordia estate complex were in ruin when the Penn family lived on the site in the early 1900s.

Carl Penn raised livestock, and worked diligently to provide for his family from the fruits of the land and sea. But, those were not easy times in the soon-to-be United States Virgin Islands. A feeling for the frustrations of the struggling St. John landholders of this era can be gained from a letter written by planter John Lindqvist, and cosigned by Carl Alexander Penn and four other St. John farmers, after the terrible hurricane that struck the island in 1916. In it, the group made an impassioned plea for financial relief from the Danish Crown:

San Jan D. W. Indies the 13th January 1917

To: His Excellency the Minister of Finance, Copenhagen

We the undersigned Planters of the Danish West Indies Island of San Jan do hereby on behalf of the poorer Planters, small land holders and Squatters of the island, beg to lay our conditions before Your Honor.

For the last fifteen years the economic state of the Island has deteriorated very much as want of capital has prevented us from cultivating the land as it should have been, and we have been compelled to limit ourselves to the raising of Cattle and Horses and in a few places Bay Leaves. The population has steadily grown poorer and after the outbreak of the War in Europe the conditions became worse for us, as our Cattle prices got reduced with about 30% owing to the stagnation in the Shipping in St.

Thomas which is our only market for Cattle, and the cost of living became more than 40% dearer.

We were practically on the brink of ruin when between the 9th and 10th of October 1916, the most terrible Hurricane broke on us and destroyed not alone the most of the Houses, but—which for us means far more—also the plantation of every description and our entire fencings. The Government has kindly granted loans, some with, some without interest to have the houses rebuild, but has not been disposed to grant us any assistance to replant our cultivations and to rebuild our fences. We have absolutely nothing in the ground to harvest, and no means whatever to plant, unless the Mother Country helps us out of our dire need by giving us as free gift sufficient money to enable us to recultivate our lands that we thereby again may be enabled to maintain ourselves and our families.

We beg to state that an amount of $25,000, twenty-five thousand dollars, will be sufficient to give us the necessary relief, and if such relief should be granted us it shall always be remembered as one of the last generous actions of our Mother Country to her suffering Children in this island.

> *Obediently and gratefully,*
> *A. White*
> *J. E. Lindqvist*
> *H. W. Marsh*
> *Carl A. Penn*
> *Carl E. Francis*
> *E. Harthmann*

Carl Alexander Penn died at Concordia in 1929. His grave lies down slope, to the north of the estate house—it is inscribed: "In Memory of Carl A. Penn." The last occupant of the Concordia house was Gladstone Mathias in the 1970s. He whimsically christened the house "The Sparrow Hotel," a name some locals still use when referring to the site.

February, 2000

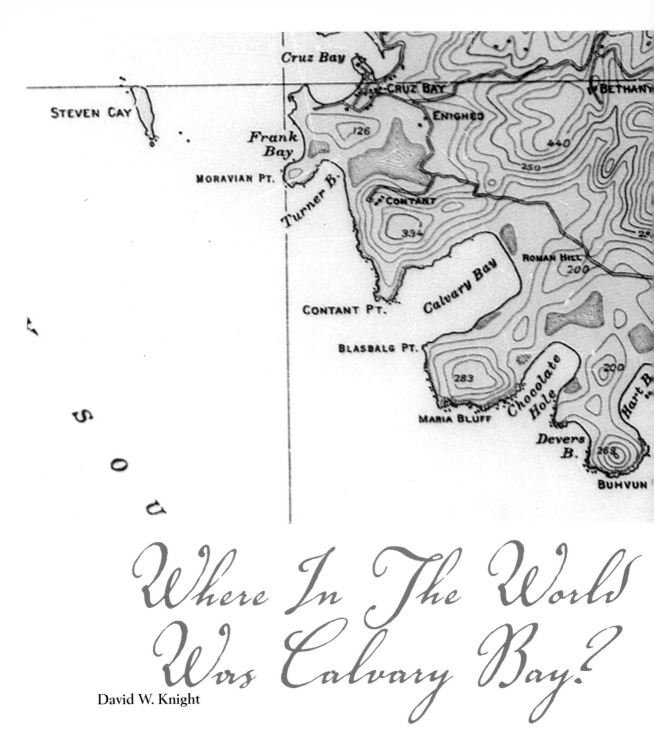

Where In The World Was Calvary Bay?

David W. Knight

Warren G. Harding, the twenty-ninth president of the United States, has consistently finished last in polls ranking the presidents. After Harding's untimely death in 1923, a variety of attacks and unsubstantiated claims left the public with a poor impression of him that has tarnished his reputation to the present day. So, why is his legacy of interest to the St. John Historical Society?

Immediately after transfer of the Danish West Indies to the United States in 1917, the first American governor, Rear Admiral James H. Oliver, sent an urgent message to the Navy Department stating that a complete geographical survey of the islands needed to be undertaken "at as early a date as practicable." Five months later, a team of engineers led by Lieut. O. W. Swainson of the U.S. Coast and Geodetic Survey office was dispatched to the

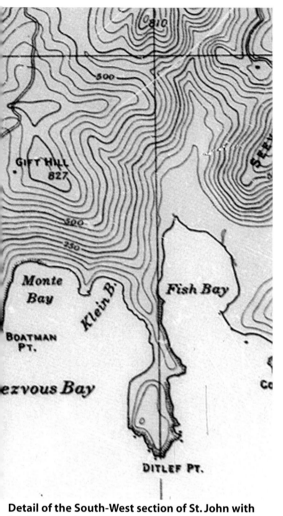

Detail of the South-West section of St. John with "Calvary Bay"

[U.S. Coast and Geodetic Survey map of St. John, 1935]

Virgin Islands to begin the arduous task of mapping the area.

Among the many problems Swainson's team encountered were the multiplicity of strange-sounding names that had come to be associated with places and geographical features throughout the islands. Indeed, under Danish rule no effort appears to have been made to standardize geographic distinctions, and in some cases the local community used a number of conflicting names to refer to a particular location. The job of sorting out this problem and deciding upon standardized names that would henceforth be utilized on all official maps and documents fell to the United States Geographic Board led by James W. McGuire.

It was to be many years before McGuire and his board, with the aid and advice from Danish scholars, regional historians, trusted informants, and local experts [including Capt. A. J. Blackwood of St. Croix, a relative of SJHS member Dan Smothergill], finalized a list of approved place names for the Virgin Islands. And, not until 1935 did the Coast and Geodetic Survey publish updated and revised topographic maps of the area utilizing McGuire's newly-standardized distinctions.

In determining place names, the Geographic Board had endeavored to avoid the use of same or similar names for different features. Therefore, *Great Cinnamon Bay* became simply *Cinnamon Bay*, while *Little Cinnamon*—or in Danish, *Klein Caneel Bay*—was officially changed to *Durloe Bay*, a reference to an early Danish settler. Similarly, it was decided that having two Cruz Bays [*Little Cruz Bay* and *Great Cruz Bay*] in such close proximity could only lead to confusion, so, seeing as *Cruz Bay* was also the name of a town, it was decided that the harbor that fronted the town would become simply *Cruz Bay*, while the name *Great Cruz Bay* would be changed.

This however led to a problem. *Great Cruz Bay* had always been called *Great Cruz Bay*, and no alternative name existed; the choice of a new name was left to an arbitrary decision by the Geographic Board. To come up with a name the Board turned to one of its advisors, President Warren G. Harding. Harding, taking the name *Great Cruz* as a reference to the Great Cross of Calvary, suggested the name be changed to *Calvary Bay*, to honor the Calvary Baptist Church in Washington DC, of which he was a member.

In the end, it seems that the name *Calvary Bay* was never widely accepted. When an updated map of St. John was published in 1958, President Harding's contribution to local place names was nowhere to be found.

February, 2002

Establishment of the Virgin Islands National Park

Bruce Schoonover

Laurance Rockefeller addressing the gathering at the dedication ceremony

(Photo courtesy of the Rockefeller Archive Center)

Fred Seton, Secretary, Department of the Interior, accepts the deeds for 5,086 acres of land on St. John

(Photo courtesy of the Rockefeller Archive Center)

Cruz Bay, St. John, VI, Saturday, December 1, 1956. It was reported that close to one thousand people gathered that sunny afternoon at the bandstand in Cruz Bay and were welcomed by Walter Gordon, the Governor of the Virgin Islands. The occasion was the dedication ceremony for the establishment of the Virgin Islands National Park. The afternoon had begun with a picnic in Cruz Bay Park for over 900 people, and had proceeded to the bandstand for the ceremony itself. The Reverend George Starling offered the invocation:

> *"OUR FATHER, we thank Thee for the occasion that brings us here today. As we see our island brought into national prominence, may we in deep humility accept it with grateful hearts. Thou hast said it is more blessed to give than to receive, therefore, give us the grace today to think not of what we can get but what we can give; that a new spirit may come into our island, with a new vision and a new purpose that Thou will delight to bless.*
>
> *Make us willing to share the good things we enjoy with all who come our way, and may this Park provide inspiration, enjoyment and recreation to all who are attracted to its shores. May it fulfill the every wish of those who caught the vision and labored to bring about this day. Keep from our shores and hearts all that would harm and mar, and help us to make this God's own country by living like God's own people, in the name of Jesus we pray. Amen"*

Thus began the formal ceremony which was the result of the federal enabling legislation that was signed into law by President Eisenhower. Importantly, the legislation provided that a minimum of 5,000 acres would need to be acquired and turned over to the National Park Service, and that not more than 9,485 acres could be included within the boundaries of the park on St. John. St. John consists of approximately 12,800 acres, so approximately 3, 000 acres was to be carved-out and reserved for private ownership.

From the beginning, the founders were adamant that the proposed park should not only benefit the nation as a whole, but should also benefit the locals, or natives, of the Island. It is for this reason that the population centers, Cruz Bay and Coral Bay, were to be outside the boundaries of the park. As Julius Sprauve, St. John's Senator to the Virgin Islands Legislature would state in a March 14, 1956 Daily News letter-to-the-editor piece, *"the remaining 3,000 acres includes all established communities, ninety percent of all arable land, all present port or boat entries and those which might be used for such purposes in the future."*

In the ceremony that day, Laurance S. Rockefeller formally presented the deeds to 5,086 acres of St. John land to Fred Seaton, Secretary of the Department of Interior and our nation's 29th National Park was formally established. This seemingly culminated a two and one-half year process. However, a closer look at the records reveals that the genesis of the park was some 20 plus years earlier.

As far back as the early 1930s, during the term of Dr. Paul Pearson, the first civilian Governor of the Virgin Islands, there was an interest in seeing St. John set aside as a park. Dr. Pearson recognized this as a way to build the tourist trade, and more importantly, help the economy. However, all these early efforts failed for a number of reasons, but it was certainly the turmoil in Europe in the late 1930s, and then the onset of World War II that would scuttle all efforts to establish a park in the 1940s.

Ultimately, there were five individuals who played pivotal roles in the establishment of the Virgin Islands National Park. They are:

Laurance S. Rockefeller (LSR), was the grandson of John D. Rockefeller, Sr., the founder of Standard Oil and the middle son of John D. Rockefeller, Jr. Laurance became known for the "three c's"—capitalism, conservation and cancer research. The Rockefeller family instituted the first medical research center in the U.S. in 1901 and LSR served on the board of the Memorial Hospital for Cancer and Allied Diseases and ultimately the board of Sloan-Kettering

Pictured (left to right) Laurance S. Rockefeller, Henry Beebe-construction engineer, Frank Stick, Senator Julius Sprauve and Reverend George Starling, c1956

(Photo courtesy Laurance S. Rockefeller Estate)

Institute for Cancer Research. In conservation, LSR and the Rockefeller family worked closely with the NPS to preserve thousands of acres of land, and they gave millions of dollars in support of numerous programs initiated by the NPS. In 1991, LSR received the Congressional Gold Medal of Honor in recognition of his lifelong contribution to the environment.

Frank Stick, was born in the Dakota Territory in 1884. He was an accomplished illustrator, conservationist and land developer. He moved to the Outer Banks of North Carolina in the 1920s and was instrumental in having land set aside for the Wright Brothers Memorial, the Fort Raleigh National Historic Site, and the Cape Hatteras National Seashore Park. He worked closely with the NPS in all these efforts.

Julius Sprauve, was a native of St. John. From 1936 to 1954 he served on the Virgin Islands' governing body—the Municipal Council—and was responsible for legislation which for the first time would make affordable land and housing widely available to St. Johnians. In 1954, Mr. Sprauve became St. John's first Senator and helped bring banking to St. John. He also improved transportation and was a

Harold Hubler is on the left and Conrad Wirth on the right, overlooking the Cruz Bay Battery, c1956

(Courtesy of Virgin Islands National Park)

tireless advocate for St. Johnians. Mr. Sprauve not only offered his own land to the Park, he was a great proponent of the establishment of the park and was the sponsor of the required Virgin Islands legislation for the Park.

Conrad Wirth's career with the NPS began in 1931 and he became its Assistant Director, Branch of Lands. In this capacity he was responsible for the evaluation of properties for future national parks and he also headed the NPS's Civilian Conservation Corp. (CCC) efforts. In 1939 he requested an evaluation of St. John as a national park. In 1951, he became the Director of the NPS, and remained so until he retired in 1964.

Harold Hubler who began his career with the NPS in 1934, was head of the CCC program in the VI in the 1930s, and he wrote a report on

making Reef Bay a territorial park in 1938. In 1939, the job of evaluating St. John as a potential future national park or recreational area fell to Hubler. In the 1950s he would update the 1939 report, and in 1957, he became the VINP's first Superintendent.

Coincidentally, Laurance Rockefeller and Frank Stick both made their way to St. John in 1952. Shortly thereafter, Laurance Rockefeller bought Caneel Bay Plantation, consisting of some 573 acres, and began renovation of the facility to make it his first environmentally-oriented resort.

About the same time, Frank Stick, along with four business partners, bought the Lameshur Estate consisting of 1,433 acres. They immediately began plans for also acquiring the Reef Bay estate and establishing a commercial venture on these properties. Within a year, Frank would abandon these plans in favor of proposing a National Park or Monument for St. John, as he had done earlier in the Outer Banks of NC. It is felt that his change of heart was due to a number of reasons, including: his age (70), his failing health (heart problems), realization of the effort and costs involved in achieving their objectives, and his son David's lack of enthusiasm about the project.

On May 30, 1954, Frank Stick wrote an extensive letter to Archie Alexander, Governor of the VI. At the same time, he proposed the park idea to LSR. It immediately resonated with LSR, and they agreed to meet. In September, meetings between LSR, Frank Stick, and Conrad Wirth were held, and it was agreed to proceed. LSR would fund and oversee the project with the assistance of his associate, Allston Boyer. Conrad Wirth would shepherd the necessary legislation through Congress, and Frank Stick would line up the options and purchase agreements for the land to be included within the park.

At a meeting in November 1954, Frank Stick surprised the group with the news that he had, in fact, obtained purchase options for sufficient property to achieve the minimum requirement of 5,000 acres. (Frank had done this at his own expense, and over the course of the next several years, consistently refused any compensation for his efforts in connection with the park.) The purchase options obtained by Stick were turned over to Jackson Hole Preserve, Inc. (JHPI) which would exercise the options on behalf of Laurance Rockefeller. It took the next two years

From Christiansfort to Calvary Bay

An aerial view of the western end of St. John, c1956
(Courtesy of the Estate of Laurance S. Rockefeller)

to do so, negotiating purchase arrangements for additional properties, passing the required enabling legislation in the VI Legislature and in Congress, and finalizing the plans for our nation's 29th National Park.

On December 1, 1956, in a ceremony in Cruz Bay Park, Laurance Rockefeller, on behalf of JHPI, turned over the deeds to 5,086 acres of land on St. John to Fred Seaton, Secretary of Interior. At this ceremony, it was reported that when Laurance Rockefeller got up to present the deeds, many of the local people got up and clapped and shouted "God bless Mr. Rockefeller." This fact was reported in a letter from Conrad Wirth to John D. Rockefeller, Jr. It appears that this was a sentiment that was widely held at the time. St. John Senator, Julius Sprauve, stated in a letter to the editor, in March 1956, the following:

"While the name of Laurance Rockefeller is mentioned in connection with the proposed national park, his past and proposed future benefactions have been too lightly dwelt upon. No man knows better than the writer, what Mr. Rockefeller's efforts so far have meant to people of St. John. I can state with complete conviction that during the past year and more, as the sole result of this generous and far seeing man's efforts, our people have enjoyed greater prosperity than at any time in the memory of our oldest inhabitants. And without these efforts, many of our people would have been in a condition approaching destitution and many would have been forced to seek precarious employment in distant lands, as has been the unhappy rule in years gone by."

According to records obtained from the Rockefeller Archive Center, JHPI paid a total of $962,100 for this initial acreage… or about $189 per acre. Following is a list of the parties that provided the initial land for the VINP:

Emily Creque....................................719 acres
Frank Stick and partners.................1,437
H.E. Lockhart Development Corp 843
Irving J. Backer 374
Frank R. Faulk 651
Julius Sprauve 225
Halvor Neptune Richards...................54
Claudia Joshua 150
Ralf Hartwell Boulon 59
Leonard and Silvia Cox.....................17
Gehardt Sprauve...............................39
Agnes and John Butler 57
Julia Chanler Laurin...........................40
Laurance S. Rockefeller 421

In a May 23, 1958 letter to Frank Stick, Laurance Rockefeller would confirm Stick's contribution to the park effort. In part, it states:

"… I greatly appreciate your outstanding contributions to the Virgin Islands National Park project. The gift of approximately $50,000 to the Jackson Hole Preserve, Inc., representing your share of the Lameshur land, was not only a generous gesture on your part but was a tangible evidence of your deep interest in the park project. You have undertaken this as a volunteer and you have consistently resisted our efforts to reimburse you for the enormous amounts of time and effort you have put into this project. Since that day many years ago when you brought the Hubler report to my attention and offered your lands, we have seen the project become a reality. I am sure that this achievement will be a lasting satisfaction to you. The Virgin Islands National Park will in the years to come mean more and more to people there and those who come to the Virgin Islands from all parts of the globe, in keeping with the hopes and expectations expressed at the time of its inception."

"Thus came into being on the Island of St. John the twenty-ninth National Park of the United States… as a sanctuary wherein natural beauty, wildlife and historic objects will be conserved unimpaired for the enjoyment of people and the generations yet unborn…" (Quoted from the dedication booklet.)

March, 2006

Chapter 2:
CREOLES AND CONTINENTALS

The Missionary and the Overseer

(The tragic story of Brother Jacob Tutweiler's visit to Mollendahl in 1744)

David W. Knight

Detail from an original print of the Moravian Mission Station of "Neu Herrnhuth" (or in English, New Herrnhut) on St. Thomas, 1757

(Courtesy D. Knight Collection)

On the sweltering summer morning of July 27, 1744, a young Swedish missionary, Jacob Tutweiler, made his way down the winding cart road to the isolated sugar plantation known as Mollendahl. Brother Tutweiler had often made the arduous journey from St. Thomas in order to carry the message of the Lord's salvation to the enslaved laborers on plantations throughout St. John, an island that did not yet have the benefit of a permanent Moravian Mission.[1]

The Mollendahl plantation was owned by the under-age heir of the deceased planter Gerhard Moll, who had been the original land grantee of the property in 1721. Although the senior Moll had been married numerous times he had left only one surviving male heir. As a child, Gerhard Moll Junior had been sent to live with his Grandparents in Amsterdam in order to receive a proper education.[2] Since his father's death in 1731, the young heir's properties in the Danish West Indies had been under the administration of his guardians, who, like the senior Moll before them, relied on hired overseers to run the plantations.[3]

As the late Gerhard Moll had been an established St. Thomas planter and wine merchant, accustomed to the comforts of his townhouse in Charlotte Amalie, his St. John property was not a place of fine amenities. Functional in design and utilitarian in nature, the Mollendahl plantation served only one purpose: to profit through the raising of sugar cane and the production of sugar. To this end, the plantation overseer aggressively drove the property's slaves in an effort to yield maximum reward for his employer. To Brother Tutweiler, the over-worked and harshly-treated slaves on the Moll plantation represented fertile ground for the sowing of the Gospel.

Upon reaching the high inland valley of Mollendahl, Brother Tutweiler sought out the property's overseer and requested permission to instruct the slaves in the word of God. Reluctantly, the overseer granted his consent and warily ordered the workers to put aside their labors so they might hear what the missionary had come to say. Inspired by this opportunity to administer to such a needy flock, Brother Tutweiler delivered a long and impassioned oration.[4]

At the conclusion of his sermon Tutweiler prepared to take his leave, only to find his way blocked by the now enraged overseer. Without warning the overseer grabbed the missionary by the arm and proceeded to violently beat him. As a stunned Tutweiler struggled to break free from his assailant's grasp, the overseer added a tirade of insults and threats to his abuses. When Tutweiler was finally able to gain his release, the emotionally shaken and badly injured Brother

beat an unsteady retreat from the Mollendahl property. Once again it had been vividly displayed to the Moravian missionaries in the Danish West Indies that while some of the colony's inhabitants believed all men were the children of God, many felt strongly that slaves were the children of but one master: the one who had laid out the silver to purchase them.

Jacob Tutweiler died on St. Thomas of "inflammatory fever" on December 10, 1744. It is not clear whether the severe beating he received at the hands of Mollendahl's overseer was in any way responsible for his death.

January, 2008

References:

[1]C.G.A. Oldendorp, (English Edition and Translation by Arnold R. Highfield and Vladimir Barac), *A Caribbean Mission*, Part 2, Book 3, Section 8, p. 404.

[2]West India and Guinea Company, Notorial Records 1713 - 1737, p. 497 - 499, March 18, 1737, [Rigsarkivet, Copenhagen, Denmark].

[3]West Indies Local Archive, St. Thomas Byfoged, Skiftaprotokol for Planters 1728 - 1735, Ltr G, p.104, July 17, 1731, [Rigsarkivet, Copenhagen, Denmark].

[4]C.G.A. Oldendorp, (English Edition and Translation by Arnold R. Highfield and Vladimir Barac), *A Caribbean Mission*, Part 2, Book 3, Section 8, p. 404.

John Wright, Outstanding Citizen of the Danish West Indies

A presentation by Per Nielsen; Summarized by Jan Frey

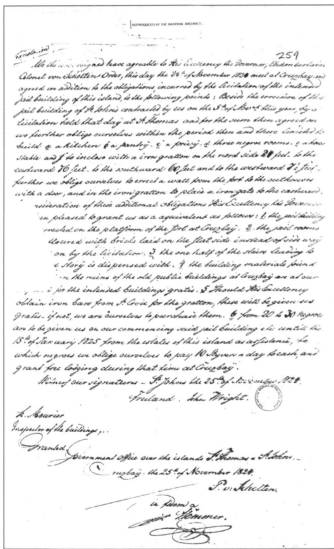

A copy of John Wright's contract to construct the Cruz Bay Battery, dated the 25th November 1824

(United States National Archives, Record Group 55, College Park, Maryland)

John Wright was an important figure in St. John and in Virgin Islands history. He was born enslaved in 1775 on St. John and worked for Pastor Sporon of the Dutch Reformed Church. Around 1796, he joined the ranks of the Free-Colored community by purchasing his freedom from wages earned as a carpenter. He later moved to St. Thomas where his presence is documented in the 1803 "Proceeding and Register of the Free Colored."

Wright owned a construction company and eventually became the fifth-largest property owner in the town of Charlotte Amalie on St. Thomas. He would buy old houses and repair them or take them down and build new ones. Professor Nielsen believes that Wright built a large number of private houses in St. Thomas, but had not uncovered any physical evidence of such construction until a written contract was unearthed in the Danish archives by David W. Knight.

Wright's work expanded to include large government contracts. He built the barracks on St. Thomas (which after the natural disasters of 1867 had to be rebuilt) that now houses the Virgin Islands Legislature. Most importantly for us, he built the Cruz Bay Battery, formerly called *Christiansfort*. Governor Peter C. F. von Scholten ordered the plans for the Battery drawn and on December 5, 1825, personally presided over the opening of the new courthouse and jail. Ruth Low, in her 1985 book *St. John Backtime*, referred to the Battery as "the embodiment of the island's historical continuity," because of association with von Scholten and as the site of all official actions on St. John to these modern times.

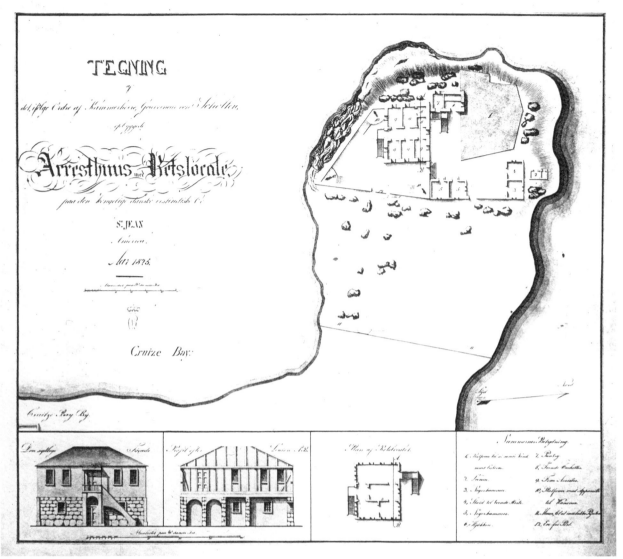

Ground plan and elevation drawings for the "Arrest-house & Courtroom" built by John Wright on the island of St. John, dated 1825

(Rigsarkivet, Copenhagen, Denmark)

John Wright fathered one daughter and two sons. Their mother was Theresa Sartorius, a "Free Mulatto" who owned a house on King Street in Charlotte Amalie. The children were sent to Moravian boarding schools in Denmark at early ages and the sons eventually followed careers in law and medicine. John Wright also bought a house in Cruz Bay for his mother, Edmuth Francis. He eventually married a woman by the name of Charlotte Sophia.

Professor Nielsen spoke of John Wright's concern for the improvement of the status of the Free Colored both in social and political standing. In 1786, the Ordinance of Governor-General Schimmelmann sought to regulate the social dress and activities of both enslaved Africans and the Free Colored. He wanted to counter the tendency to dress "fancy." The cost of such dress, he maintained, was "inappropriate to their rank and condition." Since "banquets

and festivities" given by people of color provided the occasions for the display of luxury, Schimmelmann proposed to regulate these more closely and to institute "more modest and proper forms of dress."

Accordingly all people of color were expressly forbidden to wear jewelry of precious stones, gold or silver, material of silk, brocade, chintz, lawn, linen, lace, or velvet; gold or silver braid; silk stockings; elaborate up-raised hair styles, with or without decoration; or any form of expensive clothing whatsoever. Under the Ordinance Free Colored were permitted to wear the "more modest and proper" dress prescribed for domestic and field slaves. Also permitted were wool, cotton, coarser varieties of lace, silk ribbon of Danish manufacture, a simple gold cross or silver ornament worn on the head, chest, or around the neck. The ornament was not to exceed 10 dollars in value. Pinafores of simple cambric were acceptable, as were head or neck-scarves of the same material.

At the end of the eighteenth century, the place of the Free Colored in the social order had more or less taken shape. Their numbers had grown in all three islands. The male leadership had been co-opted, and while some degree of status might have attached to ranks such as Freedman Captain, the avenues to status and economic mobility were shut. Their women folk, with marginally more access to the avenues of economic mobility, were no more mobile in status terms. The intention of the law, and the conventions as they evolved, was to ensure that the boundaries of ethnicity and class remained inviolate. The law emphasized the lowliness of all Free Colored as a status group by insisting on the "Free Brief," or certificate of freedom, but denying the "Burgher Brief," a certificate held as a matter of course by even the most inconsequential white resident or itinerant. No Free Colored held any position of trust under the Crown except as security personnel, and then largely for reasons of expediency, and their evidence was not admissible against a white person in the local courts.

The above world of the Free Colored was ably described by Neville A.T. Hall in his *Slave Society in the Danish West Indies* (University of West Indies Press, 1992).

John Wright signed and supported "The Freedman Petition of 1816," which was a long list of grievances that followed a request for privileges. It was delivered directly to the King in Denmark. The petition didn't work because the King would not accept any requests directly. The West Indians who delivered it were admonished for leaving their homes without approval of the government. It did however result in the creation of the local Fire Service staffed by members of the Free Colored community.

It is said that a definite indicator of wise men is the ability to learn from their errors. Next, the Free Colored employed the good and collegial offices of the Governor-General to carry their concerns to the King, and, this time, not as demands but praises. Governor-General Peter von Scholten was a leader of vision who not only saw the inevitability of emancipation, but also the steps necessary to obtain it. He was, however, mistaken in his perception of granting freedom. "Freedom can only be taken," as our own Guy Benjamin has so often said. Along with their requests, the Free Colored thanked the King with a proposal that he have a medal struck commemorating his approval of the Royal Ordinance of April 18, 1834. Five medals were struck in gold, which were graciously accepted by the King from the Free Colored for "We Ourselves"—as he officially referred to himself, his sons the crown princes and von Scholten. Medals were also struck in lesser metals and distributed to the leading members of the Free Colored community. This was a stupendous public relations ploy that resulted in equal status and burgher briefs or full business licenses in place of the demeaning Free-Colored identification papers.

John Wright's life was well lived and along with helping improve the lot of his fellow man he also left us the Battery in Cruz Bay, a daily reminder of his construction skills. Per Neilsen also told us of John Wright receiving the Order of Dannebrog from the King in 1834 for his role in fighting the devastating fire of 1832 in St. Thomas. Wright died in 1846 at the age of 71 and is buried in Western Cemetery on St. Thomas next to his wife Charlotte Sophia.

Per left us with a final admonition to preserve all of our cemeteries since we have important people buried in all of them. Isn't that the truth!

January, 2005

Huguenot at Lameshur: Captain Ingiald Mourier

Daniel Smothergill

Syracuse University Professor Emeritus Daniel Smothergill is a SJHS member who traces his ancestors back to 19th century St. John.

Denmark is well known for having allowed citizens of other countries to settle in its West Indies possessions. The English, in particular, took advantage of the policy and at one time owned a large number of the estates on St. John. This has special significance to me since it is part of the story of my 2nd great-grandfather William Smothergill, who owned Estate Enighed in Cruz Bay during the mid 19th century. He rather quickly went bankrupt, victim of a combination of Emancipation and a cholera epidemic. For the rest of his life he managed the estates of others on St. Croix.

Although William Smothergill was of English ancestry, he came to St. John from Ireland where his family had gone in the 17th century as part of the great historical movement known as the "Plantation of Ireland." I was reminded of these things by two articles in the splendid SJHS Newsletter.

One reported a hike around the East End and remarked that French Huguenot families once had settled there. The Huguenots were a Protestant group that found themselves unwelcome in Roman Catholic France and its colonial possessions. Large numbers left for England, North America, and Germany. Of those that went to Germany, a small contingent later moved on to Denmark. Could some of St. John's Huguenots have come from Denmark?

The same question was raised more pointedly in a second article on a trip planned to Estate Lameshur. For more than 40 years in the 19th century, Lameshur was owned by Captain Ingiald Mourier. Although the name has a

Daniel Smothergill at Lameshur Estate

(Photo by D. Knight)

distinctly French sound, Captain Mourier himself was Danish. Was his family among the refugee Huguenots that eventually wound up in Denmark?

The answer seems to be yes. Ingiald Katrik Jorgen Mourier was born in Copenhagen in 1807 to Frederic Guillaume Mourier and Louise Rothe. Tellingly, his grandparents, Frederic Moise Mourier and Marguerite Susanne le Sage de Fontenay, were married in the French Reformed Church in Copenhagen in 1757. Although the route by which the Mouriers got to Copenhagen is unknown, the main body of Huguenots in Denmark came at the invitation of King Fredrick IV in 1719.

On St. John, Ingiald Mourier owned the already combined estates Little and Great Lameshur in 1832. He appears to have transformed the plantation from cotton production to sugar. Later, in 1855, he rounded out his holdings by buying the neighboring Kabrithorn property from E. J. Weinmar.

Mourier married Catherine Ann DeWindt at Lameshur in 1833. Her half-sisters Lydia and Louisa moved in with them sometime later. The latter was to become my 2nd great-grandmother. The Mouriers themselves had 7 children, so life in the modest-sized estate house must have been somewhat cozy. How long Lydia and Louisa DeWindt lived at Lameshur is unclear. They were there in 1841. Lydia married John Smothergill in 1844, but Louisa still was at Lameshur in 1846. She married William Smothergill in 1853, probably at Lameshur. Ingiald Mourier was a testor at the wedding.

A clue, perhaps, to the as yet unborn Ingiald Mourier's military career appears in the 1801 census of Denmark. His parents and older siblings were residing then at the Artillery Institute in Copenhagen. Mourier's prominence on St. John is evidenced in the offices he held. In 1857 he was Town Captain and in 1870 Royal Cashier. He also is celebrated for having brought the news of Governor-General von Scholten's emancipation decree to St. John on July 4, 1848.

The estate house at Lameshur continues to stand to this day, providing a home for a family much as it did more than 150 years ago. That's tribute in my mind to the Huguenot Captain from Denmark who was such a part of life on St. John at that time.

April, 2007

John Gottliff: The Man Behind Buddoe

George F. Tyson

George Tyson is a SJHS member and Director of the St. Croix African Roots Project

Slavery in the Danish West Indies ended abruptly on July 3, 1848, contrary to the intentions of the Danish Government and Governor General Peter von Scholten. It ended because several thousand enslaved individuals on St. Croix staged a largely non-violent demonstration that forced a reluctant Peter von Scholten to proclaim freedom for all of the "unfree" on St. John, St. Thomas and St. Croix. This, however, is not how the story has been told in most books and textbooks.

Only recently have we begun to realize that Emancipation was a collective achievement of the enslaved, and that, moreover, it culminated decades of continuous, relatively peaceful, protest by many groups of heroic enslaved plantation laborers throughout the Danish West Indies. The story of emancipation as a popular movement began with the writings of the late Dr. Neville Hall in the 1980s. It has been continued by Dr. Svend Holsoe, who is preparing a major study of the Emancipation Rebellion from the bottom up. The path-breaking work of these scholars is based largely on testimonies of the enslaved participants recorded in the voluminous trial records compiled in the wake of the Emancipation. Their meticulous reconstructions of what took place in plantation villages and urban yards in advance of July 3, 1848 represent a necessary and important corrective to earlier histories. Thanks to this new research, men and women are emerging from the darkness of the past to take their rightful place in the historical record.

The large database of enslaved individuals on St. Croix being created by the St. Croix African Roots Project will also contribute to giving

John Gottliff, aka, "Budhoe," "Buddo," "Burdeaux" or "Moses Gottlieb"

(wood-cut rendering by Charles Taylor, c1888)

a voice and an identity to those who stepped forward in the name of Freedom. Its potential is indicated by the following biographical information about the one enslaved individual who until recently has been recognized as the only hero of 1848. I am referring, of course to John Gottliff, otherwise known variously as "Buddoe," "Buddo," "Bourdeaux," or "Moses Gottlieb."

LEANING THE YOUNG CANE ON THE SUGAR ESTATE

Cleaning the young cane on the sugar Estate, c1900

(Photo postcard by A. Duperly and Son, Kingstown, Jamaica)

John Gottliff was born enslaved on March 19, 1820 at Estate La Grange, a large sugar plantation located just outside of Frederiksted. His father's identity has not been ascertained. His mother was Maria Rosina, who had been born enslaved on La Grange plantation in 1799.

Maria Rosina was listed as a field worker in 1818, and as a member of the big gang in the censuses of 1841 and 1846. Besides John Gottliff, she gave birth to two daughters: Mathilde Petrus, born in 1829, and Leah [aka Sanchy] Petrus, born in 1832. Their father was John Peter/Petrus born enslaved on Estate La Grange in 1801. In 1846, Maria Rosina married Anthony George, a rat catcher on Estate Little La Grange. In 1850, Anthony joined Maria Rosina on Estate La Grange, where the couple lived and worked until the 1860s, when they moved to Frederiksted. Anthony George died in Frederiksted in 1873. Maria Rosina George died of a sudden hemorrhage on a Frederiksted street in 1877.

Maria Rosina's son, John Gottliff, appears in the censuses of 1841 and 1846 as belonging to the Lutheran Church and a member of the big gang. His character was described as "not too good" in 1841 and as "indifferent" in 1846. He was

imprisoned for three months in 1840 for theft and for three months in 1841 for "insolence." Obviously, he was not a submissive individual.

John Gottliff's activities on July 3, 1848 and the days that followed have been chronicled by many writers. Dr. Svend E. Holsoe has provided the most reliable account, which is based on eyewitness testimonies extracted from official court records and other first-hand accounts. Holsoe shows that Gottliff was one of several figures that stood out among the crowd on July 3rd, but that he did not appear to be directing the action. After July 3rd, instead of joining those seeking revolution or retribution, Gottliff rode around the countryside urging protesters to lay down their weapons, cease looting and property destruction and return to work. Nonetheless, after calm had been restored, he was arrested and imprisoned by the Danes as a ringleader of the insurrection.

Gottliff's role as an instigator of the rebellion is somewhat controversial. Throughout his intensive interrogations, he steadfastly maintained that he had nothing to do with organizing or leading the uprising. Holsoe has reached much the same conclusion and has identified Moses Robert of Estate Butler Bay and others as the principle organizers. But, several insurgents did identify John Gottliff as the chief organizer, and this role has been tentatively accepted by Dr. Neville Hall and, less critically, by other historians.

Whatever the truth of the matter, the Danish colonial officials decided, without a trial, to deport John Gottliff from the island in 1848. Documentary evidence has recently emerged that he was landed in Trinidad. He later made his way to New York City, where he appeared in the office of anti-slavery crusader Lewis Tappan in 1850. Thereafter, nothing further is known of him.

Among the many legacies John Gottliff left behind on St. Croix, was a daughter named Rebecca Bordeaux. Rebecca was born free on December 16, 1841. Her mother was Eliza/Elise/Ann Eliza Jackson, a free woman of color living in Frederiksted at the time of Rebecca's birth.

Eliza Jackson was born circa 1821 on the island of St. John. In 1829, she came to St. Croix from St. John with her mother Mary Ann Gutliff. The background of Mary Ann Gutliff on St. John remains to be explored. Born enslaved, she may have lived on Estate Carolina in Coral Bay, for in the St. Croix Free Colored Census of 1831-32 it is recorded that William Beech, an attorney working for the Schimmelmann's, (owners of both Estate Carolina and Estate La Grange), certified that she had been "given free."

With her daughter Eliza and grand-daughter Rebecca, Mary Ann Gutliff moved from Frederiksted to Estate La Grange in 1852. They lived and worked there until early 1860, when they moved back to Frederiksted. Mary Ann Gutliff died in Frederiksted of old age in 1877. Her daughter, Eliza Jackson died of natural causes in the Frederiksted hospital.

The fate of Rebecca Bordeaux, like that of her father, remains unclear. No one with that name could be located in the census, church or death records of St. Croix after 1860. In the 1880 census, a Rebecca "Gutlieb," born in 1841, appears as owning and living at Friedensthal No. 12, on the outskirts of Christiansted. But, Gutlieb was her married name, which she took from her husband Frederik Gutlieb, 32 years of age. This Rebecca appears as widow "Gutloff" in the 1901 census. She died in Christiansted in 1905. As far as can be determined she left no descendants. Was she Buddoe's daughter? Or did Rebecca Bordeaux leave St. Croix forever in the 1860s, perhaps to join her father in the United States? Hopefully, the answer will one day be revealed as we dig ever deeper into the marvelously rich archives compiled about our ancestors by the Danes.

June, 2006

The Life and Heritage of Carl Emanuel Francis of St. John

David W. Knight

Carl Emanuel Francis, c1905

(Photo- National Museum Copenhagen, DK)

Ebony in complexion, brash and aristocratic in deportment, zealous and public spirited by nature, outspoken, and often controversial, Carl Epolite Emanuel Francis[1] dedicated much of his life to community service and the betterment of the people of St. John. The son of a former slave, Carl Francis was born May 13, 1867, in the rural hinterlands of Denmark's West Indies colony. His rise to prominence in a period of declining fortunes and harsh social injustice is an intriguing story from any perspective. But, to fully grasp the breadth of his character, one must first explore the historical context of his development and the roots of his heritage [Holdridge, 1936; Knight, 2001; Moolenaar, 1992].

The early half of the nineteenth century was marked by increasing unrest amongst the enslaved laborers on plantations throughout the Danish West Indies. Nowhere in the colony was this situation so apparent as on the isolated estates of St. John, where one or two hired overseers were generally responsible for controlling large enslaved populations that often outnumbered them more than fifty to one. Under such conditions tensions ran high and during this period one overseer on the Annaberg sugar plantation was poisoned, while another died under suspicious circumstances. Force, therefore, was often seen as a necessary deterrent, and punishments such as detainment or restraint in the properties' stocks were dealt out liberally by the overseers. For more serious offenses, the local judge (Landfoged) was empowered, and indeed mandated by law, to take harsher measures [SJLD, 1828-56; SJPJ, 1829-55].

It was amidst these turbulent and uncertain times that a young man by the name of George Francis made the awkward transition into manhood in a sprawling slave village below the imposing windmill tower of the Annaberg plantation. Already a widower by age nineteen, George worked diligently to gain the respect of his fellow workers, as well as his influential master, Hans H. Berg. By the time the 1846 census was compiled, Francis was among the most trusted of the estates' enslaved laborers [SJR, 1835 & 1846].

Emancipation, declared in the Danish West Indies in 1848, seems to have had little immediate effect on the isolated plantations of St. John. Limited opportunity and a strict contract labor code forced most formerly enslaved individuals to remain on the estates under rapidly declining conditions. This was the case with George Francis, who by 1850 had gained the position of "driver" (the leader of the work-gangs). Sometime in or about 1845, George Francis married Hesther Dalinda, a young woman who had been born enslaved on the neighboring Munsbury plantation, where she had lived all of her life. Secure in his new position as driver, Francis felt confident that a request to allow his wife to leave Munsbury and join him at Annaberg would not be refused. And indeed, a short time later Hesther and her children, Peggy and Johannes, were all reported to be living at Annaberg [SJR, 1835, 1846, 1850, & 1855; Carstensen, 1897; SJLUC, 1850].

Over the course of the succeeding decades, George Francis encountered opportunities that in his youth must have seemed unimaginable. In the 1860 census for Annaberg, Francis's position was listed as estate "overseer," and two years later he received clear and outright title to a two-acre parcel of land on Mary's Point by the will of his former master, Hans H. Berg. But, George Francis's ambitions did not stop there. Through hard work and frugality he managed to save enough money for a down payment on the remainder of the Mary's Point property when it came up for auction during Hans Berg's probate reconciliation [SJR, 1860; STEP, 1862; SJA, 1850-1865; Carstensen, 1897].

George Frances's wife, Hesther, died only a short time after their purchase of the Mary's Point estate. The couple's possessions, itemized in Hesther's probate inventory compiled on September 29, 1864, display the relative wealth the Francis family had attained by that date:

18 Head of Cattle	1 Row Boat
40 Sheep	2 Bedsteads with Bedding
3 Asses	2 Tables
2 Horses	1 Press
1 Decked Boat	18 Chairs
'The Ester of St. John'	
1 doz. Plates, Knives, Forks, Spoons and Glasses	
[SJCP, 1864]	

A year after Hesther's death George Francis married for a third time to Lucy Ann Blydon. Together the couple lived on and worked the Mary's Point property, and in the 1870 census for the estate, Francis had the gratification of listing his profession as "Planter" [SJA, 1864-1870; SJR, 1870].

In 1871 George Frances encountered what was perhaps his greatest opportunity. After the buildings and crops on the Annaberg and Leinster Bay plantations were destroyed in the devastating back-to-back hurricane and earthquakes of 1867, the owner of the estates, Thomas Letsom Loyd, fell heavily into debt and could not afford to rebuild the properties. After enduring years of pressure from his creditors, Loyd finally "quit" the colony to evade his obligations. Upon his departure, Loyd signed over title to both Annaberg and Leinster Bay to his former property manager, George Francis, for the sum of $100 [SJA, 1865-1875; STM, 1871].

George Frances died on St. John in 1875. At the time of his death he had recently completed the construction of a small sugar factory at Mary's Point, and was endeavoring to reintroduce sugar cane cultivation on his properties. The burden of managing and maintaining George Francis' vast holdings now fell to his wife Lucy and their five children: their oldest son, Carl, was only eight years old at the time [STSJCP, 1875; SJA, 1872-1875; STR, 1870].

After George's death the Francis family valiantly struggled to maintain the quality of life they had worked so long to achieve, but with labor difficulties, diminishing revenues, and mounting debts, they soon began to feel the sting of poverty. As young men, Carl and his brother Fritz[2] were forced to leave St. John in search of economic opportunity. As was the case with so many Virgin Islanders of the time, Carl emigrated to the Dominican Republic where he found work in that country's active agricultural sector. For twelve years he diligently toiled, sending money home and saving whatever he could [STSJCP, 1875; SJCP, 1909; Moolenaar, 1992; Jadan, 2001].

By 1900, while still residing in the Dominican Republic, Carl Francis had accumulated enough capital to secure, or reacquire, much of his family's property on St. John—including Estate Annaberg, which had been put up for auction due to nonpayment of taxes. After his mother's death in 1901, Carl returned to St. John and took up his rightful place as head of household in the Francis home at Mary's Point. With strength and conviction he vigorously set out to redevelop the family's long-neglected land holdings. According to oral sources, Carl first attempted to convert much of the property to mixed agriculture, but after his fruit crops yielded inferior results he made the decision to concentrate on animal husbandry [SJCP, 1900; STM, 1900; SJA, 1899-1905; Near (Edwards), 2000; Lightbourn, 1921].

It was during this period that Carl Francis became increasingly concerned over the worsening economic conditions and oppressive disparities that plagued his homeland. Never a man to stand idly by, Carl's energetic and authoritative demeanor naturally led him to the role of community activist, for which he soon garnered the attention, and respect, of Danish West Indies authorities. One of the prominent individuals Carl Francis met and befriended was the Minister of the Lutheran Church on St. Thomas, Christian Krag, whose duties included overseeing the small Lutheran congregation on St. John. Pastor Krag served the Lutheran Church in the Danish West Indies from 1897 though 1904. Immediately prior to his return to Denmark, Krag paid one last visit to his friend Carl Francis, who had regularly assisted with church affairs on St. John. At that meeting, Carl presented the Pastor with a small photo portrait of himself, on the back of which he inscribed: "Carl E. Francis Present to Rev'd Krag. Febr 14/05 Mary's Point St. John." In 1971, this photograph was donated to the National Museum in Copenhagen by Pastor Krag's daughter-in-law (see page 60) [Larsen, 1950; Per Nielsen, personal correspondence 08/02/05].

A well established and prosperous cattle dealer by 1909, Carl Francis married Amy Elizabeth Penn in the Emmaus Moravian Church in Coral Bay, after which, the couple took up residence in a house Carl had built amidst the ruins of the former Annaberg sugar factory. In October of the following year Amy gave birth to the first of their two children, a son, Earl[3] [Moolenaar, 1992; Jadan, 2001; VIC, (1917) 1920].

Throughout these years Carl continued to be active in community affairs. While as a younger man he attended the Moravian Church and stated his religion as Moravian in the 1911 census, he later served for fifteen years as clerk and lay reader to the Lutheran Congregation on St. John. For many years Francis held the title of Maho Bay Quarter Officer, a position that carried broad responsibilities for a large section of the island, and in 1913 he was honored by Governor Helweg-Larsen with an appointment to the colony's governing body, the Colonial Council, in which he served for two decades. As St. John's highest ranking representative, it was Carl Francis who was chosen to hoist the first American Flag over government headquarters on St. John during that island's formal ceremony of the transfer of the Danish West Indies to the United States on April 15, 1917. It has been stated by one eyewitness to the occasion that Francis was "in his glee" [Moolenaar, 1992; Jadan, 2001; Larsen, 1950; Larsen, 1940; Lightbourn, 1921; Low & Valls, 1985].

Under United States rule, Carl Francis carried on his efforts to bring improved services and broader economic opportunity to the residents of St. John. Although in his later years he became notorious for openly expressing his frustration over the "laziness" of the islands' inhabitants, it is clear that he saw their malaise as a symptom of larger sociopolitical ills, rather than an inherent tendency [Lightbourn, 1921; Franck, 1920; Holdridge, 1937].

To the end Francis remained a staunch advocate for improved inter-island communications, an expanded and accessible educational system, and the establishment of an agricultural bank that would make affordable loans available to small farmers and encourage self-sufficiency. Due to failing health he retired from public service in 1933, and died on the island of St. Thomas at the age of eighty-nine on October 26, 1936 [Franck, 1920; Moolenaar, 1992].

Even today, Carl Francis's name is spoken with reverence and respect on the island of St. John: a very remarkable man indeed.

January, 2007

Footnotes

[1]For most of his life Mr. Francis used the name Carl Emanuel Francis, however, census documents record him respectively as: Carl H. Francis, at the age of three in 1870; Epolite Francis, at the age of thirteen in 1880; and, Carl E. Francis, at the age of forty-three in 1911.

[2]Fritz Francis is known to have been in Gonâve, Haiti, as late as 1902.

[3]The Francis's second child was a daughter, Carmen, born in 1917.

Primary Sources:

[SJA] Central Management Archives, West Indies Audit Registers for St. John, 1755 - 1915 (Rigsarkivet, Denmark).

[SJCP] Record Group 55, Entry 720, Case Papers Before the St. John Probate Court, 1849 - 1909 (U. S. National Archives II, College Park, Maryland).

[SJLD] West Indies Local Archives, St. John Landfoged, Diverse Correspondence, 1828 - 1856 (Rigsarkivet, Denmark).

[SJLUC] West Indies Local Archives, St. John Landfoged, Unarranged Correspondence, 1851 - 1875 (Rigsarkivet, Denmark).

[SJPJ] West Indies Local Archives, St. John. Landfoged, Police Journals, 1829 - 1892 (Rigsarkivet, Denmark).

[SJR] Central Management Archives, Registers [Censuses] for St. John., 1835 - 1911 (Rigsarkivet, Denmark).

[STEP] West Indies Local Archive, St. Thomas Byfoged, Executors' Probates, 1778 - 1868 (Rigsarkivet, Denmark).

[STM] St. Thomas / St. John Mortgage & Deed Registers, NA (Office of the Recorder of Deeds, St. Thomas, Virgin Islands).

[STSJCP] Record Group 55, Entry 647, Case Papers Before the St. Thomas and St. John Probate Court, 1870 - 1917 (U. S. National Archives II, College Park, Maryland).

[VIC] Department of Commerce, Record Group 29, Records of the Bureau of Census 1920, Virgin Islands [compiled in 1917] (U. S. National Archives, Washington, DC).

Published Sources:

A Riis Carstensen, *Over Viden Strand; Livs og Rejseskildringer* (København, Forlagt Af Universitetsboghandler G. E. C. Gad, Thieles Bogtrykkeri, 1897).

Harry A. Franck, *Roaming Through The West Indies* (New York, Blue Ribbon Books, 1920).

Desmond Holdridge, *Escape To The Tropics* (New York, Harcourt, Brace and Company, 1937).

David W. Knight, *Annaberg, An Updated Survey of the Annaberg Factory Complex, Virgin Islands National Park, St. John. USVI, With Overviews of Contributing Sites Within The Annaberg Historic District* (USVI, Virgin Islands Historical & Genealogical Resource Center [for the Virgin Islands National Park], 2001).

Jens Larsen, *Virgin Islands Story, A History of the Lutheran State Church, Other Churches, Slavery, Education, and Culture in the Danish West Indies, now the Virgin Islands* (Philadelphia, Muhlenberg Press, 1950).

Kay Larsen, *Guvernører Residenter, Kommandanter og Chefer* (Copenhagen, Denmark, Arthur Jensen Forlag, 1940).

Alberic G. Lightbourn, *Lightbourn's Annual and Commercial Directory of the Virgin Islands of the United States for 1921* (St. Thomas, Alberic Lightbourn, 1921).

Ruth Hull Low & Rafael Valls, *St. John. Backtime, Eyewitness Accounts from 1718 to 1956* (St. John, U. S. Virgin Islands, Eden Hill Press, 1985).

Doris Jadan, "Carl Francis Family Epitomizes St. Johnians' Leadership, Service," St. John Tradewinds, March 5-11, 2001 [St. John, Thomas A. Oat, Editor and Publisher, 2001].

Ruth Moolenaar, *Profiles Of Outstanding Virgin Islanders*, Third Edition (USVI, Department of Education, 1992).

Don Near, "100 Years at Annaberg Plantation," St. John Times, November 2000 [St. John, June Bell Barlas, Editor and Publisher, 2000]. Note: This article relies exclusively upon information from an unpublished report written by St. John historian Steven Edwards.

The Boulon Family

A Presentation by Rafe Boulon; Summarized by Vicki Bell

Ralf and Jane Boulon with Rafe, at Trunk Bay, 1952

(Photo courtesy Rafe Boulon)

Rafe Boulon began his family story in the early 1900s when his great grandfather was a meteorologist in Puerto Rico, starting in 1908. Rafe's grandfather met his grandmother and moved to Puerto Rico where he had a refrigeration business. In 1927, while visiting Denis Bay with the Puerto Rico Fishing Club he purchased 100 acres for $5,000 which included Trunk Bay. Rafe's father was born in Puerto Rico but grew up at Trunk Bay. His mother was born in Boston and traveled to the Virgin Islands at the age of 21 "on a lark," met his father, and the rest is history.

In 1956, the Boulon family sold approximately 59 acres of non-beachfront Trunk Bay property to Laurance S. Rockefeller, in connection with the then proposed Virgin Islands National Park. And, in 1957, they sold the beachfront property to the Park Service, keeping only the 3 acres of the "Windswept" peninsula for their own.

Rafe talked about, and showed pictures of, his "crib with a view" looking back across Trunk Bay from what is now the Ranger residence at the eastern end of Trunk Bay Beach. He recalled having Leatherback sea turtles as playmates, and how the area that is now the parking lot at Trunk Bay was a dense grove of fruit trees, supplying fruit and produce for the family guest house. Tortola sloops sailed in regularly at Trunk Bay, delivering produce, or offering a lift over to St. Thomas for the day.

Rafe noted that it was around 1955 that Colonel Julius Wadsworth, who had purchased the land at Denis Bay Beach and the adjacent hill top where the mill is located, constructed the "Christ of the Caribbean" statue at what is now called Peace Hill. The Colonel's hope and dream at the time was to gather all the leaders of the world and establish world wide peace.

Rafe's family ran a small guest house with 8 to 10 rooms at Trunk Bay. Guests on their way to Trunk Bay would be entertained by Mama Dohm at the Red Hook dock while they awaited transportation to St. John. It was sometimes a long wait, but Mama Dohm was quite affable and hospitable, and the guests enjoyed whiling away the time with her, until a boat arrived for them.

Rafe remembered being paid to gather up cigarette butts at Gallows Point for then-owners "Duke" and Kay Ellington. But, Rafe recalled that when his parents found out about this occupation they put a swift halt to it.

There were few roads on St. John, none paved, but many trails, and Rafe spent countless hours, even days, out exploring the island, often camping in old sugar mills. Fishing was big at Mary's Point, Cruz Bay Creek, and anywhere they could fish or set a fish trap. Thus the children on St. John stayed very busy exploring their island home, and catching dinner for their families.

In 1958 the Boulon family moved to Puerto Rico, but returned to build a stone house at Windswept Beach next to Trunk Bay that was used for summers and other vacations until 1964, when the family moved back to St. John. Today, Rafe, his wife Kimberly and their two sons, Devon and Revel live in a house they built at Windswept.

April, 2006

Tortola sloop departing Trunk Bay after delivering produce, mail or people to the Trunk Bay Estate Guesthouse, c1955

(Photo by Jane Boulon)

The Gibney Family

Eleanor Gibney

Robert and Nancy Gibney came to the West Indies from New York City in 1946. They were on their honeymoon, and planned to spend just a few months in the islands. Nancy had quit her job as a features editor at Vogue magazine, and Robert planned to write a novel; he was 31 and Nancy was 25.

After a few days in Haiti, then a top destination for American tourists, the Gibneys came on eastward, looking for a simpler and less populated island. They found St. John, and Robert felt immediately at home. The couple rented a tiny cottage—no plumbing or electricity—on Cruz Bay beach, then an almost imperceptible village of 80 people. Several weeks later they met Julius and Cleome Wadsworth, the owners of Denis Bay—and St. John's first part-time winter residents. When the Wadsworths returned to the states, they offered Denis Bay rent-free to the Gibneys until the following winter. Over that summer Nancy also fell in love with St. John, so when the Wadsworths came back at the end of the year there was no question of the Gibneys leaving the island. Instead, they moved to the only available housing: a shed on Henley Cay, the 11-acre island off Caneel Bay. Henley Cay then belonged to St. Thomas resident Rog Humphries, who had no immediate plans for the cay. Robert and Nancy lived on Henley Cay for three years.

Early in 1950, Robert's father died, leaving enough money that the Gibneys began looking seriously at buying land on St. John. They made an offer on the property at the eastern side of Hawksnest Bay that was then known as Hawksnest Beach (Today's popular Hawksnest Beach was then part of Caneel Bay Estate and known as Little Hawksnest). The absentee owner, Herbert Stevens of Boston, had previously rejected many offers for the land, as had his father before him. Much to their surprise, the Gibneys' offer was accepted.

The Gibney house was built of the stone, collected on the site, by Robert and a crew of St. Johnian masons. Cement and all other materials were landed by sailboats on the beach. The Gibneys soon shipped down their New York furniture and a vast library of books that had been in storage for years. Although jeeps were to arrive on the north shore within a year or two, Ed Gibney, the first child, was born just as the family moved off Henley Cay and into the barely finished house, and Nancy often recalled walking the five-mile round trip to Cruz Bay with Ed in her arms for his first check-up; the doctor came only once a week from St. Thomas, and the outboard motor on their small boat was broken.

A varied and interesting group of Robert's and Nancy's friends from the circles of New York literature, art , and fashion visited St. John over the years, and they thoroughly enjoyed the company of St. Johnians and the adventurous travelers who came and went from the island in that era. Nancy's beauty and elegance are long remembered on St. John, and Robert's formidable grasp of both practical and intellectual knowledge in many fields—from watch repair to 18th century French literature—made him popular with a wide range of acquaintances.

All three of the Gibney children were home-schooled by Robert, who preferred to work without a set schedule as general "fixer" of all manner of machinery, generators, etc. He often helped the Boulons at Trunk Bay and the Ellingtons at Gallows Point with the maintenance of those properties. Robert also worked for Caneel Bay during the Rockefeller expansion of the resort in the 1950s. He

Nancy Gibney (L) and *Vogue* magazine friend Sarah Lee at Denis Bay; Robert Gibney in Coral Bay, 1947

(photos courtesy of Eleanor Gibney)

eventually took a regular job in the 1960s as librarian in Cruz Bay for several years.

Nancy had won prizes in writing competitions as a student and in her early years on St. John, and wrote short fiction that was regularly published by the "women's" magazines such as McCall's and Redbook, under the name Nancy Ferard. She taught creative writing at what was then the College of the Virgin Islands in the 1960s, and both Gibneys were frequent substitute teachers at the Cruz Bay public school.

Robert Gibney died in 1973, Nancy in 1980. They are both buried near the sea in the Cruz Bay cemetery, a few hundred feet from where they first lived on the island.

April, 2006

Restoration at Cinnamon Bay; a Callwood Legacy

Presentation by Reggie Callwood; Summarized by Bruce Schoonover

A skilled mason and former Virgin Islands National Park employee, Reggie Callwood put in forty years of committed work to stabilize and restore historic ruins throughout the V. I. National Park on St. John.

Reggie Callwood, 1987 and today

(Photos courtesy Virgin Islands National Park and Bruce Schoonover)

Affectionately known to most folks on St. John as "Reggie," Mr. Callwood was born on Tortola but has called St. John home since the age of 16. Reggie worked for the VINP from 1958 to 1968, and then again from 1977 until he retired in 1996. During this time, he worked on stabilization efforts at all of the Park sites that are now open for public visitation, including: the Cinnamon Bay sugar factory, the Annaberg sugar factory, the Annaberg Country School, the Cathrineberg windmill, the Mary's Point (Francis Bay) sugar works, the Lameshur Bay factory, the Reef Bay factory, the Par Force estate house, and the customs house on Whistling Cay.

In his wonderfully soft-spoken way, Mr. Callwood explained the often arduous task of working on the ruins on St. John, many of which required great effort to access and bring in the needed materials. While he and his crew initially had the benefit of guidance from Mr. Fred Gjessing—a long-time employee of the VINP and an expert on colonial-era architecture—for the most part, Mr. Callwood and his coworkers were left on their own to make decisions as to how the work would be carried out.

Reggie described how his crew always endeavored to restore the ruins as accurately as possible. Their task often involved salvaging bricks, coral and other building materials

from distant sites, or retrieving heavy coppers (kettles used for boiling down the cane juice) from where they had been relocated for use as watering troughs after the sugar factories ceased operation. In some cases, traditional skills and a knowledge of historic building practices were required, such as the harvesting and hand shaping (with a hatchet) of brain coral to replace missing corners and keystones, the use of beach sand for making mortar, and the use of a donkey to carry materials to the more remote sites.

While in earlier times locally-made quicklime (coral and shells mined from the sea and heated in a limekiln to make a cement-like substance) was used as mortar, Reggie explained that he used commercial bagged cement to which he added additional lime in order to strengthen the mix and give the mortar a more authentic look. He pointed out to the group that many of the walls that appear to be of original construction have actually been totally replaced. A common technique used in the restoration work was to carefully measure and dismantle badly damaged components and rebuild them in order to achieve a more uniform appearance.

When asked if after his retirement in 1996 anyone at the Park had taken on the responsibility of continuing his efforts, Reggie indicated that, sadly, little has been done over the past ten years in that regard. David W. Knight commented that while many of the factory ruins on St. John do indeed date back to the 1700s, they have only survived because they had periodic and continuing maintenance during their operational life-spans, which, in some cases, ran well into the early 20th century. He stressed the importance of ongoing maintenance and the need for further stabilization if the historic ruins in the Park are to be preserved for future generations to learn from and enjoy.

Mr. Callwood's pride in his efforts and love of his work were clearly evident in the tone of his voice, the twinkle in his eyes, and in the stories he told. Like all of the sites he has worked on over the years, Mr. Reggie Callwood is truly one of St. John's treasures. We are honored to have had him share his knowledge and insights with our members and guests.

March, 2006

Mr. Callwood speaking at the ruins of the Cinnamon Bay Sugar Factory

(Photos by Bruce Schoonover)

A visit to the ruins of Estate Hope in the Reef Bay Quarter, c1900

(Image from "The Danish Atlantic Islands" [Copenhagen, Denmark, 1907])

Chapter 3:
RUINS AND RAMBLES

Lovango Cay Excursion

Summarized by Robin Swank

Picturesque Smith Cottage

(Photo by Robin Swank)

The motor vessel "Sadie Sea" was loaded to her (legal) gills with a cargo of St. John Historical Society members and their provisions. We were crossing a tumultuous Pillsbury Sound to Lovango Cay to see some old and some new real estate.

Toni and Wally Leopold's motley crew of canines, led by the terrifying Daisy, welcomed us at their dock. Our first explore was of the Leopold's enchanting house. Its beautifully crafted beams reclaimed from the Great Salt Lake, open living areas, eclectic furnishings, and humorous signage were wonderfully interwoven with the reality of its desalination plant, solar panels, battery farm, and a "barnyard" of cared for animals.

After touring this modern house, we walked east along the beach toward Smith House and Smith Cottage, earlier and more modest incarnations of living off the grid. The Smith House foundation probably dates from the

Lovango Cay Historical Timeline 1728-1934

Compiled by David W. Knight, *Annotated with commentary and discussion during our Lovango Explore*

1728, Oct. 18 – Deed to Lovango granted to **William Gandy,** a carpenter and planter of English Caribbean background, by the Danish West India & Guinea Company, with an 8-year tax amnesty to encourage plantation development. Gandy was a master carpenter who had worked for the DWI & GC in St. Thomas. He had previously been granted a waterfront parcel on Cinnamon Bay in 1722, which he sold to Peter Durloo, in 1728. (RA/DWIGC/SJLL, 1728-39)

1730 – William Gandy is found dead in his hammock on Lovango, believed to have been killed by his slaves. As the corpse is rapidly decomposing, he is buried immediately, wrapped in his hammock. The sole heir is his wife **Elizabeth**; the estate is valued at 300 Rigsdallers. (RA/Martfeldt, 1765)

1732 – Probate of **Elizabeth Gandy:** her daughters **Anna Maria Mauor** (married to Dedrick van Still) and **Rachel Mauor** (married to Johannes Jansen) inherit Lovango and a house in Charlotte Amalie equally (RA/VLA/SkiftePro/Ltr.B.1724-32)

Thereafter, but prior to 1751 – According to an account of the cays of St. John by Christian Martfeldt, a Danish economist, (c1765), Gandy's sole remaining heir is noted as "old Madam Other" (pronounced as in Otter Creek). He goes on: "As she could not, because of poorness, resume at the cay, it was left alone and unworked…." (RA/Martfeldt, 1765)

1751-1752 – A British subject **Conners** applies for and receives a land patent, from the General Government of Antigua, on Lovango as a deserted island. As late as 1765 he is still upholding his claim and cultivating provisions on the cay. (RA/Martfeldt, 1765)

Meanwhile (c. 1756) – The Danish Crown takes possession of Lovango late 1700s or early 1800s; as such it is one of the oldest structures in Cruz Bay Quarter still standing. It has, however, been reconstructed a number of times and one has to look hard to find its historical roots.

Smith Cottage, a mid-twentieth century structure of white Portland cement and blue shutters, with a corrugated roof, also sits ocean-side. Behind it is a very large depression in the earth, possibly the remains of a pit used either to burn coral to make quicklime, or to make charcoal, industries for which Lovango was commonly used.

SJHS member Eleanor Gibney gathered us on the beach to review the earlier history of the Cay. She began by debunking one story of the derivation of its name. It's a good touristy invention, a charter captain's story, that there was a brothel on the island, and that the name springs from Love and Go, she says, but it's not so. Pronounced and sometimes written Lu'ongo or Loango, the cay's name more likely comes from the name of an African kingdom, a trading post in the Congo, of the 16th or 17th century. The names of proximate cays—Congo and Mingo—tie in with this theory.

She reviewed the Lovango Timeline (see accompanying Lovango Cay Timeline) beginning in 1728. As her review approached the early 1900s, the timeline's telling became

more and more participatory. SJHS member Andro Childs remembered that her mother, Miss Myrah Keating-Smith, used the cay as a respite from her always being on call; Andro was left at home on the "mainland," St. John. Member Eulita Jacobs contributed lively stories about her family's tenure on or use of Lovango. How shameful we didn't have the tape recorder,

Headstone of Andromeada Child's aunt, Roselyn Smith Anderson

(Photo by David W. Knight, 2008)

as an abandoned and bankrupt estate, and then issues a deed to **Peter Durloo** (RA/Martfelt, 1765)

1780 – Peter Oxholm shows the cay as uninhabited on his manuscript map of St. John. (RA/Oxholm, 1780).

Note that on his map, the cays currently known west to east as Thatch, Grass, Mingo, Lovango and Congo, are named Teyer, Grass, Mingo, Lovango, and Kukelurse. The 1919 US Coast and Geodetic Survey (page 120) notes that the "Lovango Cays" are three islands called by the Spanish, respectively Lovango Grande, Chico, and Medio.

1788 – The 22 ton bark *Two Sisters*, owned and operated by **George Hazzel**, receives a sea pass to sail from her *homeport* of Lovango

to Charlotte Amalie. (RA/GTA/SeapssPro, 1788-1808)

1791, Dec. 16 – Lovango, noted as consisting of 200 acres, is deeded to **George Hazzel**. (RA/VLA/STJM. 1794)

Note that Lovango's acreage in the historical record is sized at different times from 60 to 250 acres; the 1919 US Geodetic Survey sizes it at almost 118 acres.

1794 – Lovango, owned by **George Hazzel**, reappears in the yearly tax rolls for St. John for the first time since 1729; it remains in the DWI tax records thereafter. (RA/VLA/STJM, 1794)

1803 – Tax rolls record that **George Hassel** (a spelling change) is residing on Lovango, with ten

acres in pasture or provision crops. (RA/VLA/STJM, 1804)

1804, Jan 18 – Probate for **Rebecca Elisabet Hassel**, wife of **Benjamin Hassel**, reveals that Rebecca and her brother **George Hassel** are joint owners of Lovango. A deed issued by Peter Hassel granted George Hassel the western half and Rebecca Hassel the eastern half of Lovango, each valued at 1000 Rigsdallers (Rd).

Rebecca and Benjamin's children are her heirs: John Hassel, 8, Anna Hassel, 24, (married to planter Joseph Sewer—sometimes spelled Sore—of Jost van Dyke), Sara Hassel, 18 (present but bedridden with smallpox), and Louisa Hassel, 14 (also bedridden with smallpox). The underage children's guardian

Gravesites at the west end cemetery proceed in an orderly fashion down to the beach. Some are indicated only by piles of stones or conch shells. The tall marker in the picture reads 'In memory of my beloved Husband, Henry Smith. Died December.'

The epitaph on this tombstone in the east cemetery reads "In loving memory of the Louis Christian Andersen. Born in Denmark June 8, 1879. Died October 1957."

(Photos by Robin Swank)

but perhaps if it had been there, we would not have heard all the stories that will now enable us to call her Miss Mandolin at the next jumpup!

Fishing was the industrial mainstay of the Cay over time. Lovango censuses from 1850 through 1917 list the predominant job as fisherman or mariner. Charcoal making and quicklime production may also have been important to a number of on and off-cay people. A June 28, 1854 *Tidende* notice placed by William James Halley, representing the three (related) families on Lovango Cay, warns: "All persons are hereby cautioned against breaking of Ballast, cutting of Wood, or otherwise trespassing on the Island of LOANGO as also the adjoining Quay called 'Congo.' Offenders taken in the act after the date of this notice, will be dealt with according to the utmost rigour of the law—St. Thomas, 21st June, 1854." As charcoaling and liming declined, fishing remained. Even now, claimed those present, the best fishing is off Congo. A number of Lovango residents were actually born in the fishing communities of the nearby cays of Mingo and Thatch. The population of Lovango rose and fell—from 0 at times, to having more people than any individual settlement on the island of St. John. The population summaries: 1804—14; 1805—8; 1815—0; 1836—16;1846—22; 1850—17; 1860—12; 1864—15; 1870—13;1901—3; 1911—24, 1917—49. By

is to be Rebecca's brother, James Hassel, a merchant on St. Thomas.

The Probate appraisal of Lovango included:

200 acres of land with 4 acres planted in cotton or provisions @ 6.5 Rd/acre), 1250 Rd.

Residence house @ 300 Rd

Kitchen @ 125 Rd

3 Negro Houses and a bake oven @250Rd

8 enslaved people, @2,625 Rd

Livestock @ under 1000 Rd

Household miscellaneous @ under 50 Rd

(RA/VLA/STJL/Reg&VurPro, 1797-1807)

1805 June 5 – James Hassel Jr. assumes two mortgages on Lovango, totaling 25,365.5 Rd. (NA/55/833/2000/PantReg, 1776-1806)

1805 – Ownership of Lovango is split in the tax rolls between Abraham Helm 100 acres, and James Hassel Jr. 100 acres. (!) There are 3 white residents and 5 slaves, with 6 acres in pasture or provision crops. (RA/VLA/STJM, 1805)

1807 – Capt. James Halley acquires J. Hassel's ½ share of Lovango (RA/VLA/STJM. 1812)

1812 – J. Anduze acquires Abraham Helm's ½ share of the cay (RA/VLA/STJM, 1812)

1815 – James Halley acquires full title to Lovango. Tax rolls list the island as 250 acres (?) and unoccupied. (RA/VLA/STJM, 1815)

1825, Aug 16 – Capt James Halley dies on Lovango. At the time of his death, tax records record Lovango as having 2 acres in pasture or provisions and 2 slaves. (RA/VLA/STJM, 1825; RA/VLA/STJL/Skifte #13, 1825)

1825, Oct 19 – Halley's probate lists a dwelling house, fishing net, a sailboat, a rowboat, household furnishings, and 2 slaves, Frank and Thimoth, all appraised for 2493.6 Rd (RA/VLA/STJL/Skifte #13, 1825)

1917 there were clearly enough children for a school.

Myrah Keating-Smith's Funeral Booklet describes the school she attended on Lovango in the early 1900s: "Classes held in the 'parlor' of Mrs. Anderson's home on the neighboring island of Lovango were attended by row boat with her headmistress, Miss Sylvanie Sewer, who left Cruz Bay in the early morning and returned late afternoon. There were 18 students in that 'parlor' school, mostly residents of Lovango. When the headmistress could no longer commute, the school was closed, and Myrah and her twin sister were tutored by their stepfather, the late Edward Moorehead, Sr...."

Because burial had to be done quickly in the tropics, the cay had its own cemeteries. We visited two of them. At the west end of the island is an older set of graves, many of which are identifiable only by the multitude of conch shells. There are a few stone markers.

At the east end of the island is a cemetery where Roselyn Smith Anderson (9/18/1889-9/22/1969), Louis Christian Andersen (6/8/1879-10/11/1957) and the more recently deceased Mr. Rudy deWindt, born on Eensomhed, St. Thomas, are buried. This plot is now surrounded by private property.

Rudy deWindt, 1960s

(Photo by George H. H. Knight)

1826 – Tax rolls record Lovango as owned by **"James Halley's Heirs."** (RA/VLA/STJM, 1826)

1836 – Tax rolls record 10 free-colored persons and 6 slaves residing on Lovango; no cultivation is reported. (RA/VLA/STJM, 1836)

1846, Oct 2 – Census for Lovango, owned by James Halley's heirs, records Peter Halley (36), William Halley (24) and Mary Halley (49), living alongside 14 other free inhabitants and 5 slaves. (RA/VLA/STJR, 1846)

Note this census is posted in the Documents section of our website

1848 – Emancipation in the Danish West Indies

1850 – Census lists **Mary Halley** and **Elizabeth M. Vlaun** as "part owners" of Lovango. There are 17 persons living on the island in 3 households (RA/VLA/STJR, 1850)

1854, June 21 – William James Halley posts a notice in the St. *Thomas Tidende (Times)*. Please see the text of the Notice in the accompanying *Lovango Excursion* article.

1860, Oct 9 – Census for Lovango belonging to The Halley Heirs lists **Mary Halley**, 64 (who states her occupation as "commander") and her sister **Elizabeth M. Vlaun**, 54, living on the island with 10 other individuals. (RA/VLA/STJR, 1860)

1864 – Tax records for the Halley heirs on Lovango show 2 acres of land in cultivation or in pasture. An agricultural accounting of the same year reports 10 goats, along with 6 women, 4 boys, and 5 fishermen living in 5 houses. (RA/VLA/STM, 1864)

1869 – Lovango purchased by "retailor" **Henry Varlak**. The land in pasture has increased to 14 acres. An agricultural accounting of the same date records 1 laborer tending 4 head of cattle and 50 sheep. (RA/VLA/STJM, 1869)

1870, Dec 7 – Census conducted by John Weinmar for Lovango, owned by **Henry Varlak**, records a population of 13 persons living in 4 households. Among them are **John McKenzie Smith** and family, who is

There was a spirited discussion of burial practices. Those present remembered that in the 1920s through 1940s the deceased was almost always prepared for burial by washing down with limejuice, then dressing the person in his or her good clothes. Then (s)he was wrapped in a sheet or some other large available cloth. It was some time before the government provided wood coffins for burial. The person would be buried the same or next day, and often the visiting, cooking, singing, and eating went on long after the person was in the ground. There was singing and crying all night, Eulita Jacobs recalled. Proper mourning, indicated by the sequence of the color of clothes one wore months afterwards, also took time; there was real grieving.

There was also lively discussion of life on the cay. Families moved between cays, and the inhabitants were recalled as feisty (rock-throwing was mentioned), but no-one could recall the genesis of Murder Rock. The housing was simpler—the Perkins' 2 storybook cottages were fondly recalled. There were memories of mid-20th century inhabitants who came and went—such as Dick and Ginny Joyce, and later the Muilenburgs and Hermon and Suzy Smith. Parties on the beach were also joyfully remembered. Tony Palmer recalled a time when a stroll on the beach meant you could say hello to everyone by name on your way to a pig roast. And if the pig happened to be too large to roast in the time allotted, well then, one had to make do with the substituted liquid refreshment!

May 2008

listed as manager, and one laborer, **Ventor Sprauve**, with his family of 4. Three other men on the island are listed as mariners. (RA/VLA/STJR, 1860)

1880, Oct 11 – Census for Lovango, owned by **Henry Varlak**, records a population of 15 persons in possibly 2 households; 5 men are recorded as fishermen. Tax rolls show that agricultural land use has dropped to only 2 acres. (RA/VLA/STJR, 1880)

1885 – Henry Varlak dies; Lovango is appraised during his probate. Among the items listed in the inventory are a 2-room house of wood, a bake oven, a little cookhouse, a house of wood with a masonry foundation, another wood house 10x15 feet, a cistern with a platform holding 114 puncheons, 60 acres of land, and about a 'tuende' of quicklime, all appraised for 738 dollars. (NA/55/728/1907, Skifte, 1885)

1885, March 8 – Lovango is sold at action to **Francois Caliste**. Other items from Lovango sold at auction are some cattle and sheep, 2 boats and a seine net. (NA/55/728/1907, Skifte, 1885)

Note that Caliste is the former estate manager of Leinster Bay during the Anduze ownership; he built the water mill near the factory ruins at Leinster Bay)

1889 – Lovango is acquired by **Henry Clen**. (RA/VLA/STJM, 1889)

Note that Henry Clen is the brother-in-law of Carl Francis and owner of Leinster Bay

1900, Mar 15 – **Clen** dies on St. John; Lovango is appraised in Clen's probate as follows: A house on the bay @125, a house on the hill @10, a cistern and trough @200, 60 acres of land in grass or bush @180, 2 stone wall fences dividing the island @100, 2 boats and 1 seine net @55, 12 coconut trees @10, for a total of $680. (NA/55/720/1903, Skifte #2, 1900)

1901 – Lovango census lists 3 individuals on the island—**John Smith**, 31, a fisherman born on Thatch Cay, **Charles Smith**, 9, his son born on Mingo Cay, and **John George**, 41, a fisherman born on Lovango (RA/VLA/STJR, 1901)

FOR TRUE

Did you know that Lovango Cay was once part of the British Virgin Islands?

For many years historians have puzzled over the lack of references to the island of Lovango in early Danish West Indies records. This mystery may be explained by a little known account of the Virgin Islands' past, penned by a Danish visitor around 1765.

According to St. John tax rolls, in 1729, the island of L'Oango [AKA: Lovango or Loango] was the possession of William Gandy, a carpenter and planter of English Caribbean background. After Gandy was killed in his sleep by his slaves in about 1730, his widow and two stepdaughters were left in poverty. Unable to afford to cultivate their Lovango plantation, the Gandy heirs abandoned the property and the island was dropped from the yearly Danish tax records.

This situation soon prompted a British subject by the name of Conners to apply to the Government of the Leeward Islands in Antigua for a patent on the cay. According to the visiting Danish economist Christian Martfeldt, Conners was still occupying Lovango and cultivating food crops there in the mid 1760s. By virtue of the fact that Conners' English land patent predated a deed issued to Peter Durloo by the Danish Crown, Lovango was technically part of the British Virgin Islands throughout this period.

1905 – Lovango is purchased by **Louis C. Andersen** (RA/VLA/STJM, 1905).

Note that Andersen came to DWI from Denmark and had been a policeman on St. Thomas. He married Roselyn Smith. Also note that the censuses spell AndersEn, but Roselyn Smith's headstone and other references use AndersOn.

1911 – Lovango census records the island as jointly owned by **Henry Smith** (buried in the cemetery on the west side of the bay) and **Elsa Poulina Anderson**, daughter of Louis and Roselyn Anderson (all of whom are buried in the eastern cemetery). There are 24 persons living on the cay in 7 households. Smith, Andersen, Birch, and George are the most common names. (RA/VLA/STJR, 1911)

1916 – A hurricane destroys Lovango, leaving only the Smith House foundation.

Note: Interestingly, this hurricane is very well documented as occurring on the night of October 9 running through the day of the 10th. De Booy and Farris said, "The last hurricane, on the night of October 9th, 1916, was perhaps one of the most destructive ever experienced." In Matilda Marsh's taped interviews with elders, all remember the hurricane very well. However, it goes unmentioned in NOAA's exhaustive list of "Tropical Storms and Hurricanes which passed within two degrees of latitude of Puerto Rico and the Virgin Islands from 1515 to Present."

1917 – A public school is opened on the island. (USC&GS, 1919) Census for Lovango records a population of 49 persons in 19 households. Smith, George, Andersen, Aubrey, DeToy, and a few other family names are present. (RA/VLA/STJR, 1917)

Note that during the period 1900-1930, the DWI/USVI population dropped from 33,000 to 22,000.

1934 – Cattle census of St. John district lists **Louis Christian Andersen** as owner of "½ Loango" with 19 head of cattle; **Henry Smith** owner of "½ Loango" with 11 head of cattle; and **L.C. Matta** of "Loango" with 15 head of cattle. (NA/E4/56/1932-34)

A Hike on the Old Danish Road to Estate Sieben & Mollendahl

Presentation by David W. Knight; Summarized by Robin Swank

On December 15th a group of hardy SJHS members and guests met for the last hike of the calendar year. The day was cool and the trail was slippery, with occasional raindrops keeping the guts flowing. Our destination was the south-side estates of Sieben and Mollendahl. These once active sugar plantations are sheltered from the north wind by "Camel Mountain" (AKA: Camelberg), once thought to be the highest point on St. John. David W. Knight led us down the Sieben Road, which was once a major thoroughfare of the Danish-Colonial period. The hike was long and beautiful,

On his 1800 map, Oxholm labels Sieben as "Mollendahl," the two estates were merged at that time.

(Rigsarkivet, Copenhagen, Denmark)

the overgrown ruins proved to be rich time capsules, and the information overload daunting. Here are just a few of the gems:

The Estates

The first plantation encountered along the road is **Estate L'Esperance**. L'Esperance, David tells us, was formed in 1736 by the merger of two properties: one granted jointly to Governor Erik Bredal and Amsterdam-based merchant Claus Tonis, in 1721, and a 2/3 portion of another plantation granted to Capt. Christopher Krabbe in 1720. We stopped at the cutoff to the L'Esperance ruins where we could barely see the remains of an old bridge across the overgrown gut. David took this opportunity to point out that the Danes were adept road engineers. For example, until a land bridge was built that spanned the "Defile"—the "Rift" or fissure that splits the island in two at the head of the Reef Bay trail—east-west travelers on anything but foot would have to use trails down to the coastline to cross the island overland. The Sieben/Mollendahl Road, therefore, was an important thoroughfare as it connected the port of Cruz Bay with a number of occupied plantations in the Reef Bay Quarter (Sieben, Mollendahl, Little Reef Bay, and Parforce); it also continues on past Reef Bay to Great & Little Lamesure, (the other) Mollendal, Salt Pond, Johns Folly, and on to Coral Bay. To this day, it remains a substantial trail—although it hasn't been drivable for many years now.

The property known as **Estate Sieben & Mollendahl** was formed by a merger of the remaining 1/3 of the Krabbe property and four other estates owned respectively by: John H. Sieben (granted 1721), Elizabeth Friis (granted 1721), Adrian Charles (granted 1721), and Gerhard Moll (granted in 1720). The date of full consolidation of these properties was c1756.

Sieben, Mollendahl, and L'Esperance are truly landlocked. Most successful plantations of the colonial era had access to a bay for the collection of resources such as seafood, sand and coral, as well as easy shipment of their produce and importation of supplies. If an estate had no shoreline they usually tried to acquire adjoining properties to gain access to the sea. This is indeed the case with the landlocked properties along the Sieben & Mollendahl road. By 1793, all three estates (Mollendahl, Sieben, and L'Esperance) had come under the common ownership of Dr. D'Juno Vriehuis, who also purchased the waterside estate of Parforce on Reef Bay. However, after Vriehuus's death in 1808 the estates were no longer linked by common ownership, and, partly as a result of the added transport burden, L'Esperance, Sieben and Mollendahl soon ceased sugar production. The remains of the sugar factories found on these estates today, therefore, are true relics of the early-colonial sugar culture on St. John.

In 1805, all planters or estate managers were asked by the Danish West Indies government to write "elucidations" concerning their properties on a special census taken throughout the colony. The plantation census was primarily an effort to determine the labor situation on the estates after the Danish Crown's mandated cessation of the trans-Atlantic slave trade in 1802 (illicit and legitimate slave trade did, in fact, continue throughout West Indies well into the 1880s). As it turns out, these plantation censuses contain all manner of historical information not available to us in other official documents. For example, on the census for Annaberg the estate overseer noted that it was during James Murphy's ownership that a modernized factory and windmill had been constructed on the property, a fact disclosed only in these elucidations.

David handed out transcribed excerpts from one of these handwritten plantation reports by Dr. D'Juno Vriehuis, dated January 12, 1805. Setting aside descriptions of soil types, noxious insects (borer, blast, grub), and diseases (he was a physician as well as a planter), they read in part:

L'Esperance—

"The Estate is situated on the (Westend) of the island……. Two small rivulets run through the estate where of one waters the works and has not been dry 30 years that I have been here. It has agreeable to the opinion of those who understand it, water enough to supply a water mill which I have not been able to build on account of the heavy debt which rested on the estate when I bought it, the want of (laborers) on it, dry years and lastly hurricane."

Mollendahl and Sieben—

"The land of these estates are situated on the South side of this Island ….there are two sets of convenient works [sugar factories] on them. That these Estates do not at present yield more sugar in a better proportion to their number of Negroes, is owing to some of the Negroes have worked a couple of years in the lands of my Estate L'Esperance, which lie contiguous to, and are better than these lands. … To cultivate all the good land, 60 to 70 more [Negroes] would be required. ….."

"As men have wives, and women husbands upon this Estate, the husbands go generally to their wives where they live. Such as live in matrimony on the Estate occupy one house inhabited by a pair and their children…."

"The Buildings and Negro houses of Sieben are on the side of a hill open to the East and South winds. Those of Mollendahl on the side of a hill facing West. The Negro Houses are in general 20 to 24 feet long, and 10 to 12 wide. Those of the house Negroes and Tradesmen are larger…. (They) have in good weather not only provisions enough for their own subsistence, but also to dispose of for money; to that, a few negroes excepted, I need not buy for the others any other but salt provisions. That they may keep their grounds in order, I give them out of crops one day in the week to work for themselves, which they prefer to being fed…"

Dr. Vriehuis goes on very directly addressing the amelioration question and identifies the inhibitors of a self-sustaining labor population— the spread of VD; sterility caused by polygamy, too-hard labor conditions and guilt-induced abortions; and the government mandated redirection of the labor force to the making and repairing of roads instead of sugar.

The Estate Sieben baobab tree still stands, now protected by a large hive of bees… As Mr. Elroy told us, "the tree is easier to find if you just look up."

(Photo by Robin Swank)

As David passed around a copy of the original text of Vriehuis' elucidation, he passed on a primary research tip learned from his friend and associate Garry Horlacher. In undertaking translation of Danish archival materials it is not only helpful to be able to decipher Gothic script, but also to know some contemporary Norwegian, as in many cases today's Norwegian is closer to old Danish than is modern Danish.

At the slippery turn-off to a Baobab Tree on estate Sieben one of our members takes a nasty tumble; but we do find the baobab tree!

We stop for several stories along the way, tales which bring the people of the period alive for us. We hear about Alexander Frazier, who was the owner of Estate Sieben during Emancipation. He was one of a small group of English planters on Tortola who relocated to the Danish West Indies to broaden ownership opportunities for his mixed-race children. Alexander Frazier was a friend of A. C. Hill; he was also the Quarter Officer for the Reef Bay Quarter of St. John. Despite his responsibilities

and the prodigious amount of documentation he collected on every facet of his official life (every bill, note, correspondence, troop drill, etc), he died without leaving testament regarding his own possessions. Therefore, all were invited to submit claims to his estate at his death. As a result, his probate records are voluminous! Interestingly, claimants were not interested in his plantation, which was valued at only $400, but in the compensation due from the Danish Crown for his emancipated slaves, which were valued at $50 each. Because of his dying intestate, Frazier's intended St. John heirs, all born out of wedlock, were left with no claim to his property.

The Sieben estate was devastated in a major hurricane in the 1830s; most of the buildings we find there date to after that event. As is common in multi-generational sites, the later-period house was rebuilt incorporating elements of what had previously been the sugar factory. (During that hurricane it was reported that fruit trees were uprooted, sheep killed and the coffee crop destroyed at L'Esperance.)

We then head farther down the trail to the Estate Mollendahl, where the humid air is scented by abundant bay rum trees (*Pimenta racemosa*). The estate was named by Gerhardt Moll for his son, who was sent to Holland for his education. Gerhardt was blind; we know this because his wife Maria, who inherited the estate as guardian in 1754, tells us so in an inscription she had engraved on his gravestone located in St. Thomas's Western Cemetery. Maria led a troubled life—her son died before reaching his majority, so she remarried, passing title of the lands to her second husband, Governor & Commandant John van John, a duplicitous type who died in office. She tried again with Captain Wencel Kass, with whom she had two daughters before the plantation was sold.

While at Mollendahl we observed remnants of a community of in-holdings where tradesmen and bay rum leaf harvesters once lived. These plots held by the free community were legitimized in the 1870s and 1880s. We see one of about 12 houses, some partially intact; the early craftsmanship is still evident.

David informed us that bay rum oil was originally used as lubricating oil. At full strength it will burn your skin; it is diluted at various strengths depending on its intended use. SJHS member Chuck Pishko noted that pure bay oil

Wide boards on a foundation of field-stone and rubble, set with quicklime mortar are remnants of a comfortable 2 room house among the Bay Rum trees. The detail of the house's careful construction is worth a picture-taking visit.

(Photos by Robin Swank)

is diluted 1 in 500 parts, e.g., when used as a scented oil/toilet water. The St. John bay leaves were distilled into oil by families with names like Marsh, White, Bornn and Lindquist, and then the oil was shipped to St. Thomas where it was manufactured into bay rum.

We reluctantly leave the cool canopy of trees for the trek back uphill, which was almost as much fun as the hike down. I'm certain many of us will be taking this hike again, to make sure that these time capsules are still intact.

January, 2008

Among the bay rum trees hike members view an oven, created with gathered stones and brick, and placed well away from the house.

Estate Misgunst Meander

Presentation by David W. Knight and Eleanor Gibney; Summarized by Robin Swank

Detail of Estate Misgunst (noted as "Kervink") from a map by Peter L. Oxholm, 1780

(Rigsarkivet, Copenhagen, Denmark)

The sugar works at Misgunst are crude and date to the early settlement period on St. John. They were in place by 1736 and were probably upgraded around 1769, when the property was purchased by Dedrich Kervink, who also owned Maria's Hope and Pasquero.

On approaching the estate from the Bordeaux road by a downhill path, in part an old Danish cart-road, you first spy the factory ruins to the right of the trail as two flat areas. It appears that there were two horse mills. The earlier horse mill, built on higher ground, was later replaced by a second mill directly below it. The first mill was then dug out (the wild pigs love it here and are still digging it out!) and quick-limed in an

Timeline History of Estate Misgunst in the Reef Bay Quarter of St. John, c1724 – 1910
Compiled by David W. Knight

1724 – A land deed is issued to **Riis David** by the Danish West Indies government for a plot of land in the Reef Bay Quarter of St. John measuring 3000 X 1500 Danish feet.

1728 – First St. John tax rolls record that Riis David lives on St. Thomas and has 10 slaves (with no overseer) at work on his St. John plantation.

1730 – Tax rolls record that the David plantation is now owned by **Riis David's widow**.

1733 – Plantation is sold to **Josias Valleaux**. In the slave uprising of that year the dwelling house and

warehouse on the plantation are burned.

1736 – Tax rolls record that Josias Valleaux, his wife, and daughter, Susanna, are living on the plantation, which has a "good sugarworks" and 10 slaves.

1739 – Tax rolls record that the plantation is now owned by **Josias Valleaux's widow**.

(NOTE: No tax records exist for St. John for the period 1740 through 1754)

1755 – Tax rolls record that the property is now being developed into an active sugar plantation under

Johannes vonBeverhoudt Janzoon's ownership. vonBeverhoudt and his wife are residing on the property along with 82 enslaved laborers.

1761 – Tax rolls record that the property is a sugar plantation worked by 65 slaves with no overseer. vonBeverhoudt and his family are now residing on St. Thomas.

1763 – Tax rolls record that the property is now owned by **Johannes vonBerverhoudt's widow**.

1769 – Plantation is purchased by **Dedrich Kervink**. The property is inventoried for his mortgage. The effort to store water for use in processing sugar & rum. It may be, David Knight conjectures, they were collecting water from the runoff of the field system above the works. The steep topography and the speed of water cascading through the gut when it rained probably dictated the need for such a reservoir.

The dwelling house, located on a knoll south of the factory, measures out at close to the 27 x 16 Danish feet that is documented in an early inventory. A portion of Misgunst's works remain standing; it was noted in 1769 to have 4 copper kettles, a molasses tank, and the equipment for sugar making. An animal mill on the site was noted as "new."

The estate inevitably failed as a sugar plantation. When it was bought at auction by John Jennings in 1780, there was only one more year of sugar production. After Mr. Jennings died in bankruptcy in 1782, the estate was sold to Frederich deBreton. After that date it appears that the Misgunst works were never rebuilt or repurposed. DeBreton did what many consolidators did at the time: he purchased the estate not for the land but for its salvageable equipment and its slaves, assets more valuable than the land.

There were several inland estates in this area of St. John—Maria's Hope, Hope, Bordeaux, Mary Simpson, Pasquero, Josie's Gut and Misgunst. All eventually failed as sugar plantations. Misgunst was among the first to fail. Having no access to sustainable fresh water for planting, nor to the sea for shipping, the estate was of little value. Most estates in the upland areas of Bordeaux Mountain eventually diversified into coffee, cocoa and livestock, or were later used as provision grounds or planted with bay rum trees, but on the whole during the colonial period, the inland estates on Bordeaux Mountain were doomed by their 'iffy' conditions for growing both cotton and sugarcane.

It is in 1782 that the estate name "Misgunst" appears in the written record for the first time. Estates were often named after their owners or family members, such as "Annaberg"; for desirable virtues, as was the case with "Hope"; or, for site characteristics, like "Lameshur." It's easy to imagine that "Misgunst," a Danish word meaning *unfavorable* or *misfortune*, may have been commonly applied to the property as an epithet. After the first three owners (Riis David, Josias Valleaux, and Johannes vonBeverhoudt Janzoon) died quickly after taking ownership, it could easily have been perceived as a risky investment to own or reside on the *Misgunst* estate.

condensed extract of mortgage inventory follows:

August 23, 1769 – "The plantation is situated in the Reef Bay Quarter between Baron Schimmelmann, to the east; Agent Johs. Wood, to the west; Landfoged C. F. Weyle, to the North; and, Daniel Overton to the South.

The Plantation is 3000 X 1500 feet. Some of the plantation is in bush and 9 pieces of land are planted with sugarcane, provisions are cultivated.

There is a dwelling house, 27 X 16 feet. It is wooden and the roof shingled. A store house 20 X 16 feet, wooden and a shingled roof.

A boiling house 40 X 20 feet. The southern wall is brick-built, the others wooden, and the roof is shingled. Inside there are 4 kettles of copper, a molasses tank and the equipment for sugar boiling.

There is a new animal mill, a still with 2 copper kettles, one of 80 gallons and another of 40 gallons, and all equipment necessary. 36 Negro houses, 29 Negro men, 24 Negro women, 15 boys, 15 girls and 11 mules…"

1775 – Tax rolls record the plantation is now sold to **Adrian Kervink**, who is living on the property with his wife and 2 daughters. It is noted as a sugar plantation with 35 slaves.

1777 – The plantation is once again listed in tax rolls as owned by **Dedrich Kervink**. A white man and woman are reportedly living on the property with no slaves.

1780 – The plantation is purchased at auction by **John Jennings**.

1781 – John Jennings property is once again noted as a sugar plantation with 1 white man and 48 slaves. It is the last year sugar is produced on the property.

1782 – John Jennings dies in bankruptcy and his plantation is put up for auction.

A translated excerpt from the auction documents follows—it is the first time the name *Misgunst* was found in the archival record…..

"*March 8, 1782…Carl Friderich Weyle, appointed bailiff and auction administrator on St.*

Red *Canavalia nitida* seeds, found rarely in the V.I. litter the estate grounds. Also found were bay trees, and amarat, which, along with white cedar and casha, would have been burned for charcoal.

(Photo by Eleanor Gibney)

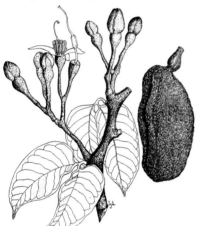

Red locust (*Hymanea courbaril*) is a multi-purpose tree—its pods are edible, the resinous sap produces a natural medicine (copal), and the wood makes admirable timber; it is found in abundance at Estate Misgunst.

(Image from Common Trees of Puerto Rico and the Virgin Islands [Little & Wadsworth])

In 1798 Misgunst, then abandoned and unworked, was purchased by Louis Michel, the owner of the neighboring Bordeaux and Hope (also called Patience) plantations. Louis Michel's wife died at Hope in 1802, leaving a 14-year-old son, John, and a one-year-old daughter, Johanna. After the death of his wife, Louis Michel began a relationship with Margaret Catherine Braithwaite, a former slave who had been the mistress of the previous owner of Estate Bordeaux, Reverend Thomas Braithwaite. Michel died in 1838 leaving the bulk of his properties to his grandson, John William Weinmar, except for a ten-acre parcel of land and the estate house at Misgunst, which he formally gifted to his long-time companion Margaret Catharine Braithwaite and their daughter Catharina Michel.

Margaret Braithwaite lived at Misgunst at least through 1850. Her impassioned appeal to Judge Henschell in Cruz Bay [see page 85] to intervene on her behalf shows that she was nearly impoverished, but quite literate and assertive at that date. Her daughter, Catharina, at the time was in no condition to help her, as she was herself isolated and impoverished on her own property in Little Reef Bay. In 1863 Margaret's grandson, John Knevels, reported the death of Margaret Braithwaite at his home in Coral Bay. Depending on the source, she was anywhere between 96 to 119 years old, and, if

John makes public that March 8, 1782 in his office according to Danish and Norwegian ordinance of Dec. 19, 1693, he has sold the following:

A sugar plantation Misgunst on which is a residence house, a cook house with accessories, still with pipes & basin, also Negro houses, 18 Negro men, 18 Negro women, 7 Negro boys, 8 Negro girls, 5 mule asses and one stone-ass.

...The said plantation with its livestock was sold to St. Thomas [resident] Herr Baron Friderich de Bretton for 19,120 Rd., with co-signer John deWint.
St. John, date above written
C. F. Weyle
No minor's inheritance is found to this estate.

St. John Upper-guardians Aug. 2, 1783
P. D. Wint D. J. Vriehuis"

1782 through 1798 – Frederich deBreton, who owned other plantations throughout the DWI (including *Adrian and Trunk Bay* on St. John), appears to have purchased *Misgunst* for the slaves and whatever equipment he could salvage. Throughout his ownership, tax rolls record *Misgunst* as vacant, with no land use. The property also ceases to be recorded as a sugar plantation during this period.

1798 – The abandoned un-worked property, *Misgunst*, is purchased by the owner of neighboring *Hope* plantation, **Louis Michel**.

1802, Sept. 17 – Louis Michel's wife, Anna Elizabeth, dies on the *Hope* plantation. As there are 2 underage heirs (a son, John, 14; and a daughter, Johanna, 1) a probate is carried out to appraise Michel's properties. The probate inventory shows Hope to be a well developed sugar plantation with a complete set of works, 2 residence houses, 62 slaves, 2 horses, 15 mules, 4 oxen, 1 cow with calf and 18 sheep. *Misgunst* is noted in the inventory as planted with some sugar, but devoid of buildings or occupation.

1805 – Louis Michel states on a plantation census that he has no slaves on *Misgunst* and estimates that he would require at least 50 able slaves to work the property.

Ruins and Rambles

To the Honorable, Judge Hanschell

Honored Sir:

It is not from a desire of mine that I am now about to address you, (trusting that you will excuse the liberty I have taken,) but my necessities demands that I must make known to you my grievancies.

I am laying in a big [bed?] of sickness, from which I dare not hope ever to leave; my hole support, is the eight dollars a month that the deceased Mr. Michele left me and without that I must inevitably starve so that I am compelled to request that you will please speak to Mr. Weimar [Weinmar] for me as it is now entering the fifth month since last I have a stiver from him And I am in a state of depression, not knowing where to seek for the common necessaries of life but I trust to your interference will bring me some support; likewise a barrel of sugar I am to get each year from Mr. [Weinmar]. I have sent to him for it, but he has refused giving it until the latter end of this year, wherein I am so much in want of it even now; hoping that your honor will intercede for me.

I remain your honor's most humble servant

Margaret Braithwaite

1833 – **Louis Michel** acquires the adjoining *Bordeaux* plantation from the heirs of Reverend Thomas Braithwaite.

1838 – Louis Michel dies with his only legitimate son, John (who died 1832), having predeceased him. Michel's properties, *Bordeaux*, *Hope* and *Misgunst*, are inherited by his grandson (his daughter Johanna's son with husband John Mathias Weinmar), **John William Weinmar**. As per Louis Michel's will, a 10-acre parcel of land on *Misgunst* is divided out of the property and gifted to Margaret Catharine Braithwaite and her daughter, Catharina Michel.

An excerpt from the registration of their deed follows:

Malprotocol Book A, 1838

According to a gift of January 1, 1838, Louis Michel gives Margaret Braithwaite and her daughter Catharina Michel the place called Misgunst, *matriculated under the sugar plantation* Hope *in Reef Bay Quarter, St. John. Witnessed on September 27, 1841*

September 15, 1847 – J. W. Weinmar attests that he has sold the "closed-down plantations Bordeaux *and* Hope *(with the remainder of Misgunst) to his "now deceased cousin"* **Peter Evald Weinmar** *on August 28 of that year.*

1848 – Slaves are emancipated in the Danish West Indies. The owner of record of the abandoned *Bordeaux*,

Hope and *Misgunst* properties is the deceased P. E. Weinmar.

Margaret Braithwaite is living alone at the former estate house of the *Misgunst* plantation.

May 5, 1850 – 90-year-old Margaret Braithwaite writes an impassioned appeal to Judge Henschell in Cruz Bay to intervene in her support (See the original and the transcript of her letter).

1854 – The "dismantled estates, *Misgunst*, *Hope*, *Pasquereaux* and *Bordeaux*" are auctioned off during the reconciliation of Peter Evald Weinmar's probate. The properties are purchased by Hans H. Berg. Notice of the auction reads as follows:

the 1860 census of St. John is correct, she had been born in Africa.

What happened to Misgunst? Around 1910 Count Castenkjold purchased Margaret Braithwaite's ten-acre parcel from Thomas Francis, the remainder of Misgunst, Hope and Pasquero from William Henry Marsh, and Cabrithorn and Great and Little Lamesure from Richard Penn. This vast consolidated property eventually became one of the first large tracts of land given over for the creation of the Virgin Islands National Park.

April, 2009

RECYCLING ~ *an Old Idea*

There were four well-documented industries practiced by St. Johnians during the Post-Emancipation era. Raising cattle and fishing/seamanship were two. Working the land for provisions or for charcoal was a third category—as several coal pits along this trail to Misgunst attest. The fourth was recycling old ruins for resale to the building trades. Hardwood timber, scrap metal, machine parts, and old brick and coral block were primary targets. By comparing the 1769 inventory of Estate Misgunst with what we see on the ground 240 years later, it's clear much of the infrastructure has been dismantled. The 1769 mortgage inventory for the property notes a 40' x 20' boiling house. Lief C. Larsen's translation of the inventory notes that the southern wall of the boiling house is built of brick (or possibly he meant masonry) and the others are wooden; the roof is noted as shingled. What we encounter on the site today is only the bare outline of this boiling house, as there are no remains of the wooden walls. The brick, tile, boiling pots and rum still, along with any other recyclables, have long since been carried away.

Auction in St. John 1854

At the request of the Dealing-Court of St. John will be put up for sale at three public Auctions, in conformity with the ordinances of 22 April 1817, the dismantled estates and tracts of land, viz:

Hope, Misgunst, and Pasquereaux with Josygut, situated in Reefbay Quarter No. 5, 6 and 7, containing some old buildings and about 450 acres of land in wood and pasture valued all together at $250.

Bordeaux with adjacent Hammersgut, Mary Simpson, Yocomana, and Cabrithorn, situated in Coralbay Quarter No 5 and Reef bay Quarter No 1, containing all together about 500 acres of land in wood and pasture valued at $250, all belonging

to the Dealing of Peter Evald Weinmar Esq. Deceased.

1860 – Hans H. Berg sells *Bordeaux* and *Cabrithorn* to **Ingjald C. Mourier**, owner of the *Great & Little Lamesure.*

1863 – John Knevels reports the death of **Margaret Braithwaite**. According to the 1831 Register of Free Colored, Margaret Braithwaite would have been 103 years old in 1863—her age was given as 70 in 1831. The 1831 register additionally states that she was unmarried and a member of, and confirmed in, the "Mission church." She had been born enslaved on Tortola and given her freedom by Thomas Braithwaite on March 27, 1797. At the time of registration (1831) she had been on St. John 35 years.

NOTE: *Margaret Braithwaite's age given in DWI census documents are as follows: 83, in 1850; 100, in 1855; 100, in 1857; and, 116, in 1860.*

1865 – Margaret Braithwaite's 10 acres of *Misgunst* are sold to **Thomas Francis**.

The remainder of *Misgunst, Hope* and *Pasquero* are sold to the new owner of neighboring *Parforce,* **William Henry Marsh**.

c1910 – Thomas Francis sells the former Margaret Braithwaite parcel to Count **Castenskjold,** who also purchases the remainder of *Misgunst, Hope, Pasquereau* and a parcel of *Parforce* from W. H. Marsh, and *Great & Little Lamesure* and *Cabrithorn* from Richard Penn.

Mary's Point Hike

Presentation by David W. Knight and Eleanor Gibney; Summarized by Robin Swank

David W. Knight welcomed about thirty SJHS members to our hike on Mary's Point. We met at the Francis Boiling House on what was once the Betty's Hope plantation, which straddles a strategic isthmus separating Mary's Creek and Francis Bay. At the outset David informed us that he was going to lead us to several little-known sites, some of which were reused and built over throughout history. He proposed to share available documented historical fact, but cautioned that he would interweave it with sound conjecture—necessary because, although there is much existing data, there has not yet been a committed effort on the part of the land owners (the National Park Service) to uncover the full story of these sites and the people who occupied them.

Betty's Hope and Mary's Point appear to have been parcels of land originally held by high Danish West Indies and Guinea Company officials during the early years of Danish settlement on St. John. Balancing the desirable east-west coastal shipping access of the isthmus with Mary's Point and the general unsuitability of the land for agriculture (dry, windy, steep), it wasn't until the 1720s, after the best planting grounds were taken up and a new generation of Danish settlers needed additional land, that the area began to be parceled out.

Already resident, the van Still family was given the first controlling landholding on Mary's Point. By 1733, there were 2 established plantations in the area. The *Betty's Hope* estate, which had its own house and factory complex, straddled the south side of the isthmus between Mary's Creek and Francis Bay, and the *Mary's Point* estate, which bounded the isthmus to the north and controlled the Mary's Point peninsula. Both were eventually merged as part of Annaberg by 1786-87.

Detail from the 1800 Oxholm Map of St. John
(Rigsarkivet, Denmark)

While a "Free Colored" population had long been established on St. Thomas, the owner of the Mary's Point estate, Franz Claasen, was among the first "Free-Colored" plantation owners (c1738 – 1780s) on St. John. How did the Mary's Point parcel pass from the van Still's in the 1720s to Franz Claasen? The van Still family held the property through the 1733 slave rebellion. As originally reported by Pierre Joseph Pannet in his 1733 "Report on the Execrable Conspiracy Carried Out by the Amina Negroes on the Danish Island of St. Jan in America" (translated from the original French and published by Aimory P. Caron and Arnold R. Highfield in 1984), a band of rebels were headed to ravage the van Still plantation. However, a loyal estate slave headed them off, saying he had already killed the owners. Jacob von Still, who was ill and bedridden at the time, thus had the opportunity to gather his family and escape by boat, delivering the first word of the St. John rebellion to St. Thomas. After the rebellion, c1738, the Company's records show that "a loyal negro" was given a parcel of land "in return for his help during the Rebellion." Franz Claasen's deed to the property was recorded August 20, 1738, by Jacob van Still and is corroborated by numerous archival references.

"Rediscovered" several years ago within the bounds of the Mary's Point estate and identified as a separate, earlier site by historian George Tyson, the Classen plantation is shown on the 1780 Oxholm map. The original land deed clearly defines the boundaries of the estate as across the Mary's Point isthmus "sea to sea" and following the coast-line. Oxholm's map also displays that the adjoining beach at "Francis Bay" was originally named for the property owner, Franz [aka: Francis] Claasen.

Francis Boiling House

(photo courtesy of David W. Knight)

Now skip forward ¾ of a century……to another story…

Post emancipation, poor economic conditions and the plantation owners' reactive contract labor code had contrived to keep most former slaves on the estates. In the 1848 census, George Francis was listed among Annaberg's most trusted enslaved laborers, but in the 1860 census his position was listed as "overseer." By this time he had married Hesther Dalinda (c1845) from the Munsbury/Frederiksdal Plantation and moved their family to Annaberg. Hans H. Berg, Annaberg's owner, passed away in 1862, and granted George Francis outright title of a 2-acre parcel on Mary's Point. When Mary's Point came up for auction during Berg's probate reconciliation, George Francis bought the remainder of the estate. By the 1870 census, he was listed as "planter." In 1871 he purchased both Annaberg and Leinster Bay at a post-hurricane bankruptcy sale.

Why was a man named Francis again on Francis (Franz') Classen's ground? Is George Francis's last name a place-name rather than a family name? Was George Francis a descendant of the man who gave Francis Bay its name? David points out, as he talks through several possible answers to this question, that knowledge of local naming practices is key to documenting history and genealogy. Unlike in the British colonies, where a plantation owner's name was often taken up as a surname by estate laborers, this practice was not widely adopted in the Danish West Indies except in the cases of a blood relationship. Also, names taken-up by both poor, or disenfranchised European settlers, as well as persons of African descent, were often based on designations of profession (Cooper), of places (Allberg), or whimsy (deWint [the Wind]), and, particularly in the case of the enslaved, a child would often carry his or her mother's given name. Or, perhaps, the name Francis could simply be a contraction, designating an individual of French heritage, or the name might identify a place of specific interest to a person's lineage—which could well be the case in George Francis' situation. The truth is, we simply do not know.

We do know that the stone boiling house and chimney at the current Mary's Point parking lot where we begin our hike, were constructed by George Francis in 1874 soon after his purchase of the broader Annaberg Estate. Three cut coral plaques with the 1874 date are imbedded in the walls. This may well be the last true sugar factory constructed on St. John, a scaled-down version of the one at Annaberg. Tax records reveal that sugar cane was indeed grown at Mary's Point by George Francis, but whether or not sugar was ever produced at the Francis boiling house is unknown, as George Francis died soon after completing construction of the facility. A fourth cement plaque, bearing a 1911 date, commemorates the conversion of the boiling house to another use, possibly as a more generic farm building.

As we walk north and uphill toward the boundary between the Betty's Hope and Mary's Point estates, David informs us that after George Francis's death management of his property was left to his third wife, Lucy, and their 5 children. The estate remained largely in pasture through the 1960s when, Eleanor Gibney remembers that there were wild horses to be caught and broken, even though no-one would buy them. A small and active community developed on neighboring properties in the second half of the 19th century, after Hans Berg gave as gifts numerous small parcels of land to his loyal labors in his will. Ethel McCully's book,

Grandma Raised the Roof, and some of Karen Olwig's research document that community's history.

Pink-blossomed Coralita, a Mexican creeper, suddenly flows across the path. This sun-loving "pretty pest," Eleanor informs us, was used to insulate earth-covered piles of wood being turned into charcoal. The ruins of the Creque family summer house, which appear to be a second or third generation structure built over the older Betty's Hope estate house, are covered with this plant. The older yellow bricks, the more recent green, cream and coral tiles and several toppled decorative cement balustrades peer out from beneath a collapsed second story. The abandoned Creque commissary freezer and batteries lie side by side with concrete around the cistern that appears to be the same vintage as the house. There are outlying buildings, possibly old servants' quarters built prior to the reclamation of the original estate house. Behind the house and around the path the re-growth of bush reminds us that time obscures both the history and physical sites from human memory, and that we had best hurry to gather the recollections of our living historians.

We continue upward onto Mary's Point. Through the thick bush we need to look closely to see that the whole ridge has been manipulated by man since the early 1700s. The rock flats, ledges, and open spaces need to be interpreted into the industrial plant it probably once was. Once this land was the site of an active and well-developed cotton plantation, indicated by the remains of stone-built slave cabins, house foundations and a storehouse (magazine) needed to keep the cotton dry after ginning. There is a large cistern, possibly constructed with recycled stone, with gravity feed for the lower house and plantings. There is a large flat area, possibly a "bleach," where laundry was laid out to dry. One can well imagine that the bush still holds many unseen components of industrial structures associated with activities such as the grazing of livestock listed in the estate rolls—cattle, sheep and goats—and the planting and processing of cassava and other provisions required to feed the estate.

As for Franz Claasen's estate house itself, a stone ring-wall foundation is all that remains, but it was most likely constructed with daub and wattle or half-timber upper walls and a palm, sugar-cane thrash, or grass thatch roof—all of which would have been plentiful. The image of the "grand estate house" is clearly wrong here, but the main house was two or more times greater in size than most of its contemporaries. In comparison to his peers, Franz Claasen was in all likelihood quite well-off, embedded in the upper strata of the Free Colored society of the time. According to his probate documents, upon his death in 1780 he owned 9 enslaved people, who appear to have been living as family groups on his plantation.

The entire area is difficult to interpret, David points out, because it is more "organic" than a European-style straight-line plan; rock

This eighteenth-century grave could be the final resting place of plantation owner Franz Claasen

(Photo by Bruce Schoonover)

outcroppings are used strategically, areas cleared and materials gathered for one use have been reused. The whole process speaks loads about the ingenuity used to live lightly with the land—everything was recycled.

After Franz passed away, his wife and his daughter were given a prominent Free Colored curator, Peter Tameryn, to handle their estate. However, despite this and the matriarchal orientation of the Free Colored community, the lack of a son made it difficult for the family to retain their landed status. It is probable, David conjectures, that Claasen's genealogy reflects the trend of the time, where the daughters of Free Colored families often "married up" into the Creole or white plantocracy, thereby diminishing, rather than perpetuating Free Colored land ownership.

The headstone of Hesther D. Francis, 1826-1864

(Photo by Bruce Schoonover)

Continuing our walk, now staying strictly on a path through the sucker-cactus strewn ground (a sure sign of previous cattle-grazing, says Eleanor) and dancing around the fire ants, we visit two partial burial sites. The older grave is a quite formal raised European-style (i.e. not the flatter Moravian-style) marker of imported red-clay tiles. This could be the gravesite of Franz Claasen's first wife, but is more probably the gravesite of Franz Claasen himself. The more recent formal red-brick structure is the grave of George Francis's second wife, Hesther Dalinda Francis, dated by a loose (rather modern) stone tablet—April 20, 1826-September 9, 1864. These two markers are possibly indicative of a large, now overgrown, multi-generational cemetery—but that is yet to be determined.

Full of information, we trek back to our automobiles. Driving home, we mull over all the things we have learned and are intrigued by how much we still don't know. So, David… just who was Betty of Betty's Hope anyway?

Many thanks to the following bush-cutters who made our journey back in time a little less perilous—John Achzet, Peter Burgess, Larry Boxerman, and Weldon Wasson.

January, 2007

The Trail from Hermitage to Brownsbay

David W. Knight

A walk along the Brown Bay trail is indeed a trip back into St. John history. Beginning on the shores of Borck's Creek, named for Dr. Edmond Borck, the owner of Estate Hermitage c1779 through 1800, the trail heads north and ascends rapidly. Along this first part of the journey the sprawling ruins of the primary residential complex of the Hermitage estate are clearly visible on the ridge-line to the east of the trail.

Cresting Moore Hill above Borck's Creek, the trail crosses over the Hermitage Estate boundary and leaves the East End Quarter. As you begin the long descent to the North Shore, the trail enters Estate Brownsbay, the easternmost property in the administrative district known as the Maho Bay Quarter.

Among the plantation properties of St. John, the history of Estate Brownsbay is perhaps one of the most compelling. From the 1728 Danish tax rolls, we know that a tract of land formally deeded to Jacob Thoma in 1725 had previously been the possession of one "Jan Bruyn" [John Brown]. Jacob Thoma died prior to 1728, leaving his Brownsbay plantation to his two daughters, Elizabeth and Maria, both of whom were killed in the 1733 slave revolt.

March 2003

Looking out over Estate Hermitage and Borck's Creek from Moore Hill on the trail to Brownsbay, c1900

(Photo by Clare E. Taylor [D. Knight Collection])

Exploring Lieven Marche Bay

Presentation by David W. Knight and Eleanor Gibney; Summarized by Robin Swank

30 hikers ascend the Brown Bay Trail… probably not the route of the historic trail depicted on the 1800 Oxholm map

Many of the hikers who joined David W. Knight and Eleanor Gibney on our exploration had already visited Brown Bay, but only a few were previously aware of the Hermitage or Mount Pleasant estates, or of the earlier subsumed and less-documented estate houses and industrial plants that remain along the coral-strewn north shore of the St. John's East End.

Before setting out on our hike David explained that British immigrants from the Eastern Caribbean began to take up failing plantations in the area of East End in the mid 1700s. Earlier, this section of St. John was known as the "French Quarter," because it had been originally settled by French Huguenot families—Constantin, Loisan, Bordeaux, Castan, and Marche—who sought refuge from religious persecution in the liberal, Protestant, Danish colony. British settlers from the Eastern Caribbean, with family names like Moore, Coakley, Turner, Sewer, George and Borck, represent a second wave of Danish-sanctioned settlement in the area. Most of these

English families migrated from Anguilla, Peter Island and Spanish Town (Virgin Gorda), where depleted soil, poor climate and geographic isolation had made it nearly impossible to eke out a living. Accustomed to life on the edge, these hearty Creoles readily settled on marginal lands that wealthier sugar planters shunned as unsuitable for agriculture.

David pointed out that one theme apparent throughout St. John is that successive waves of settlers used and re-used existing resources. Most structures and landforms were built over, recycling materials and building sites from earlier times, thus disrupting any cleanly-layered chronological history. Early estates in this area appear to have raised cotton, later converting to mixed agriculture, fishing and cottage industry, along with the grazing of a Creolized breed of sheep and other livestock. Among the diverse activities engaged in during this period was the tanning of hides to meet the huge demand for leather goods (gloves, holsters, bridles and saddles, etc.) stimulated by the Napoleonic conflicts at the turn of the 19th century. The ruins of a tannery or rendering plant at Lieven Marche Bay, our destination for the day, are notable in that they appear to be the only such facility constructed on St. John exclusively for this purpose. (The Caroline's Lyst Estate on Water Island, off of St. Thomas, also appears to have been similarly engaged.)

We trek up the Brown Bay trail to Moore Hill, pausing only for sips of water. Once over the crest of Moore Hill, we take a vote on our route, and then adventurously descend directly to Lieven Marche Bay through the bush. With the ruins of Marche's Mount Pleasant estate house and laborers' village above us on the right, we trek down a gut, still damp from last night's showers, through scattered catch 'n' keep and genip

An eighteenth-century tanning factory

(Dederot's Pictorial Encyclopedia of Trades and Industries, France, 1751)

trees. Along the way David calls our attention to the remains of terracing that line the hillsides around us, evidence of past agricultural land use and an important element of St. John's rapidly diminishing cultural landscape.

A few large genip and tamarind trees provide a shady canopy that helps minimize the brush underfoot. These are old enough, Eleanor Gibney notes, to have been specimen trees when the landscape was cultivated or grazed. As we now better understand the real growth rates of our native plants, it's certain much of St. John was not clear-cut (up until 1800 large sections of St. John were still bush), and it makes sense that some trees were left for shade, shelter, or for the fruits and medicinal resources they provided. Many of our stands of trees could not possibly have grown this large in less than 300 years, Eleanor informs us.

Soon the land flattens out and the gut empties into a mud-packed crab pan near a brick and stone well and watering trough, less than 50 yards from today's beachfront. Wildly varying rainfall, then as now, required water management techniques to store it (in cisterns, ponds and reservoirs) and to access or distribute it (via aqueducts and wells). Although much of the island's water-intensive sugarcane support infrastructure has eroded off the landscape over time, wells and cisterns were particularly reused. Not far away from the first well we encountered is a second one with a semi-circular watering

trough, dated as mostly late 1800s by its beach-sand and quicklime-mortar construction. This well of 1800s-sized brick may have used a wind driven pump, David conjectures, but we can only surmise, as we have lost knowledge of a lot of the technology either imported or developed here. (At Leinster Bay, there appears to have been an ingenious automated wind-driven pumping system at the estate's sugar works from a very early period). We noted with interest the practice of reuse of earlier materials in both wells on the site.

Although we didn't see it in our downhill bush-trek, David describes the area as littered with remnants of cattle grazing through the early 1900s—watchmen's shacks and barbed-wire fence lines are laid out as pens and chutes to route cattle to the watering troughs on the beach and over the hill to Hurricane Hole where they were loaded (and/or unloaded) into lighters for transport.

Also scattered in the bush are ruins of smaller subsumed plantations. A practice incidentally helpful to clarifying timelines was the founding of large estates by the merger of several smaller ones. The conversion factor was generally 3:1, David tells us. Lieven Marche's Mount Pleasant was a huge estate for its time, an extraordinary 4800 feet in width, formed by the acquisition and merging of at least 3 earlier land holdings. By following the pattern of taking the most prominent old estate complex as its primary, and abandoning the others to bush, these forgotten settlements became important time capsules, that is, if not cannibalized for re-use, demolished by fire, wind and weather, or ransacked by those wanting archaeological souvenirs of their St. John visit.

We walk a short distance, still close to the beach, to a mid-1700s site which, David states, has been previously described as an abattoir or slaughterhouse. However, David believes that the cumulative evidence of the site points to its multi-faceted industrial use as a rendering plant, rather than to a mere slaughter-and-eat strategy. While meat was surely butchered and sold for immediate consumption, or dried and salted for future use, the primary function of the facility was certainly a tannery, where hides were prepared for export. Animal fats may also have been extracted here as by-products for use in the production of soap and other fat-based commodities.

The walls of the structure hold early yellow Danish "Flensberg" brick and recycled rubble, overlaid with irregular red brick dating to the mid-eighteenth through early-nineteenth centuries. The existing window openings appear to be lined with a more standard-sized brick of the mid-1800s. These walls clearly indicate reuse of the building over a prolonged time period.

Compelling evidence to support the building being a tannery includes the site location. "History is not so mysterious," David muses. "If you want to know how things were, simply look at how they are today; patterns of life and man's necessities are constant." In places like Brazil and Paraguay, for example, small tanneries resembling the ruins at Marche Bay are still in operation, and they are always situated at waterside where buildings can be easily sluiced down several times a day—sea water or river water serve equally well for this purpose. Fresh water is also necessary to the tanning process, hence the two nearby wells and a pond (reservoir) on the Marche Bay site.

Quicklime was another key element in the process—tanning requires lime for curing hides—and here again the Marche site had ready access to this material. Lime would have been produced on-site by burning the abundant beach-dried coral heads to a powder. A substitute for Europe's geological limestone, the discovery that quicklime could be produced from coral in the West Indies provided not only an inexpensive renewable hide-curing resource to fuel an industry, but also provided an inexpensive and readily available mortar-hardening agent to facilitate building with brick and stone. It was a discovery which enabled stone houses, windmills, and other more permanent estate structures to be built throughout the colony.

Inside the building curved brick liners below floor level look as if they once supported two heated vats. The remains of a small furnace and chimney can be observed from the outside. There is no evidence of any alternative industrial use: no crushing mill, molasses catchments or rum still, and no documented estate activity of sugarcane—and the site's suitability for sugarcane is wrong in any case.

As our group straggles back up to the Brown Bay trail—some straight up an informal trail marked by discarded clothing left by illegal immigrants, and some taking the longer route by way of the Brown Bay ruins and Johnny Horne trail—Society members begin their post-hike conjectures, and more questions begin to pop up. We always learn so much, and then we always realize how little we know!!

February, 2007

Detail of Lieven Marche's Bay from Peter L. Oxholm's 1780 manuscript map of St. John

(Rigsarkivet, Copenhagen, Denmark)

Ruins and Rambles

Hike to Estate Retreat

Presentation by David W. Knight and Eleanor Gibney; Summarized by Robin Swank

David introduced us to Estate Retreat as we stood along the East End Road. "Retreat is a site intriguingly remote and obscure, even by St. John standards," he tells us. But, how did this estate come to be, and why is its history so obscure?

By about 1725 nearly all of the good lands on St. John had been parceled out and settled. The East End, however, was still largely underdeveloped, as it was considered marginal planting ground due to its arid nature. After the 1733 slave revolt it was even harder to encourage local planters to attempt to make a living here. Many plantations on St. John were failing, and as they did an immigration opportunity presented itself. This situation opened the doors of ownership to a group of struggling settlers from places like Peter Island, Spanishtown (aka Virgin Gorda), or Anguilla, who were seeking land on which to escape poverty and elevate the positions of their creolized families. They were accustomed to eking out a living on dry remote islands, were comfortable with a seafaring life and with hustling for a modest living, so they immigrated to the challenging central East End of St. John—then called the "French Quarter." Families with names such as Richardson, Moore, Brown, Coakley and Sewer, eventually displaced the earlier French Huguenot settlers in this area during the 1760s through c1800.

Retreat's history is obscure partly because of its location outside the mainstream of the Danish system. It sits between the seafaring East End community and the plantation-based Coral Bay community. It was a large estate, though not one necessarily viable from the point of view of the structured economy of the time, which planted and paid taxes in sugar and cotton. Rather, it was a property that found a niche, and with its neighbors, contrived to live passably well.

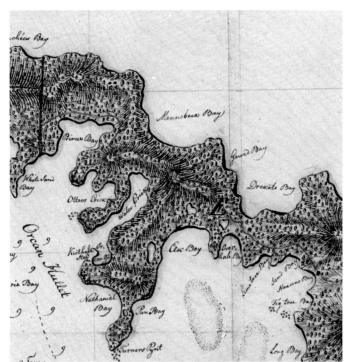

Retreat was granted to the Dane Niles Anderson in 1728. It was briefly merged with Hermitage by Dederich Kervink between 1779 and 1782. The owner of Mt Pleasant, Joseph Coakley, acquired Retreat in 1805, merging it into his property. They remained merged thereafter, minus a few in-holding sales, until their 1910 sale to A.H. Lockhart from St. Thomas, who speculated that Germany's intent to build a naval base in Coral Bay would increase the value of his investment.

(Detail from the 1780 Oxholm Map showing the area of Estate Retreat and Hurricane Hole [Rigsarkivet, Denmark])

It is also obscure because of its intermittent habitation and serial mergers with other properties (such as estates Mount Pleasant and Hermitage). Because of its changing ownership, Retreat's documentation is fragmented, located in far-flung probate proceedings, or as part of other estates' tax documents, as it merged

The mysterious *Solanum conocarpum*, long thought to be extinct but rediscovered on St. John in the 1990s. It has been thriving in cultivation, but is still only found growing wild on the island's eastern half.

(Photo by Robin Swank)

through marriages or split off by sales; records are both in English and Gothic scripted Danish.

Armed with historical background, we ascend the steep eastern flank of Mt. Pleasant from Princess Bay. As Eleanor Gibney has pre-flagged our route, it is an easy walk up through a well-recovered area of 100% native forest. Where cattle have grazed, Eleanor tells us, plants such as casha, catch and keep and maran bush flourish (as the cattle ate everything else); we find those in small measure near the top of the hill.

Those of us in sandals also find "suckers," (finger sized opuntia cacti), additional signs of grazing. Here and there are remnants of pinguin, (wild pine) "fences," which would have met the Danish government's requirement for a vegetative barricade to supplement a wood post fence. Prickley pear (also called Blyden bush), was also used as barricade, as was catch' n' keep, our "country policeman." There are a few trees that would have been field trees. There is amarat (*Acacia muricata*), a dark green twice-pinnate spineless acacia tree good for soil building, used for charcoal and as building material.

A white cedar (*Tabebuia heterophylla*), which is neither white nor cedar, was sporting its pale pink trumpet-vine like flowers. Its wood was excellent boat building material. Eleanor also points out a few young multi-trunked lignum vitae (*Guaiacum officinale*), a self-lubricating wood used for bearings and blocks, it would also have been a welcome planted resource. We also

spot maubi, or snake bark (*Colubrina eliptica*). No doubt every tree, vine, bush or weed was used for something!

Also on our path is a tree once thought extinct from its original narrow range of the eastern end of St. John—the *Solanum conocarpum*. "It is so rare it doesn't have a common name," Eleanor informs.

Everyone asks the ages of trees, but Eleanor reminds us that tree rings do not represent annual growth in our environment—and there are no postcards or photos of Retreat to help the dating process.

There is less of a carpet of artifacts, David tells us, than in his youthful island meanderings. One hiker finds the base of a black glass English port bottle dating to the late-eighteenth or early-nineteenth century, a utilitarian bottle that would have been used, reused, and possibly transported—so finding just one is not a good clue for pinpointing date of occupation of the site. A single piece of chaynee (blue and white porcelain pottery, aka chanee or chinee) is found. Conchs, possibly once adornments of graves, are scattered. Being good National Park guests and historians, we are careful to leave everything *in situ* as we find it.

It would have been a simple life. David read from an "Evaluation" of Retreat's land and buildings belonging to John Richard Richardson, found in his wife's Probate dated July 9, 1800. It says in part "the plantation lies in this island in the East End quarter, planted with a little cotton and provisions. Hereon is a new dwelling house of American shingles and a little magazine and a few Negro houses." This description is in keeping with the modest footprint of this and other plantations in the area that were not involved in large-scale sugaring or cotton raising; it was valued at 5,512 Rigsdalers (Danish West Indies currency).

We walk past large fruiting tamarinds (*Tamarindus indicus*), which may have been planted near the cleared ground as social meeting trees. We also pass small stands of torchwood, *Amyris elemifera*, a citrus-y plant whose common name is ascribed to this and other plants that will burn when green and can be used as disposable flashlights. Then at the crest of the hill, we come upon the "magazine," the storehouse or barn used to keep cotton and any 'Indian provisions' (cassava and corn) dry.

Ruins and Rambles

The roots of a huge loblolly or water mampoo (*Pisonia subcordata*) sprawl on the north side of the magazine.

The foundations of the house, possibly once a two-story structure with two rooms up and two down, sits on the crest of the hill collecting breeze from the north and east. The foundations slope away from the wood-post and shingled walls, keeping the house dry. David notes that there is no evidence of a water storage facility—there may have been large earthenware jars to collect rain from the roof, although wells in the valley below were most likely the primary water source. We do not find all the buildings we would expect from a standard footprint. There must have been nearby outbuildings for slaves. The kitchen, remains of which are in a debris field down slope to the north, would have been accompanied by an oven, now only rubble. In keeping with the estate's merger history, the house was probably lived in only a short time. After Mr. Richardson's death, his wife probably relocated to her much grander family home at Brown Bay.

East of the site, Mennebeck Bay may have been the north landing spot for Retreat's boats. Major shipping, however, would have transpired through the Hurricane Holes, where, David recalls, he once snorkeled over a sunken lighter. The water is deep enough along the shore there that cattle could easily have walked from a sand spit onto a lighter for transport.

Homesteaders on Retreat and nearby estates lived in times of increasing interaction and cross migration, as social and political circumstances evolved. David notes that they did business mostly with their British "cousins" in nearby Tortola communities, avoiding, or perhaps evading, the longer "required" Danish trading routes through St. Thomas. With the passage of the British Slave Act of 1783, significant cross migration between Tortola and St. John began; British restrictions on Free-Coloreds' rights led to much relocation *to* St. John. Then, the British colonies abolished slavery. The Foreign Slave Act of 1825 stated "…any persons arriving in any of his Majesty's Colonies from any foreign island or state where they were lawfully held in slavery, were not to be sent back thither as slaves, or to be dealt with as slaves." Any enslaved persons reaching Tortola could declare themselves free. With this Act, there was a sharp upturn in attempted escape *from* St. John.

David read an excerpt from *Reminiscences of the West India Islands*, a collection of stories of the Methodist Missionaries, wherein a regular shopping foray from St. John to Tortola and one of these attempted escapes by two slaves is recounted; one is named Harry. When we turn to an excerpt from Hester Coakley's Probate, which lists the land and slaves of Estates Hermitage and Mount Pleasant, c1799, there is the highly valued Harry!!! (The full account of this caper and a look at raising turtles in kraals, [another niche-y approach to survival], can be found elsewhere in this volume.)

Our short "200-year" hike over, we turn back toward Princess Bay. A few turpentine trees (*Bursera simaruba*) have dropped zillions of seeds and as we crush the seedlings, they flavor the air. We thank Eleanor and David for giving us an appreciation of how homesteaders made a unique living here, and alerting us of our need to learn at least two dead languages—Latin and Gothic-scripted Danish.

April, 2008

Lamesure Bay Explore

Presentation by David W. Knight and Eleanor Gibney; Summarized by Robin Swank

Yawzi Point's Great Lamesure Estate House. It's rounded entry steps overlook the cotton magazine.

(Photo from the SJHS Archives, c2007)

Seventy-eight hikers met at the Virgin Islands Environmental Research Station to join David W. Knight and Eleanor Gibney for a tour of the physical remains of three contiguous estates, Great Lamesure, Little Lamesure, and Bowe, which were consolidated in the latter half of the 18th century to form a single Lamesure Bay estate. David shared the available historical record of these plantations and invited us to conjecture upon what is not yet fully documented.

Lieutenant Ullerup's plantation situated on Great Lamesure Bay is the oldest of the three Lamesure estates; it was deeded to him in 1720. Situated on a dry and windswept ridgeline on what is today called Yawzi Point, the estate house foundation, with at least two gravesites on the west side of the house, overlooks the ruins of what appears to have been a cotton magazine (warehouse), necessary to keep the fragile harvested cotton dry. Farther inland are the remnants of the slaves' compound. Because the grounds were cleared last year by the Sierra Club, the outlines of the estate's primary structures depicted on Peter Oxholm's 1780 St. John map can be clearly distinguished in the bush. To date, David has not found documentation to verify local stories that this site was once used as a quarantine station,

and he urged anyone with solid references to support this claim to share that information with us.

A second plantation on neighboring Little Lamesure Bay was deeded to Johannes Uytendael in 1721. This appears to have been a more developed property, having an overseer and seven enslaved laborers on site by 1733.

The third plantation at Lamesure, known as Bowe, was deeded to Lt. John Stiwell in 1725. Unlike the other two estates, structures associated with this property do not appear on the 1780 Oxholm map, and history documents it as mostly unoccupied. Nor is there evidence of the Stiwell house today. David speculated that it may have been the small site that fell to the bulldozer when the modern road over the hill to Lamesure was built some years ago. We may never know, for all that remains of that site today is a suspicious bunch of aloe and other usually domestic plantings on both sides of the road.

Early histories of these sites share the common themes of cotton cropping (probably accompanied by grazing and the self-sufficiency requirements of liming and provisioning), transitions of the land from one owner to another due to early death, sales at auction because of debt, and damages during the 1733 slave rebellion.

Cotton was the primary crop on the dry south side of St. John in this early period. It is believed cotton was already planted on St. John, possibly initially by Amerindian textile weavers, by the time the first permanent Danish-sanctioned colonists arrived. It was sea isle cotton, noted for its oiliness and valuable for sail making. It could be sold either as stone cotton (with the seeds), or ginned (free of seeds). As a crop, cotton harvesting required only a modest degree of wealth for the purchase of slaves designated not strong enough for sugar work (i.e. macrons).

Macrons could also comb or gin the cotton, yielding the seed for future plantings.

Another valued commodity of the time was quicklime, which was not available in mineral form here, but made by burning dried coral heads. In one historical inventory of the Lamesure estate, bags of lime are among the most highly assessed product on the property. Was Lamesure named for the chalk-white cliffs (lime shore) these settlers hoped were made of limestone? Or was it named for the "limes ashore" planted by earlier seamen? Eleanor Gibney pointed out probably not the latter, as citrus would have been called "lemons" in that era. So, how about Lemon-shore?

Consolidation of the Lamesure properties occurred c1755, when Gowert Marche (the owner of Great Lamesure since c1732) purchased the neighboring Little Lamesure and his son-in-law Mathias Bowe purchased the former Stiwell parcel. But, by 1769 the holdings began to fragment to multiple Marche heirs. It was not until 1776 that all three properties came under the undivided ownership of Gustavious Nibbs of Tortola.

The Nibbs family appears to have found no success with the Lamesure estate. After a devastating hurricane laid waste to the property in 1793, all of the Great and Little Lamesure properties were sold at auction to the owner of the adjacent Bordeaux estate, Reverend Thomas Braithwaite, who was actively consolidating his holdings in the Danish West Indies. David pointed out that many of the wealthier British planters who had mixed-race children, like Braithwaite, A.C. Hill and Alexander Fraser, purchased holdings in the more liberal Danish West Indies to establish their Free-Colored heirs. British law in this era forbade them from passing on homeland properties to non-white offspring. It is estimated that at Emancipation nearly 40% of St. John estate owners were members of the island's rapidly growing Free-Colored population.

Upon Reverend Braithwaite's death his Free-Colored mistress retained tenancy at Bordeaux, while their daughters inherited the Lohman estate in Coral Bay, while his *in absentia* white British heir, Elizabeth Threlfall, got the Lamesure property (and later Bordeaux as well). It appears that Miss Threlfall never set foot on St. John and that Lamesure lay fallow throughout her ownership.

In 1832 Ingjald C. Mourier, a Danish citizen, purchased Estate Lamesure and immediately set out to develop it into an active sugar cane plantation. It appears to have been Mourier who built most of the industrial structure now visible along Lamesure Bay and the estate house atop the hill. This house is the longest continually-occupied estate house on St. John. It is currently owned by the National Park and occupied by a very gracious Park Ranger, who invited all of us to tour the inside. According to estate inventories, Mourier's new masonry

According to a survey conducted by James McGuire published in 1923, there were both a bay rum still and a limejuice still on the Lamesure estate. There is also a separate ruins of a rum still associated with the sugar works on the site.

(Photo by Robin Swank)

and tile-roofed dwelling had an attached and fireproofed cookhouse (the latest thing!), and a fire engine (a pump on a cart), just in case.

Mourier's estate growth can be tracked through tax records and a series of "appraisements," probably required because he had outstanding loans. The estate's enslaved population of 22 tripled at the height of his ownership; he created the water source needed for sugar production by digging out a pond near the bay and quickliming it to create a leak-proof reservoir. His property was valued in 1843 at 27,274 Spanish pieces-of-eight, the preferred currency of the time because its assayed intrinsic value was true, unlike that of the Danish Rigsdaler, which was made of inferior "German silver" or silver-plate over a copper core. You have to wonder in this period of sharp economic decline if Mourier's ability to pay the taxes on his increasingly valuable property kept pace with the profits he could generate from sugar and raising sheep! By 1847, the year before Emancipation, of the

Count and Countess Castinskjold on the steps of the Lamesure Estate house c1905

(Image from the Det Kongelige Bibliotek, Copenhagen, Denmark)

235 acres on the estate, only 24 were planted in sugar cane.

After Mourier's tenancy, Lamesure was purchased by Richard Penn, a cattle breeder who acquired all the southern lands between Salt Pond and Lamesure. In 1905, Penn sold the Lamesure estate to the Count and Countess Castinskjold.

The year 1905 shows the first donkey ("ass") in an inventory for Lamesure! According to a description read by Chuck Pishko, the Countess Mogeens "Daisy" Friis Castinskjold was "an elegant and wild girl," who would "thrill at the possibility of total ruin." Quite possibly

she married her totally acceptable Danish Ambassador as a family accommodation. Remarking on the picture at left, one knowledgeable SJHS member among the hiking group said—"That was more clothes than she was ever known to wear."

This hike goes to prove that the SJHS are a hardy bunch! We covered a lot of educational territory as well as a lot of physical ground. We owe a huge thank you to Randy Brown, the VIERS team, and Clean Islands International Co. for providing our midday food and drink, and for hosting us at VIERS, providing us with an additional educational experience.

What's In A Name?

Do you know how Yawzi Point got its name? A 1794 Lamesure inventory lists a "sickhouse" on the estate. Was this structure on Yawzi Point? Is the name Yawzi Point derived from the disease yaws? Or is it derived from some other source?

Yaws is a disease thought to be of Caribbean origin; it is a chronic infectious disease which first exhibits symptoms of open sores, caused by a spirochete that enters through cuts or scrapes; it then attacks the bones and joints. Today one injection of penicillin cures it. Most at risk are children under 15. The derivation of the word is obscure; the Carib word "yaya" is the word for "sore"; alternatively the African word "yaw" may have meant "berry." Yaws is also, therefore, called *frambesia tropica*. (Summarized from *www.Medicinenet.com*)

In the early days of Lamesure diseases like yellow fever, smallpox, and cholera would have been common, and the isolation of Yawzi Point at or near an abandoned estate house might have been an ideal quarantine station. Perhaps young children with yaws were also housed there.

April, 2007

Detail of Great & Little Lamesure Bays from Peter L. Oxholm's 1780 manuscript map of St. John

(Rigsarkivet, Copenhagen, Denmark)

Ruins and Rambles

The Lameshur Bay Estate of the 1950s

Bruce Schoonover

Consolidation of properties has always played a huge role in the ownership of estates on St. John. By the late 1700s, we have seen that what we now think of as the Lameshur Estate was, in fact, composed of multiple former estates—consisting of something less than 500 acres. This same consolidation continued right up through the mid 1900s.

According to the research of Crystal Fortwangler, after the ownership of the estate by Count Castinskjold from 1904-1920, there was a quick succession of owners. This was followed by the acquisition of the property by Herman O. Creque in 1922. He held the property until his death in the late 1940s, at which time title was transferred to his wife, Mrs. Emily Creque.

It was Mrs. Emily Creque who sold the Lameshur Estate, now consisting of some 1,433 acres and composed of Bordeaux #5, Cabrite Horn #1, Great and Little Lameshur #2 & #3, Hope #5, Misgunst #6 and Packero (sic.) #7 to Frank Stick in May of 1953.

Actually, Frank Stick never officially owned the Lameshur Estate. Title to the property was held in the name of David Stick, Frank Stick's son, and his wife Phyllis. However, David explains that he and his wife simply served as a "strawman" and ownership rested with his father and four business partners, all stateside friends.

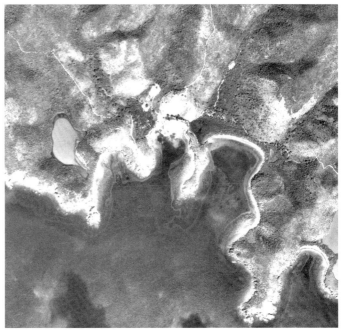

Lameshur Bay, January 1954

(USGS Aerial Survey of St. John, 1-28-1954 [US National Archives])

On January 1, 1955, the 1,433 acres of the Lameshur Estate was transferred to the Jackson Hole Preserve, Inc., the non-profit conservation entity of the Rockefeller family. Finally, on November 21, 1956, this land was transferred to the United States Department of Interior as a part of the establishment of the Virgin Islands National Park, our Nation's 29th National Park.

April, 2007

Count and Countess Castinskjold at Lamesure Estate house c1905

(Image from the Det Kongelige Bibliotek, Copenhagen, Denmark)

Chapter 4

THE IMAGE MAKERS

A History of Local Postcards

and the People Who Made Them

David W. Knight

The near total devastation of the physical and economic infrastructure of St. Thomas and St. John by the hurricane, earthquakes and tsunamis of 1867, and yet another hurricane in 1871, marks an important turning point in the fortunes of the Danish West Indies. Gone were the days of wooden sailing ships, the wealthy sugar planter, and the independent merchant trader. Massive black-iron ships driven by steam would soon inherit the seas. The Age of the Industrialists had dawned, and within their design the islands served little other purpose than that of a convenient fueling station for their coal-hungry ships filled with passengers and cargo bound elsewhere. For St. Thomas, the future of her port now lay in massive heaps of coal brought from the mines of Cardiff and New Castle; and, for her town, it lay in the increasing numbers of transient visitors. The days of tourism had inadvertently arrived, and with them came a sharp demand for small, easily-transportable keepsakes. Soon, the streets of Charlotte Amalie bustled with shops and emporiums, all competing for a share in the market for Panama hats, bay rum products, and photo souvenirs in the form of photogravures, stereo-views, and postcards.

THE PHOTOGRAPHIC GALLERY.

OPPOSITE THE STORES OF

Messrs. KREBS & PRÆTORIUS,

Has been reopened under the management of

MR. CORTE REAL.

Cartes de Visites Portraits at $4 per dozen.

Large size PHOTOGRAPHS $4 for the first impression and $1 for duplicates.

CARTES DE VISITES VIGNETTES, *AMBROTYPES & MELAINOTYPES,* all at very reasonable prices.

STEREOSCOPIC VIEWS OF

St. Thomas.

60 different views of the most picturesque parts of the Town and Harbour,

AT $4 PER DOZEN.

The Gallery being in possession of all the Negatives taken by Mr. GRAY and Mr. BJERRING, all persons wishing copies of their own portraits can be supplied with them.

St. Thomas, 2nd May, 1863.

Advertisement for the Photographic Gallery of Mr. Corte Real

(St. Thomas Tidende, May 2, 1863 [Rigsarkivet, Copenhagen, Denmark])

It is not known for certain who the first commercial photographer to set up shop in the Danish West Indies was, but on May 2, 1863, an individual with the unlikely nom de guerre of "Mr. Corte Real" placed an announcement in the *St. Thomas Tidende* newspaper for the reopening of a photo gallery previously owned by "Mr. Grey and Mr. Bjerring." Along with the usual services of producing both "Ambrotype and Melainotype" portraits, "Stereoscopic views of St. Thomas" and "60 different views of the most picturesque parts of the town and harbor" were offered. It is intriguing that the date of the opening of this photo gallery corresponds with the arrival on St. Thomas of two men who would become known as the premiere purveyors of local postcards, Dr. Charles E. Taylor and Edward Ferdinand Fraas.

A native of London, Charles Taylor came to the Danish West Indies at the age of twenty via Canada, the USA, and Cuba. Largely self educated, he was an unabashed promoter of himself and his "Spiritualist" beliefs. While not known to have been a photographer himself, Dr. Taylor was an early advocate of St. Thomas as a tourist destination and an active supporter of local photographers. Although his first visitor-

"LUMPS OF COAL."
(COAL WOMAN OF ST. THOMAS, D.W I.)

One of a series of postcards of "Coal Woman" published by Dr. Charles E. Taylor, c1900

(D. Knight Collection)

CRUZ BAY, ST. JOHN, D.W.I.

A view of Cruz Bay by Clare E. Taylor believed to be the first photo postcard of St. John, c1900

(Mike & Jane Sheen Collection)

Market. St. Thomas W. I.

Market Square on St. Thomas by Edward F. Fraas, c1900

(D. Knight Collection)

oriented publication, *Leaflets from the Danish West Indies*, published in 1888, contained no photo images, some of the illustrations in the book were credited as having been rendered from photographs by local photographer Edward Fraas. However, Taylor's second publication, *An Island Of The Sea*, published in 1895, may well be the first locally-published book to exclusively feature photographs of the Danish West Indies. In his preface to the book, Taylor relates that all of the illustrations were reproduced from "photographs by our local artists"—although none of the photos are credited to their creators.

After relying on the works of independent local photographers in his early publishing ventures, Charles Taylor next turned to his own family. Near the turn of the twentieth century, postcards and photo books published by Taylor's Book Store on Main Street, St. Thomas, exclusively showcased the photography of his son,

Clarence (Clare) E. Taylor. Born on St. Thomas in 1875, Clare was both an accomplished illustrator and a prolific photographer. The images on his many photo postcards are some of the most recognizable and longest-published photographs of the Danish period—particularly those of the "Coal Woman." His work is also noteworthy in that it is believed that an image by Clare Taylor was used on the first postcard ever produced of the island of St. John.

While Charles and Clare Taylor may hold the honor of being the great, early promoters of the postcard in the Danish West Indies, it is surely Edward Fraas who best deserves to be known as the Father of the local photo postcard. Born in Denmark, Peter Edward Ferdinand Fraas came out to the Danish West Indies in 1863 at the age of twenty-five. Once established, he married Malvina Weinmar of Cruz Bay, St. John.

Fraas's postcards clearly stand out among his contemporaries'. They not only display

Teaching basket making at the Emmaus Mission in Coral Bay by Johannes Lightbourn, c1900

(D. Knight collection)

Sugar being produced at the Parforce Estate in Reef Bay by Johannes Lightbourn, c1900

(Det Kongelige Bibliotek, Copenhagen, Denmark)

the photographer's fine sense of depth and composition, but also an appreciation for the cultural significance of a scene. His images are notable for their vibrancy: always full of life and movement. Upon Edward's death in 1913, Malvina took over the running of the Fraas Photo Studio and Postcard Shop on Main Street, St. Thomas. The business was still in operation as late as the 1920s.

But, If Edward Fraas is to be known as the "Father" of the Danish West Indies' photo postcard, and Charles and Clare Taylor are credited with being the "great promoters" of the local photo image as a tourist item, then an individual by the name of Johannes Nathaniel Lightbourn must be recognized as the most prolific publisher of Danish West Indies postcards.

A printer and journalist by trade, Johannes Lightbourn came to St. Thomas in 1864 at the age of twenty-four. Born in Bermuda, Lightbourn worked for many years in a local printing office before taking over the business in the early 1900s and diversifying its publishing activities to include newspapers, almanacs, books, photogravures, and photo postcards. Like Charles Taylor, Lightbourn's publications included images by various photographers, including himself and his son, Donald Lightbourn.

Terms:

Deltiology – Postcard Collecting: The third largest collecting hobby.

Post Card – Cards printed by a government postal service, which include postage.

Postcard – a privately produced card with no affixed prepaid postage.

Timeline:

1861 – First privately printed postcard produced by John P. Charlton in Philadelphia.

1870 – First post card issued by the Austria-Hungary government.

1875 – General Postal Union formed in Europe. Cards begin to be sent outside of their country of origin.

1877 – The Danish Postal Service prints the first post card for local and international use for the Danish West Indies.

By 1890 – Postcards with decorative illustrations, photos or advertising have become common.

1900-1915 – The "Golden Age of the Photo Postcard."

About 1907 – Divided Back postcards introduced.

In the Danish West Indies the direct predecessor of the photo postcard was the "brevkort" (letter-card), first issued by the Danish Postal Service in 1877.

(D. Knight Collection)

Tourist day - Chs DELINOIS and Co - Panama Hat Store - St Thomas D. W. I.

Advertising postcard of Charles Delinois' Panama Hat Store in St. Thomas, c1907. The Delinois family purchased estates Adrian, Cathrineberg and L'Esperance in 1848.

(D. Knight Collection)

As a photographer Lightbourn is unique in the fact that he ventured into the rural areas of the colony in search of images to a greater degree than any of his counterparts. He was also the only one of the Danish West Indies' photographers to publish a series of photo postcards of the island of St. John, all of them portraying cultural scenes or local industries. Historically important and most notable of these images are scenes of basket making at the Moravian Mission in Coral Bay and the only known picture of a working St. John sugar factory taken at Estate Parforce in Reef Bay.

To the list of pioneers of St. Thomas-based postcard producers one lesser known photographer is clearly worthy of inclusion in the group, Arturo Giglioli. Giglioli and his wife, Elvira, were born in Leghorn, Italy. They emigrated to the Danish West Indies in 1880 where they purchased a home at #64 Queen's Street. In the 1901 census Giglioli stated his age as sixty-one years and noted his profession as "music master." Giglioli's photos appear to all be of an early date as the majority of the postcards that carry his images have undivided backs. As was the case with most photographers of the era, Giglioli also produced photo portrait cards. It was popular in this era to have your image reproduced as a personal card to present

to friends and family as a keepsake. Only a few of the portrait cards produced by local photographers are known to still exist, and rarely can the individual in the picture be identified. A portrait card by Giglioli with the image of Carl Francis of St. John is a notable exception (see: *The Life and Heritage of Carl Emanuel Francis of St. John* on page 60).

In closing, it must be mentioned that a number of local merchants also published postcards in this period, either as advertising or to be sold in their shops. Unfortunately few if any of these cards give credit to the photographers. Among the most common of the local merchants' cards are those produced for A. H. Riise & Co., but cards published for G. Beretta & Co., Charles Delinois, The Danish Fruit Company, The East Asiatic Co. Ltd., H. Michelsen and Bornn's Bay Rum can also be found.

By the 1920s, US Navy photographers and visitors taking snapshots with their own cameras had undermined the profitability of shops dedicated to the sale of photo souvenirs. Photographic supplies, as well as developing

An early postcard for Caneel Bay Plantation, c1948

(D. Knight Collection)

and printing services, were now offered and few new photo postcards of the now Virgin Islands of the United States were produced in the period. Nearly all of the postcards of St. John published in the early post-transfer era appear to be reprints of photos taken during the Danish period. It was not until the onset of US tourist-oriented development in the 1930s and early 1940s that photo postcards of St. Thomas and St. John began to become more common. Since that time, many thousands of postcard images of the Virgin Islands have been produced.

January, 2004

These stereoscopic images taken at the Cruz Bay Battery in 1898 are among the oldest known photographs of St. John.

(Det Kongelige Bibliotek, Copenhagen, Denmark)

Moravian Mission Fields — Mission der Brüdergemeine No. 40

Station Emmaus (St. Jan.)

Verlag der Missionsbuchhandlung, Herrnhut

A rare early postcard of the Emmaus Moravian Mission Station in Coral Bay by an unknown photographer, c1900

(Image courtesy of the Eleanor Gibney Collection)

In the Cotton field at „Lamesure", St. Jan, D. W. I.

A color-tinted photo postcard of cotton pickers in the fields on Estate Lamesure by Johannes Lightbourn, c1900

(Image courtesy of the D. Knight Collection)

The Image Makers

Coral Bay, St. Ian, Danish W. I.

A color-tinted photo postcard of Fortsberg and Usher's Cay in Coral Bay by Johannes Lightbourn, c1900

(Image courtesy of the D. Knight Collection)

St. Jan, D. W. I., and a group of the Virgin Islands.

A color-tinted photo postcard of Maho and Francis Bays taken from America Hill by Johannes Lightbourn, c1900

(Image courtesy of the D. Knight Collection)

The Image Makers

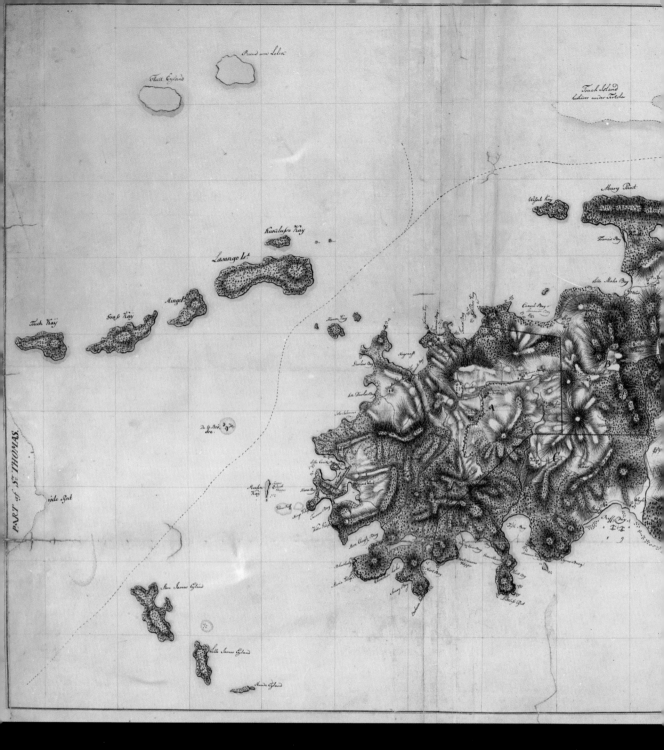

St. John and its Five Quarters

Lt. Peter L. Oxholm executed two versions of his St. John map: his 1780 manuscript version (shown above), and a slightly revised version published in 1800. While neither version of the map denotes individual estate boundaries, both do delineate the boundaries of the five administrative districts of the island, known as "Quarters" (A—Cruz Bay Quarter, B—Maho Bay Quarter, C—Reef Bay Quarter, D—Coral Bay Quarter, and E—East End Quarter). There are, however, some noteworthy differences in the two Oxholm maps.

In addition to the obvious difference of the manuscript map being rendered in hand-painted color, and the later printed map being simply a line drawing, the method of identifying property ownership was changed. On his 1780 manuscript map Oxholm wrote the name of each property owner over, or near, small black or red squares depicting the layout of each estate's primary residential and industrial compound (black squares for estate houses and plantation structures; red squares for the houses of

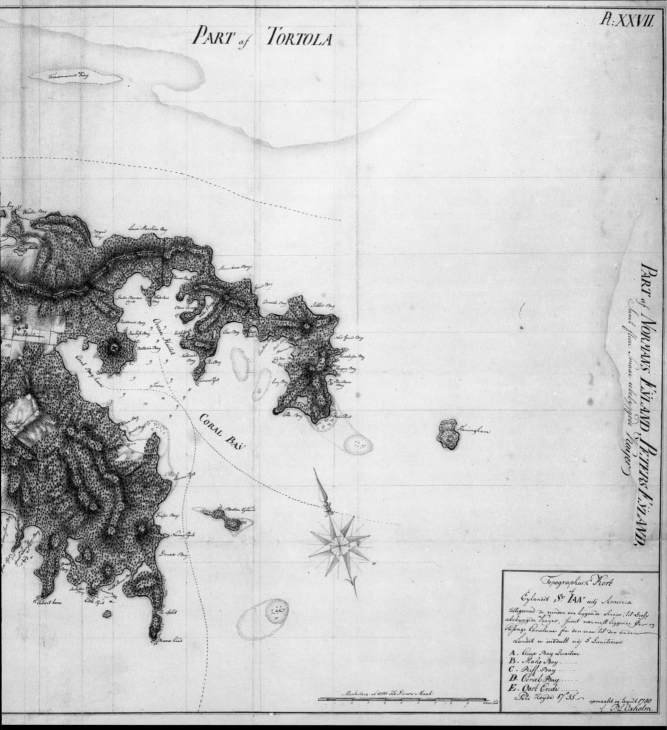

Hand-drawn manuscript map of St. Jan (in English, St. John) in the Danish West Indies, by Peter L. Oxholm, 1780 (Rigsarkivet Map Collection, Copenhagen, Denmark)

enslaved laborers). On the printed 1800 map, the names of owners were replaced by estate names (when available) along with numbers that corresponded to local tax rolls, compiled yearly throughout the colony. Further, the 1800 version included some updating of the physical components of individual properties and an inset of demographic notes and population statistics from the period. These updates to Oxholm's map highlight the importance of the document as an invaluable administrative tool to a Danish home government struggling to come to grips with the difficulties of overseeing its distant overseas colony.

Based on what we know today it is apparent that Oxholm did not actually visit and survey all of St. John, as several estate buildings and features of the landscape are improperly represented. Areas where there are notable differences between what is on the ground and what is on the map include the northern coast of East End and St. John's southeastern shoreline between Sabbat Point and Drunk Bay. Nevertheless, given the tools at hand, Oxholm's maps are an amazing accomplishment.

Going to Market, St. Jan, Danish W.I.

A color-tinted photo postcard of women on their way to market on St. John by Johannes Lightbourn, c1900

(Image courtesy of the Eleanor Gibney Collection)

Teaching Basket Making, St. John, V.I. of U.S.

A color-tinted version of "Teaching Basket Making" at the Emmaus Mission Station in Coral Bay by Johannes Lightbourn, republished in color, c1918

(Image courtesy of the D. Knight Collection)

The Image Makers

RUINS AT CANEEL BAY RESORT, ST. JOHN, VIRGIN ISLANDS   7A-H589

An early "Linen" postcard showing the sugar factory ruins at Caneel Bay—typical of the type of color postcards produced throughout the mid-1900s

(Image courtesy of the D. Knight Collection)

One of the earliest-known Kodachrome postcards of St. John is this image by Dr. George H. H. Knight of the Danish Training Ship "Danmark," anchored off Caneel Bay, c1940

(Image courtesy of the D. Knight Collection)

The Image Makers

A Kodachrome postcard of Cruz Bay taken from Lind Point by Ronald Morrisette in the early 1950s

(Image courtesy of Brion Morrisette)

Ushering In a New Era: This Kodachrome postcard by Dr. George H. H. Knight shows the Kungsholm anchored off of Cruz Bay in the early 1950s. The Kungsholm was the first cruise ship to make regularly scheduled stops at St. John.

(Image courtesy of the D. Knight Collection)

The Image Makers

Lieutenant Peter L. Oxholm and the Mapping of St. John

Douglas V. Armstrong, Mark W. Hauser, David W. Knight and Stephen Lenik

A fascinating aspect of Danish West Indies history is that no formally sanctioned maps of the tri-island colony were produced until 1780. In 1776, a Danish ship anchored off the fort in Frederiksted, St. Croix, was seized by a British naval vessel. The Danes were outraged, but, more importantly, they felt threatened by how easily their trade-based economic system could be interrupted by a belligerent foreign power. In consequence, the Danish government began to investigate the colony's defenses. As part of this assessment, a series of maps was commissioned by the Chamber of Customs. In a report to the Chamber of Customs, General Huth indicated that the islands were "of all together too great commercial importance for the colonial administration to be without accurate maps of them." Huth recommended that a survey be carried out by Lieutenant Peter Lotharius Oxholm, who had worked with him on the Eider Canal Project in Denmark.

Funding was soon approved to send Oxholm to survey all three islands. The dominant theme in Oxholm's orders was the need for details on defense against possible attacks by other nations or raids by privateers. Also of concern was the possibility of a slave uprising and the protection of water supplies in the event of a siege. Oxholm was given explicit orders to document and evaluate each island's fortifications. He was to draw all forts and batteries, "together with the harbors and stretches of land lying immediately adjacent, all in plan and profile." Along with these drawings, Oxholm was ordered to write a report on conditions, including detailed suggestions for improvements.

Peter Oxholm arrived in the Danish West Indies on March 14, 1778. After quickly determining that an earlier map of St. Croix drawn by J. M. Beck (c1750) was relatively accurate, he set about the task of producing plans of the island's fortifications and harbors. But, in contrast to the relatively flat lands of St. Croix, the rugged islands of St. Thomas and St. John represented perplexing cartographic problems. Oxholm's initial notes include the observation that these islands are "nothing but mountains and cliffs, where it is almost everywhere impossible to survey or prepare a geographic large-scale map." He therefore asked for permission to finish work on the forts and return home. Fortunately for us his request was rejected, and he continued on to produce the first concise map of the island of St. John.

Oxholm's field notes and reports are replete with details pertaining to the cultural landscape of St. John. Included among the documents he submitted to the Crown was the draft of a coastal survey of St. John dated 1777 and schematic representations of the island's fortifications. One of Oxholm's most detailed drawings is of the fortification at Cruz Bay (see: *St. John's Historic Christiansfort* on page 14). At the time, this was a newly constructed battery completed at a cost of 9,000 Rigsdaler, but funds had not been sufficient to complete the guard house. Oxholm suggested that completion of the project could be funded by selling the barracks to a private individual for use as a storehouse. With respect to the old fort at Coral Bay, Oxholm commented that the location of this fort was good for defense but that the remains of the building he visited were inadequate. He went on to lament the recent expenditure of funds on the less strategic fort at Cruz Bay while the fort overlooking Coral Bay remained in a state of ruin.

Ultimately, Oxholm opted not to map plantation boundaries on St. John, as it would simply have required too much time and expense to perform the cutting of bush needed for a proper survey. From his map and notes we learn that even near the apex of sugar production on the island, the proportion of cleared lands for sugar production represented only a small portion of the overall acreage. Oxholm did, however, document the location of quarter boundaries representing the administrative division of the islands into five groups of estates.

The decision not to map the boundaries of each estate reflects the lack of formal demarcation of property boundaries at the time of Oxholm's survey. General boundaries between estates were apparently understood among the owners, but in many cases the interior boundaries were forested and within difficult terrain and thus never formally defined—at least through survey. This lack of finite boundaries indicates the low relative economic importance for such specific divisions and demarcation on St. John.

In submitting his 1780 map, Oxholm noted that it was not quite finished but that "the work on paper corresponds in every way to the endless difficulty I had with the surveying." While Oxholm might not have been satisfied, the Royal Court gave praise to this effort noting: "In particular, the large topographic map of St. John, which is the first single map available of this island, distinguishes itself among this handsome collection of maps." Danish records indicate that in addition to his agreed-upon salary and expenses, "the King rewarded Oxholm with a douceur of one thousand rigsdaler."

November, 2008

Plan of the Danish fort at Coral Bay drawn by P. L. Oxholm, 1780

(Rigsarkivet, Copenhagen, Denmark)

References:

Condensed and edited from: *Maps, Matricals, and Material Remains; An Archaeological GIS of Late-Eighteenth-Century Historic Sites on St. John, Danish West Indies* by Douglas V. Armstrong, Mark W. Hauser, David W. Knight, and Stephan Lenik (Archaeology and Geoinformatics-Case Studies from the Caribbean, edited by Basil A. Reid [The University of Alabama Press, 2008]).

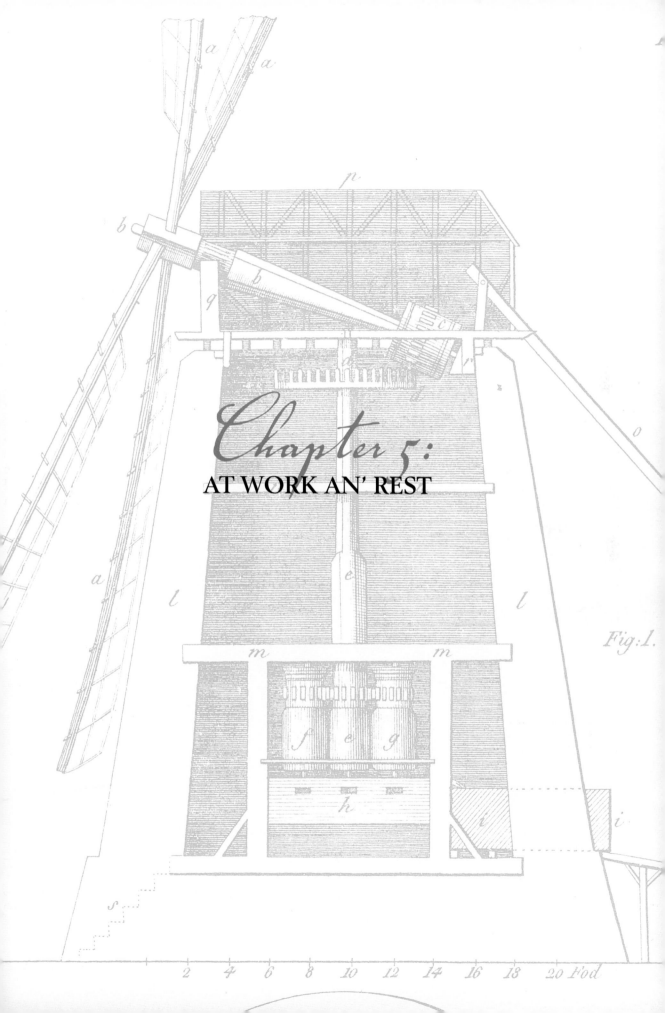

Chapter 5:
AT WORK AN' REST

A Brief History of Sugar and Sugar Production in the West Indies

David W. Knight

A 17th Century Sugar Plantation in the West Indies

(Engraving from the book *Description de L'Universe* by Allet Mallet, 1683 [D. Knight Collection])

A native to southern Asia, sugar cane has been nourishing man since prehistoric times. It is not known for certain what culture developed the technique of converting sugar cane juice into crystalline sugar, but as the earliest known written reference to the process appears in Sanskrit in about 500 BC, historians have long credited northern India as the place where sugar cane juice was first rendered into a refined end-product. As with other tropical crops of Asian origin, such as bananas and mangos, sugar cane cultivation is believed to have slowly fanned outward from India into China and the Middle East over the course of many centuries. By AD 600 it had become well established in Persia, and within a century sugar cane had reached the shores of the eastern Mediterranean and North Africa where the first great economic sugar boom occurred.

Although Europe had long been aware of sugar as a valued commodity of the eastern trade, it was not until the Crusades of the eleventh and twelfth centuries that western Europeans first encountered sugar cane under cultivation on the Mediterranean islands of Cyprus and Sicily. Attempts were soon made to introduce the crop further northward, but it was found that the properties of sugar cane were adversely affected by even the slightest frost. It therefore became apparent that the Mediterranean demarcated the far northern limit of sustainable sugar cane cultivation. For the next 400 years or so, the Mediterranean region continued to hold a near monopoly on the European sugar trade. But, as the age of Atlantic exploration dawned, sugar cane was among the first crops to be introduced into Europe's newly-acquired tropical colonies—first into the eastern Atlantic islands, and later into the West Indies and the Central and South American mainland. By 1450, sugar produced on Madeira had already begun to reach Europe, and by 1490 sugar from São Tomé (a Portuguese island possession in the Gulf of Guinea) had begun to enter northern markets as well. While the introduction of sugar cane into the eastern Atlantic islands surely had a negative impact on the long-established Mediterranean sugar trade, no single event would serve to more severely erode the Mediterranean's dominance of the industry than the proliferation of sugar cane throughout the New World.

Having quickly perceived the possibilities for sugar cane cultivation in the West Indies, Columbus brought sugar cane to the island of Hispañiola on his second voyage in 1493. In the early sixteenth century subsequent Spanish expeditions carried the crop to Puerto Rico, Cuba, and Jamaica, then on to the American continent near Vera Cruz, Mexico, where it was reportedly under cultivation as early as 1525. However, nowhere in the New World was sugar cane found to thrive better than in the humid environs of coastal Brazil. After King Manuel I of Portugal issued a royal order to introduce sugar cane cultivation into that region in 1516, the Pernambuco area quickly became the veritable epicenter of sugar production in the Americas. The long-depleted soils and drier conditions of the Mediterranean were no match for Brazil's optimum climate for sugar cane cultivation, or for its abundance of fertile, well-watered, arable lands, and the ready availability of enslaved laborers. The era of the Mediterranean's nearly one thousand-year dominance of the sugar industry rapidly drew to a close. By the end of the sixteenth century, the focus of sugar cane cultivation and sugar production had shifted across the Atlantic Ocean to the Americas; sugar cane had become nearly exclusively a New World crop.

While Spain and Portugal were the first countries to introduce sugar cane into the Americas, it was the Dutch who were largely responsible for its proliferation throughout the Lesser Antilles. Having learned the skills of sugar production during their takeover and occupation of Pernambuco between 1629 and 1654, savvy Dutch mercantilists set out to introduce the crop into the Eastern Caribbean, most notably on Barbados. By 1680, sugar was being produced on nearly all of the British- and French-held islands of the Caribbean, and sugar cane had become the dominant crop of the region [Ligon, 1673; Galloway, 1981; Watts, 1987].

It was during this period of rapid expansion of the West Indian sugar industry that Denmark first set out to establish a New World colony. Backed heavily by Dutch capital, in 1672 the Danish West Indies Company was finally successful in establishing a tenuous foothold on the island of St. Thomas. Soon after the arrival of the first Danish settlers, the colonists were joined by a small band of displaced Dutch planters and their families, who had been expelled by the British from the neighboring island of Tortola upon the outbreak of the Third Dutch War. With them, the Dutch refugees had not only brought sugar cane slips from the plantations that they had been forced to abandon on Tortola, but also the skills of sugar cane cultivation and a firsthand knowledge of the process for converting sugar cane juice into its valuable refined end-products: sugar, molasses, and rum [Knox, 1852; Westergaard, 1917; J.O. Bro-Jørgensen, 1966].

Despite the introduction of sugar cane into St. Thomas at the very outset of the colonizing effort, a lack of suitable land and the island's limited fresh water resources retarded the growth of the sugar industry in the Danish colony. As late as 1715, only about one-third of St. Thomas's plantations were planted in sugar cane, and no more than thirty-two properties were reported to have sugar processing facilities [STLL, 1715]. In the hopes of expanding the Danish West Indies Company's share in the increasingly profitable sugar trade, a decision was made to extend Denmark's colonial holdings to the neighboring island of St. John. In 1718, when Governor Bredal first laid out a set of guidelines for the occupation of that island, one of the six requirements was that a sugar works be erected on each plantation within five years on penalty of the confiscation of the property [BD, 1718]. While it was later realized that not all of the land holdings on St. John were suitable for sugar production and the order was never enforced, any planter with the necessary capital and appropriate location was clearly encouraged to plant sugar cane [SJLL, 1728]. It was not, however, until the turbulent decades that mark the turn of the nineteenth century that St. John's low-yield plantations began to be merged and developed into large-scale, agro-industrial sugar estates.

April, 2002

References:

J.O. Bro-Jørgensen, *Vore Gamle Tropekolonier, Dansk Vestindien Indtil 1755*, vol. 1 (Fremand, Denmark, 1966).

J.H. Galloway, *The sugar cane industry: An historical geography from its origins to 1914* (Cambridge, Cambridge University Press, 1989).

John P. Knox, *A Historical Account of St. Thomas in the Danish West Indies* (New York, Charles Scribner, 1852).

Richard Ligon, *A True & Exact History Of the Island of Barbadoes* (London, Frank Cass Publishers, 1970 [First printed London, 1657]).

David Watts, *The West Indies, Pattern of Development, Culture and Environmental Change since 1492* (United Kingdom, Cambridge University Press, 1987).

Waldemar Westergaard, *The Danish West Indies Under Company Rule* (New York, The Macmillen Company, 1917).

[BD] West Indies and Guinea Company Archives, Letters and Documents, 1674 - 1754 (Rigsarkivet, Denmark).

[SJLL] West Indies and Guinea Company Archives, St. John Land Lists, 1728 - 1733 & 1736-1739 (Rigsarkivet, Denmark).

Quicklime: An Essential Material of the Colonial Period

David W. Knight

Five materials were the basic components of sound construction during the early Danish colonial period in the West Indies: brick, stone, sand, timber, and limestone, from which "quicklime" for mortar and plaster was produced. Of these, only brick was initially imported, arriving in great quantities in the holds of incoming Northern European ships as ballast. While its consistency of form and geometric configuration made brick a perfect medium for leveling courses and precise detailing in corners or around windows and doorways, it was expensive when compared with other materials that could be harvested locally. For this reason, bricks were used sparingly in anything except high-end construction.

Among the resources the islands of the West Indies possessed in great abundance were stone and sand, and it was some time before the readily-available sources of these commodities became depleted to the point where it was necessary to travel any great distance to acquire them. Timber and limestone, on the other hand, were quickly depleted.

While the northern Virgin Islands are not known to have possessed any great quantities of geologically formed limestone, it had long been known that sedimentary coral-based sand stone, coral, storm-strewn coral debris, shells, and even some beach sands, which the islands did indeed possess in abundance, could be utilized in the same manner as true limestone to produce quicklime. It can therefore be stated with certainty that the Danish term "kalkstien" (limestone), when used in the context of the Danish West Indies colony throughout the eighteenth century, refers not to a specific

(Photo from "These are the Virgin Islands," by H. Cochran [Prentice Hall, New York, 1937])

Limekilns, native Virgin Islands style, stacked with coral and ready to be fired (top) and European Style.

(Photo by D. Knight)

substance but to a mélange of locally available high-calcite materials.

When coral, chalk, or limestone (calcium carbonate) are heated to temperatures of 1652° to 2012° F (900° to 1100° C) carbon dioxide is driven off leaving calcium oxide, a powdery substance, more commonly known as quicklime. Quicklime reacts thermally when brought into contact with water, producing calcium hydroxide. This substance continues to react with the atmosphere and eventually re-solidifies back into calcium carbonate; thereby completing the cycle from a solid mass, into powder, and back into a solid form.

The origins of lime production can be traced back to prehistoric times. Evidence of stone furnaces for lime burning have been unearthed in Khafaje in Mesopotamia dating to as early as 2450 BC, and we know that lime mortar was used in Crete in the Middle Minoan period, about 1800 BC. In Europe and Great Britain, large quantities of lime were utilized in the construction of the great churches, castles, and palaces of the middle ages. Still, it was not until the turn of the seventeenth century, when the use of brick became commonplace in vernacular construction, that the demand for lime mortar and the trade of the limeburner became widespread.

During the establishment of the Danish West Indies in the late seventeenth century, a limekiln would necessarily have been among the first structures to be erected before any substantial development could begin. Brick and stone, set and bonded with lime mortar and then sheathed with a lime-paste plaster, were the primary elements of sound construction throughout the colonial period: utilized first and foremost for the construction of fortifications, and later, as development progressed, for the erection of watch towers, warehouses, processing facilities, and residences.

As a spin-off of the lime business in the West Indies, brain coral also became an important component of local construction. Hoisted from the sea floor into ships, coral was easily sawn or chiseled into shape when freshly harvested, but upon exposure to the atmosphere, it quickly hardened into a highly-durable building material with exceptionally high compression strength. For this reason it became a prized and valuable substance, utilized almost exclusively for corner and keystones. Coral culls from the shaping process were used as pointing material to fill and strengthen stone walls, while any leftovers were added to the limekiln for conversion to quicklime.

The importance of quicklime and coral to the islands' developing infrastructure can not be overstated. Even half-timber buildings and rudimentary wattle and daub structures, which were erected by both enslaved laborers and the colony's less affluent free citizens, required large quantities of lime-based mortar to construct. Packed lime floors and lime-based whitewash were also common features. Beyond its use as a construction material, quicklime had several important agro-industrial applications. It was applied as fertilizer to cane fields, used as a clarifier in sugar and indigo production, and as a drying agent in the tanning process. In short, quicklime was far more than a simple commodity. It was an ongoing necessity of colonial life.

February, 2006

St. John's Indigo Years

Don Near

This article first appeared in the summer/fall 2004 edition of the Kapok Chronicles, the official [bi-yearly] newspaper of Virgin Islands National Park. Don Near, editor of the publication, is an Interpretive Ranger with the National Park Service on St. John.

The word indigo may conjure up a state of mind as in Duke Ellington's blues song "Mood Indigo," an "aura color" in New Age spirituality, or even a source of traditional folk medicine in the treatment of everything from fevers and headaches to convulsions and boils. But most people would probably equate the word indigo with a blue dye, reportedly the only natural source for blue and said to be the oldest dye of mankind. Today it is most commonly seen, in varying shades, in an estimated 2 billion pairs of blue jeans and other blue denim fabric world-wide.

While used for one reason or another in ancient cultures for thousands of years, the dye became commercially valuable in the Western hemisphere at the same time that the Caribbean islands were being colonized by Europeans in the 17th and 18th centuries. While short-lived, indigo production, along with tobacco, cocoa, coffee and ginger, dominated the plantation economies from Barbados to Hispaniola a hundred years before sugar and cotton would become the most lucrative crops in the region in the mid 1700s. On St. John, the time period was even shorter as the island was not formally settled by the Danes until 1718. At the Danish West India Company's plantation in Coral Bay, indigo plants and the infrastructure for processing it were started in 1722.

Where exactly does indigo dye come from? There are hundreds of plants that will eventually

Illustration of Typical Indigo Works

(Denis Diderot, L'Encyclopédie, ou Dictionnaire des Raisonné des Sciences, des Arts et des Métiers [First published in 1752])

produce this particular blue color (and all its gradations), distinct from purples, violets and other shades of blue. In medieval England and northern Europe the woad plant and Dyer's Knotweed were lucrative sources of the dye. In warmer climes including Italy, India and Eastern regions, *Indigofera tinctoria* was the primary species used while in pre-Columbian Central and South Americas and the Caribbean it was *I. suffructicosa*. Woad yielded an inferior color, so that when the Caribbean was being colonized, the shift to the better *Indigofera* species took place in those locales. Often the *tinctoria* species was imported to replace the lesser-valued native *suffructicosa*.

What may surprise you, however, is that whatever the dye source might have been, be it for fabrics, African or Mayan face painting, tattoos, or other uses, there is actually no blue color in any of these indigo-bearing plants. The green leaves (and sometimes stems) of "indigo" plants yield a yellow or greenish color that turns blue with the magic of oxidation, especially as induced by man.

Although the growing and harvesting of the plants was not particularly hard work, the processing was neither a pleasant nor healthy enterprise. On St. John and in other tropical areas bundles of un-bruised leaves were submerged in a large vat of clear warm water for several hours to a few days until the water "boiled" in the rapid fermentation of the plant material. This vat's water was drained off and the rotting, stinking mash of fermented leaves was transferred to a second vat of water whereupon it was beaten by paddles or whisked with sticks or by hand in order to bring oxygen to the mix. In this stage the resulting vapors given off by the foul water were particularly nauseous and noxious. Repeated long-term exposure is now known to be extremely caustic to the respiratory system and can cause cancer.

The oxidation begins the precipitation of color from the mash that settles to the bottom as a deep blue sludge. Another draining followed by soaking in a third vat leads eventually to a final draining, as more of the blue pigment sinks to the bottom. The sludge was then filtered through thick woolen or coarse canvas bags to remove impurities. The pulpy mass is compressed to remove as much moisture as possible before it is shaped into blocks ("cakes") or balls of pure indigo dye. Dried in the air, they become hard and shiny.

But the fun doesn't stop there. This newly created indigo is not water soluble and must be put through even more hoops to become utilized as a dye. The hardened indigo units are immersed in water in which several possible fermenting agents are added to yield an indestructible blue color. Fermentation by adding such things as bran, herbs, iron compounds, potash, lime soda and an old-time favorite, aged human urine, turns the solution to the color of untarnished copper. To dye a fabric blue, oxidation again comes into play. It is dipped in for a few minutes and when raised out of the solution and into the air, the cloth turns from yellow to blue. The concentration of the indigo doesn't determine the intensity of the blue. A darker shade of blue can only be achieved by repeated immersions for the same cloth.

It is arguable as to whether the replacement of indigo production in the Caribbean by more profitable sugar and cotton was any healthier for the enslaved people doing all the work. The fumes and cancer might have been gone, but the latter crops were far more back-breaking and intensive overall. Local historian David W. Knight theorizes that the scarcity of water may have been a further consideration for the profitability of indigo growing on St. John—not for the growing of the plant, but for the large amounts of water needed in the fermentation/precipitation process. In any event, by the 1900s the bulk of commercial indigo was produced synthetically by using chemicals instead of plants. Developed by the German company BASF, the artificial process was quicker, easier, and healthier for human producers and yielded a dye more uniform in concentration than natural indigo.

These days, natural indigo use is mostly limited to artists, craftsmen, textile conservationists and historians, or for traditional medicines. There is nonetheless increased interest in returning to the old ways. Cottage industries for the natural dye still persist in Central America and Mexico (the smaller quantities involved are less toxic to workers) and a fast growing segment of the fashion industry is one that purports the use of natural fibers using natural dyes. Indigo can even be obtained nowadays in powdered form which, according to a recent edition of the New Agriculturist magazine, not only speeds up the dying process by eliminating the extraction phase for solubility, but greatly decreases the hazardous solid and liquid wastes involved in the dye fermentation/precipitation vats, which saves human health and the environment.

In the future, the increasing markets for natural indigo could include use in inkjet printers, which currently use environment-unfriendly ink that unless recycled ends up in landfills. The European Union, which aims to satisfy 5% of the galloping European (and world) indigo market with natural sources by 2005, could incite a whole new wave of indigo plant growing in the Caribbean and other tropical areas. Perhaps in a few years an indigo species will once again prevail on St. John as a legitimate agricultural crop rather than as a common roadside weed that it is here today.

April, 2006

Charcoal

Eleanor Gibney

Charcoal Burners at work in the Danish West Indies

Charcoal Burners at work in the Danish West Indies

(Photo by Johannes Lightbourn, c1900 [D. Knight Collection])

One hot afternoon a year or two ago, I was driving to Coral Bay from the north shore. Turning off the one-way and heading up the Fredriksdal straight-away, I drove into a smell of smoke. Wood smoke, certainly, but not a little campfire, not the chimney smoke of a cool windy evening in the North—this was heavy and hot, but not unpleasant, permeating my lungs and clothes even as I drove through it and away. Charcoal, I said, astonished: someone is making coal at Annaberg, in that big pit below the garden, and I haven't smelled that in <u>years</u>! It was a smell that was always in the air when I was small—thick and slightly acrid—as was also the lighter and more appetizing aroma of the coal being used. My parents cooked the fish we caught in our fish-pots on our coal-pots, even long after they got a gas stove. Charcoal was always called " coal" here, even through mineral coal had been very familiar in St. Thomas during the steamship era.

I had often thought about coal burning over the years: as I studied the forests and plant communities of the island, the effects of coppicing in some forests were still evident decades after the last coal-pit was gone; I had seen photos of the Tortola Wharf on St. Thomas piled high with the crocus bags (burlap sacks) of charcoal coming in from the BVI and St. John. I'd explained to many visitors its former importance as a cottage industry,but never had a good answer for their most frequent question: Why charcoal? Why not just burn wood?

There are, it turns out, two main advantages to using charcoal as a cooking fuel, and both have to do with energy. Charcoal is wood that has had the moisture and volatile substances evaporated out, thus what remains will burn far hotter—

by about 40%—than unprocessed wood; it is also far lighter in weight than wood, no small consideration in the days before mechanical transport!

Humans were using charcoal some 30,000 years ago; at least using the charred remains of fires to draw on the walls of caves. The endurance of the medium is worth reflecting on. The first use as fuel began at least 5500 years ago, perhaps earlier, and greatly influenced the development of civilizations—the smelting of some metals was dependent on the heat of charcoal. In fact, the production of bronze (from alloying copper and tin) and iron would have been impossible without charcoal. As the Bronze Age yielded to the Iron Age in Europe, charcoal began to fuel the first large scale smelting operations—to such an extent that deforestation became a concern. During the Roman occupation of Britain, the system of coppicing grew to include many thousands of acres. In coppicing, hardwood trees are cut back, but not killed—they will re-sprout with multiple trunks, and these will grow rapidly with the support of the mature root systems beneath. In England's moist and temperate climate, wood could be harvested again in 5 to 12 years—and again, and again. As the centuries went by, almost all of Western Europe's forests were converted to agricultural land—except for the coppices that supplied the

iron smelters and glass blowers. Eventually, by the mid-1500s, England passed laws prohibiting the felling of mature trees by charcoal burners (or colliers, as they were called), which encouraged further coppice management.

As is so often the case, a new technology was developed as the pressure on existing resources became unsupportable. Mineral coal, anthracite, had long been known, but the volatile components made it unusable for cooking or iron smelting. A process to heat the coal to remove these problems was developed in the early 18th century; after heating, the coal became coke, capable of smelting and available in huge quantities, and so…the industrial revolution.

Before we leave the global history for the local, we may reflect on another use of charcoal: it is one of the three ingredients of gunpowder, invented by the Chinese in the 10th century.

The native forests of the West Indies are predominately hardwoods, ideal for charcoal, and obviously the techniques of charcoal burning were well known to European colonists of the region, but charcoal appears to have been a fairly late product of island forests. References and records of "firewood" are found in the literature, but it isn't until the 19th century that charcoal is mentioned, and it's apparently not a major factor until after emancipation. With

The Estate Enighed Fire

On Tuesday, May 2, 1899, the following report was sent to the St. John magistrate by officers F. A. Thomas and Henry Clen:

"We the undersigned hereby report to his Honor the Judge, that yesterday afternoon at 2:30 as we stood in Christiansfort's [the Battery's] courtyard we saw the house on Estate Enighed on fire, and at our arrival at the place we found the entire house burning. We together with others who came to our assistance, tried our best to extinguish the fire by means of the fire-engine, but we did not succeed. The fire originated from a spark that came from a heap of bushes that were set on fire by a man named James Howell, who is a coal-burner on the estate. The fire was set at a distance of 67 feet from the house and there was a strong southeasterly wind. The house was not occupied. It was a wall-building with wooden roof, no other house is near. A few pieces of the wood are still burning; no danger. By order from the Judge, James Howell was arrested and placed in detention."

(Rigsarkivet, Denmark)

the decline of the sugar industry, most of St. John's large estates converted to cattle, a far less labor-intensive industry, and wage employment became almost non-existent on the island. By that time, the large populations of the towns of St. Thomas and St. Croix had effectively used up the available fuel resources of their islands. St. John and the BVI, with declining populations, capitalized on this need. Records were not kept of goods shipped from St. John to St. Thomas in small local vessels, but the amount of charcoal exported from the BVI in the mid-1800s is staggering: almost 340,000 barrels between 1848 - 1887, an average of over 8000 barrels a year.

The large St. John estates remained in the hands of a few owners, many of them based on St. Thomas. Many of St. John's small-landholders and struggling "squatters" had agreements where they could access and use estate forests for charcoal burning, the edges of cleared land for growing crops or grazing animals, and the shorelines for fishing and/or lime burning. In return, the estate owner could expect sacks of coal, or strings of fish, from time to time. Almost everyone did whatever they could to feed their families or make a little money, but fishing and charcoaling were primarily men's work.

A variety of local woods were used, since only a handful are *not* suitable for charcoal: a few soft woods, like mampoo and turpentine; and probably the toxic (crabwood) or highly resinous (torchwood) were shunned, and some were too valued for other uses.

Casha (*Acacia macracantha*), puckhout (*Coccoloba microstachya*), black, white and red mangroves (*Avicennia germinans, Laguncularia racemosa, Rhizophora mangle*) buttonwood (*Conocarpus erectus*), genip (*Meliococus bijugatus*), amarat (*Acacia muricata*), and dozens more were commonly used. Some trees, prized for other reasons—like the ancient tamarind trees—with their deep shade and refreshing fruit in the driest areas—simply had their branches trimmed for the coal pit on a regular basis, which may have actually benefited the trees; there are great examples of this repeated branch-lopping on the massive East End tamarinds.

Coal-pits were often dug in the loose sandy soil close to the shore—anyone who has dug a hole anywhere on St. John can easily tell you why—but you can see coal-pits all over the hills of St. John, and many people made small quantities close to their homes.

Once the wood was cut and trimmed to reasonable dimensions, it was stacked in the coal-pit. Stacking was either in a rectangular form, or, in later years, a low circular cone. The wood was next covered by a thick layer of green vegetation: vines, or leafy branches, often soaked in seawater; a layer of soil was finally spread over the top. A hole was left to ignite the fire from below, and later plugged, another hole was made as a vent or chimney that was also gradually shut off. The pile was let smolder for 5-10 days, tended carefully, and by the time it was opened the fire should have pretty much gone out. The coal was then raked and bagged in burlap sacks. Occasionally coal that should have cooled did re-ignite. Edmund Roberts tells a story about his grandfather walking down the long straight Estate Carolina road with a sack of fresh coal on his head, oblivious to the smoke trailing behind him—until the top of his head started heating up!

A lot of St. John charcoal was sent to St. Thomas on local sloops and schooners between 1850 and 1960. Sometimes schooners from Puerto Rico would also pull in, to buy up as much as was available. A large coal-pit could yield about twenty bags, each weighing 50-75 pounds, and a bag sold on the St. Thomas wharf for 20 to 80 cents from the 1920s to 1950s. The captains and selling agents (often the same person) took more than half this sum, so the coal-burner got 10 – 40 cents a bag (and the empty bags were always returned). These low prices help put the exports to St. Croix in perspective. The only statistics I have found on charcoal shipped inter-island in the current Territory are from Zabriskie's *The Virgin Islands of the United States*, where it shows that in 1915, St. Croix imported $992.02 worth of charcoal from St. Thomas (probably all actually from St. John), and $370.17 worth from "other foreign places" (probably the BVI), for a total of $1362.19. Not a very impressive sum to us today, but at 25 cents per 60 pounds, this represents 240 pounds of charcoal per dollar, or 326,925 pounds going into St. Croix that year!

So how was all this charcoal being used? In the town bakeries, in big charcoal ovens; in the homes, mostly in coal-pots. Coal-pots were so familiar to me growing up, it never occurred to me that they were a uniquely West Indian necessity. A portable cast iron brazier with

A charcoal iron, known as a "goose," was used on St. John well into the 20th century

(Photo by Lolly Prime)

a very pleasing shape, easily portable and impervious to everything but rust. You can cook anything on a coal-pot, including bread, once you know how. Similar pots are still made out of clay on islands like St. Lucia, but the iron coal-pot seems to have totally disappeared. An exhaustive internet search led me to only one good image of a coalpot—on our own St. John Historical Society website.

A small amount of coal was also used in the necessary goose, the hollow charcoal-heated iron. Even when many on St. John might have been seen as impoverished, good clothes—Sunday clothes—were always immaculate and beautifully ironed. I imagine many young girls burnt their fingers repeatedly before they became skillful with the goose and live coals. The rusty remains of gooses (geese?) were everywhere on the island in the 1960s, in every ruin and house site I explored.

The twenty years between 1950 and 1970 brought enormous changes to St. John—and rural St. Thomas—and most families that entered that era with a wood house, coal-pot, and donkey emerged 20 years later with a concrete house, electricity, gas stove and a car. Older people continued to enjoy the flavor of coal-pot cooked food, but gradually the production of coal dwindled away. There is now a resurgence of interest in natural charcoal across the developed world, as people realize that packaged briquettes are not necessarily something you want associating with your food—but that's another story.

October, 2009

References:

British Virgin Islands Reports 1955-1962, Her Majesty's Stationery Office, London 1958-1964

Dookhan, Isaac, *A History of the British Virgin Islands 1672 to 1970*, Caribbean Universities Press 1975

Kemp, Bernard A. and Guy H. Benjamin, *The Economic Way of Life of East End, St. John*, Unpublished Manuscript., St. John 1989-2003

Little, Elbert L, Jr. and Frank H. Wadsworth, *Common Trees of Puerto Rico and the Virgin Islands*, Agriculture Handbook No. 249, US Forest Service, Washington, DC 1964

Olwig, Karen Fog, *Cultural Adaptation and Resistance on St. John, Three Centuries of Afro-Caribbean Life*, University of Florida Press 1985

UK Agriculture, *The History of Charcoal*, www.ukagriculture.com/countryside/charcoal_history.cfm

Zabriskie, Luther K, *The Virgin Islands of the United States*, G. P.Putnam's Sons, New York and London 1918

Estate Concordia and the Free Working-Class Landowners on St. John

in the Eighteenth and Nineteenth Centuries

David W. Knight

Situated atop a prominent knoll overlooking Salt Pond Bay, the crumbling remains of the Concordia estate complex languish in obscurity: silent testimony to a little-known aspect of St. John's historic past.

Intriguingly, the modest remains found on Estate Concordia are in many ways more indicative of St. John plantation properties throughout the Danish colonial period, than the grand sugar-producing estates that are most often associated with the era. Even at the height of the great sugar boom at the turn of the nineteenth century, more St. John properties were dedicated to the raising of livestock or the growing of cotton and provision crops than were engaged in sugar cane cultivation. According to tax records, in 1805 only twenty-three of the sixty-nine estates on St. John were "sugar plantations." This figure continued to decline throughout the remainder of the colonial period, and by the time the Danish West Indies were sold to the United States in 1917 only Henry Marsh's Parforce estate in Reef Bay was still growing sugar cane—and even there less than ten of the estate's five-hundred acres were under sugar cultivation.

Early on, much of the land lying in St. John's arid east, southeast, and southwestern sections had been found to be unsuitable for sustained large-scale agriculture. Once various plantation crops had been attempted and failed, less

A rural working-class household in the Danish West Indies

(Photo published by Dr. Charles E. Taylor, c1890s [D. Knight Collection])

profitable properties, such as Concordia, began to be taken over by working-class individuals, many of whom were West Indian Creoles of mixed racial heritage.

While some of St. John's working-class landowners managed to eke out an existence from the soil, most made their livings by trades other than that of "planter." Although they all maintained small provision plots and grazed limited numbers of livestock, the island's free middle class engaged in a broad range of industrial activities and service trades that filled a gap in the largely singular plantation-based economy of the colony. Some men hired themselves out as overseers on sugar plantations;

others were fishermen, shipwrights, seamen, carpenters, masons, salt harvesters, or lime- and coal-burners. Women and children also did their share to support the family. They cultivated food and herb gardens, tended livestock, did sewing and needlework, engaged in small-scale merchandising, or were midwives or caregivers.

Yet, in one respect, the struggling colonial middle class had one paramount thing in common with their wealthier plantocratic neighbors: they relied on the system of slavery to maintain their somewhat precarious economic equilibrium. Regardless of racial distinction, in the years prior to emancipation nearly all of the working-class land holders on St. John possessed at least a small enslaved labor force. These laborers worked the estates' grounds, assisted the owners in their trades, served as domestics in the households or were hired out for the benefit of their owners.

It has been suggested that slavery was not as harsh on the marginal properties, as owner and enslaved alike often lived and worked side-by-side. While this may have been the case on some properties, it is evident that treatment and living conditions varied greatly from estate to estate, and being bound to an agriculturally unproductive property, no matter how benevolent the master, could have done little to ameliorate the situation of the enslaved.

From a historical perspective, the harsh realities of daily existence for St. John's marginal landowners stand in stark contrast to the lives of the well-heeled plantocrats of the colonial period. The struggling working class of St. John are among the most enigmatic and least recognized members of colonial society. They represent a silent free majority, who laid the stones, but did not live in the mansions; sailed the ships, but seldom owned the cargoes; stitched the gowns, but were not welcome at the balls.

In the end, for all their efforts, most of St. John's free working class and their descendants were destined to fall into complete and utter poverty. The impact of emancipation on this group was eloquently expressed by Reverend John P. Knox in his book, *A Historical Account of St. Thomas in the Danish West Indies* (New York, Charles Scribner, 1852), where he wrote:

> *...Small estates, especially those without sugar cultivation, and where owners maintained themselves and families by a small stock of*

> *cattle, cutting wood, and depending upon other meager resources, are now almost worthless, the owners and laborers picking up together a scanty subsistence as mutual companions in misfortune; and some have been entirely abandoned...*

So how did the family that resided at the now crumbling ruins of Concordia above Salt Pond Bay fare through this period?

After the death of Jacob Eno Sr. in 1828, his son and daughter inherited equal shares in the Concordia estate. Together, the Eno siblings and their heirs continued to reside on and work their inherited property, eking out an existence by planting small provision crops, raising goats, charcoal making, salt harvesting and fishing. But, after emancipation was achieved in 1848, the family found it increasingly hard to make a living from the land.

In 1863, Jacob Eno Jr., the last of the Eno clan to live at *Concordia*, died bankrupt and impoverished on the estate. A short note sent to the town judge in Cruz Bay by Jacob's neighbor and cousin, David Evans, vividly relates Mr. Eno's situation at the time of his death:

> *Dear Sir,*
>
> *The rainy state of the weather has prevented me from writing you before respecting the property of the late deceased Mr. Jacob Eno as you requested me. I beg here to inform you the only property that Mr. Eno was in possession of: the half of the Salt Pond, and a small rowboat. He had no furniture whatever, not so much as a chair to sit on. This is all I am aware of.*
>
> *I remain your most Ob. Servant,*
>
> *(Signed) D. Evans*

February, 2000

Cruz Bay, St. John, c1917

(Image by Clare E. Taylor [D. Knight Collection])

St. John, 1921

(From the 1921 Issue of *Lightbourn's Annual and Commercial Directory*, Page 113)

The Island's National Song:

St. Jan, this is my native land,

And well I love its ground,

For there unnumbered blessings smile

And circle it around!

And there is not a spot on earth

That I like half so well

As this dear land that gave me birth,

The island where I dwell!

This island was settled in 1717 [*sic.*], according to Westergaard, by 20 planters, 16 Negroes and 5 soldiers. In the height of its prosperity it had 92 estates, whereon, besides sugar, cotton was cultivated, for which the soil is well adapted. Today there are probably not more than a dozen estates, with a total population of about 1,000 souls on the island.

Politically the island is united with St. Thomas, being represented in the Colonial Council of the latter island by one Appointed (by Government) and two Popular (elected by the people) Members, a ratio of one to every 300 inhabitants, while the number who enjoy the electoral franchise in the island do not probably reach 50.

Perhaps the most promising of the islands, having a supply of water requisite for agricultural pursuits, St. John is today the most abandoned of the group of the three islands, although it should be otherwise, as it has a soil adapted to a varied cultivation. The land under cultivation hardly reaches 500 acres. The "bay leaf" tree (*Pimenta acris*) is not cultivated to the extent that it may be; fortunately, it grows abundantly spontaneously. The only effort to utilize the land is the cultivation of limes, from which concentrated lime juice is made, while the woods of the forests are ruthlessly sacrificed to the manufacture of charcoal for the markets of St. Thomas and St. Croix and even Puerto Rico. The raising of cattle, to which large areas of the land are devoted, and the manufacture of straw baskets on a small scale are the only other industries of the island.

Tho there are several good bays—one of which, Coral Bay, at least rivals if not surpasses St. Thomas harbor—no steamers nor vessels call at St. John, as trade conditions do not warrant it. All importation is made thru St. Thomas in small quantities and at frequent intervals.

About the only paid officials on the island are a police assistant, with residence at Cruz Bay, a doctor, residing at Coral Bay, and a

Making baskets on East End, St. John, c1900

(Postcard by Johannes Lightbourn [D. Knight Collection])

few policemen. The climate of St. John is exceedingly healthy and the temperature is a trifle lower than in St. Thomas. On account of its more bracing air the island has been growing steadily in favor as a health resort with the people of the neighbouring islands and there is no doubt that in time and with some attention to the necessary requisites for a modern resort, St. John will become a great favorite of our continental citizens also.

OFFICIAL LIST

C. G. Thiele, with residence at St. Thomas ....Judge

A. A. Richardsen ....Government Representative

M.S.N. Pierre..Resident Doctor and Registrar

J. E. Lindquist, Dennis Bay; Carl Francis, Annaberg;
A. White, Contant; E. Marsh, Coral Bay; A. Roberts,
East End..Quarter Officers

E. Moorehead and Victor Jurgen ....Policemen

Public Schools and Teachers

George F. Penn .... Inspector

    Bethany—Miss Anne Benjamin,
    Principal; Miss Rosa Thomas

    East End—Misses Maud Shennery and Ingeberg Henry.
    Emmaus—Miss Edna Joseph, Principal; Misses Olive Sewer,
        Maria Thomas, and Consuela Stevens.

At Emmaus there is also a night school conducted by Mrs. A. L. Penn, while the basket industry is taught by Mr. Ernest Sewer.

Churches
Moravian

Rev. George F. Penn, at Emmaus .... Minister in Charge

R. P. Jacobs, at Bethany..Catechist

    Services: Sundays, 11 a.m. and 7 p.m. Sunday School at 2 p.m.
    Societies attached—King's Daughters and Benevolent.

Lutheran

"Nazareth" Chapel at Cruz Bay

Carl Francis .... Church Clerk

    Services: Sundays, 12 noon. Sunday School, 2 p.m.
    A benevolent Society is attached to this church. Monthly fee 10 cents; Sick benefits
    50 cents weekly.

                                               At Work an' Rest

The "Judge's" privy at The Creek in Cruz Bay, c1900

(Det Kongelige Bibliotek, Copenhagen, Denmark)

On the Cruz Bay dock, c1898

(Det Kongelige Bibliotek, Copenhagen, Denmark)

Boys' Reformatory

Mrs. Sophia Clen.. Matron

This institution was established on July 1, 1917, by Government, and is situated at Leinster Bay. There are about 8 inmates at present, who are given an elementary education with instruction in Agriculture. Gymnastics will also be added.

Directory

Bay Leaf Growers:

G. Bornn, J. Lindquist, E. Marsh, V.A. Miller & Co., J. Westbrooke.

Bay Oil Distillers:

G. Bornn, M. Marsh, E. Marsh, J. Westbrooke.

Bay Rum Manufacturers:

G. Bornn, P. Thorsen.

Cattle Dealers:

Carl Francis, A. H. Lockhart, Ernest Marsh, Monroe Marsh, V. A. Miller & Co., C. Penn, L. Stakemann, J. Westbrooke.

Industries

Fancy Baskets and Table Mats are made extensively in East End, the principal manufacturers being Misses Zelma Roberts and Elizabeth Boynes.

Rattan Baskets, used chiefly in the coaling of steamers, are made by Ernest and Philip Sewer.

Native Chairs of strong quality are manufactured by Ernest Sewer.

The Seed Work industry is largely carried on by Misses Nellie Williams and Georgianna O'Neal, in East End.

Boat Building is done in East End by Carl Roberts. The workmanship and construction being of excellent quality.

Post-Plantation and Pre-Tourism:

Life and Work on St. John in the early 20th Century

Crystal Fortwangler

Crystal Fortwangler is a member of the SJHS. Her dissertation research focuses on protected area politics and relationships on St. John.

After the collapse of the plantation system, a "broad-based provisioning economy" emerged on St. John. It included a diversified agricultural economy, subsistence farming, craft industries, small-scale forest industry, and cattle estates. Although only a few people owned most of the land and hired others to work for them, the emerging communities acquired small lots purchased, transferred, or gifted from the plantations. They cultivated gardens and farmed. They crafted and manned sailing vessels, became skilled fishers and maritime traders, made charcoal, participated in the bay rum industry, and made baskets, mats, and chairs. There was a strong exchange network on St. John, including gift giving and work clubs for farming and charcoal burning. Although money was used (especially when on St. Thomas or Tortola), giving goods and labor through exchange was considered important and essential to being a St. Johnian. This system continued through the transfer of the islands from Denmark to the United States in 1917 and lasted to varying degrees until the island's transition to a tourism economy and increased government employment in the 1940s, and the opening of the National Park and Caneel Bay in 1956.

Fishermen off duty St. Jan, D. W. I

"Fishermen off Duty" on St. John, Danish West Indies, by Johannes Lightbourn, c1900

(Image courtesy Eleanor Gibney Collection)

At Work an' Rest

A look at the 1917 Census of the U.S. Virgin Islands and the 1930 U.S. Census provides insight into life and work on St. John in the early 20th Century. Relying on census data, however, requires caution. For example, the census provides space for only one occupation. But we should interpret this as the primary occupation. For example, men who worked on farms or fished also burned coal, and many people could make baskets. Moreover, all St. Johnians worked to maintain the household—tending provision grounds, cutting bush, gathering fruits and lobsters, raising chickens, cooking and baking, washing clothes, burning coal for home use, and so on. Also women and children are usually listed without an occupation but worked both inside and outside the home. Keeping these cautions in mind, we can glean a basic understanding of living and working on St. John.

In 1917, according to the U. S. census, there were 959 people on St. John. The island had recently become part of the United States and experienced a devastating hurricane. Over seventy percent of the population lived on the eastern half of St. John. Most were born on island or on nearby islands with 3.5% born elsewhere. Occupations were listed for 452 people.

Over half of all working men were laborers on agricultural and cattle farms. Only a few men were farmers, managers, or overseers. Even those with other primary occupations worked on farms when work was available (as did some of the 48 coal burners—28 men, 20 women—living on Bordeaux). The bay rum industry was also booming on St. John. Although the census does not list anyone specifically working as bay rum pickers or manufacturers, we know from numerous sources that people worked when leaves were ready to be picked. Men also worked at sea. Forty-four men listed sailor or seaman as their occupation, the majority in East End and Coral Bay. Of the 30 fishermen most lived in Cruz Bay quarter and on Lovango Cay. Other men worked as carpenters (most at the East End shipyard), masons, police officers, a pastor, a tailor, a physician, a saddler, a school monitor, and a cigar maker. The average male worker was 34.5 years old. Fishermen were a bit younger (29.3) and coal burners a bit older (36.8).

Most adult women were married and worked as housewives, a rigorous and time consuming daily domestic occupation. Some of these 109 wives listed additional occupations. For example, eight of nine wives in Bordeaux listed

coal burner. Other women listed farm laborer, seamstress, and laundress. Sixty-five adult women were heads of their own households. Most of these were single or widowed and held jobs, many as laborers outside of the home.

Both young men and women worked as "servants." Twenty-nine youngsters, most under 21, lived with and worked for a family. A few were relatives but most were not. Seven were immigrants to the island, two worked for a pastor, one for the physician, one for a police officer, two for older persons, and a few for large families.

By 1930 the population dropped to 765. Most residents still lived on the eastern part of the island—just fewer. As opportunities increased off-island and in the continental United States, many were lured away from St. John. Six percent of the population was not born in the U.S. or British Virgin Islands. Occupations were listed for 386 people.

Cattle (stock) farming had exploded on the island, reaching its peak in 1930 with 1,583 head on 14 large farms. Most cattle were in Maho Quarter and Carolina. Forty-seven men worked on cattle farms and fifty-seven on non-cattle farms. Maritime work was still a foundation on St. John with 35 men listed as sailors and 31 as fishermen. Some men provided transportation boat services, especially on East End. There was a noticeable decline in men listed as carpenters. Other men worked as basket makers, cooks, servants, police officers, a basket teacher, an artist, government dispatcher, fish club caretaker, and a beekeeper (from Cuba).

Women's work remained similar with most women listed as housewives or laundresses. Thirteen were servants, eight public school teachers and six basket makers. A few women cooked and five worked on farms. One woman was a farm manager and another was listed as a farmer. Fifty-five women headed households.

Although only eight persons (6 men, 2 women) on the census are listed as charcoal laborers, we know from other sources that coal burning continued. These workers may have been listed as general farm laborers or it went unmarked because it was part of household work. Working as a bay leaf picker, however, was not nearly as common, because oil output had dropped in part as a result of hurricane damage to trees.

CCC Work Crew, Calabash Boom, June 1938

(U. S. National Archives)

A new form of work came with the arrival of the Civilian Conservation Corps in the late 1930s. CCC projects employed young men in tree planting, building and repairing roads, digging drainage facilities, combating soil erosion, and helping eradicate animal ticks.

This was the way of life on St. John until the transition days of the 1940s and 1950s. Life on St. John would never be the same again.

This short article draws upon the works of Earl Shaw, Karen Fog Olwig, George Tyson, Bernard Kemp, Guy Benjamin, and Doug Armstrong. All census calculations are by the author.

January, 2005

At Work an' Rest

The Bordeaux—Barbershop Connection:
ST. JOHN BAY RUM

Eleanor Gibney

Although St. John was always the most undeveloped of the three former Danish West Indies, there was once a product that gave our island preeminence—not merely at the local level, but across much of the world.

A century ago, most Americans knew what bay rum was. In the era before the popularization of the safety razor, urban men of the middle class were shaved daily by barbers, and the barbershop aftershave of choice for many decades was bay rum, a cologne made from the oil extracted from leaves of the West Indian bay, or bayrum, tree. This tree, *Pimenta racemosa*, is a member of the myrtle family: *not* related to the bay laurel leaves sold as seasoning throughout the world, but a very close cousin to allspice(*Pimenta officinalis)*, and a little more distantly related to cloves, guavas, eucalyptus, and hundreds of other aromatic or edible myrtles.

The exotic bracing scent was not just an aftershave. Bay rum was also used as a headache remedy and as an ingredient in soaps and in smelling salts, required to revive Victorian ladies from frequent fainting. At the height of bay rum's popularity it was firmly believed—probably with good reason—that the world's best-smelling bay leaves grew on St. John.

The Virgin Islands lie almost in the middle of the tree's apparent natural range from Cuba to Trinidad, and in that range many varieties of the species occur, with aromas that range from cinnamon to lemon. All the bay leaves on Tortola are distinctly citrus-scented, and that variety is found in one small area of St. John, but most of our bay trees are robustly bay rum scented, smelling like nothing but their glorious selves. Even without the intense aroma of the leaves, the trees would be noted for beauty, with a pleasing contrast of pale, smooth, bark and deep green and glossy foliage; and for their very hard and heavy wood.

Bay trees were so intensely cultivated on St. John that some botanists have debated whether the tree was originally native here, and we may never know the whole story. What is certain is that we are in the tree's native area, and that the tree was known here very early in the colonial period. The Dutch Creole name "caneel"—meaning cinnamon—was applied to this tree. Unfortunately it was also used for two other aromatic native trees here (not one of them is related to cinnamon…), so it gets speculative pretty fast.

That blessedly prolific recorder of these islands in the 1760s, Moravian missionary C.G.A. Oldendorp, described what is undoubtedly bay: "The wild caneel tree grows so tall and thick, it can be used as a sturdy construction timber. It yields excellent spice pepper, the so-called allspice, …its leaves, which are as tough as leather, have a very spicy taste and are used to flavor food …these leaves can be used to diminish strong odors, by covering the floor with them…"

Between the mid-1700s and 1870, islanders began using the leaves and berries more for medicine and less for flavoring. The first bay rum was probably made by simply crushing leaves and berries and soaking them in strong rum, then using this as a rub for sore muscles, headaches and rheumatism. It's likely that some mid-19th century visitors to St. Thomas were smitten by the fragrance and carried a few bottles away with them. The port of Charlotte Amalie had been one of the busiest in the Americas, but a rapid decline was setting in by 1870. St. Thomas merchants would have been quick to capitalize on any potential export. Some credit A. H. Riise

A Bay Oil Distillery Danish West Indies.

The Marsh Bay Oil Distillery at Estate Carolina in Coral Bay, c1900

(Postcard by Johannes Lightbourn [D. Kight Collection])

and Sons for the initial development of bay rum manufacture, and this seems logical enough; Riise was THE apothecary on St. Thomas, with a Danish government-granted monopoly (this was predictably controversial on the island). He certainly had one of the first and largest bay rum stills on St. Thomas, where he "double distilled," first distilling the oil from the leaves, mixing it with cane alcohol, then redistilling the mixture. Riise was the first to exhibit bay rum in the U.S., at Philadelphia's Centennial Exhibition in 1876.

Charles Taylor, writing from St. Thomas in 1888, reported that "…The bay rum manufacture (which threatened to be nearly extinguished in 1883 owing to the scarcity of leaves…) is now in full activity, several of our enterprising merchants are turning out thousands of bottles annually…In view of the increasing importance of this manufacture, and that houses in America are dispatching agents to these islands in order to buy up…the bay leaves for their own purposes, would it not be wise if proprietors of estates would devote a little more attention to it…? It is a …fact that it has been almost exterminated on St. Thomas by

indiscriminate gathering…" So, that's where St. John came into the picture. Between 1890 and 1910 several St. John estates began to actively plant and cultivate bay trees. The trees didn't do well everywhere, by any means, thriving only in well-watered and protected sites, on deep soil. The successful cultivated areas are still very discernable today, and the majority of those 100+ year-old trees are still very much alive—at Cinnamon Bay and Hawksnest/Denis Bay on the north shore; Mollendahl high above Fish Bay; and in extensive tracts of the Bordeaux ridge, descending the Reef Bay and Lameshur watersheds to the south. Many of these old trees are now about 3 ft in basal diameter.

By the time of transfer to the United States in 1917, bay rum was a very big deal. Luther Zabriskie wrote then that "The cultivation of the bay tree, and the extraction of oil from its leaves, provides for …St. John its most important industry" and the manufacture of bay rum gave St. Thomas "its only article of local manufacture and most important of its exports." Zabriskie said about 4000 quarts of bay oil were produced on St. John annually, most of which went to St. Thomas, which exported about

Workers on the Bay Tree Estates, St. John, c1917

(Photo by Clare E. Taylor)

60,000 cases of the finished product—of 12 bottles each. That is 720,000 quart bottles, so about 180,000 gallons. That's a lot of cologne. (Way too much, perhaps—another chronicler said that a mere 47,000 gallons were shipped out yearly in this period.)

In 1917, the leading bay oil producers on St. John were: E.W. (Ernest Waymouth) Marsh, A.White, G. Bornn and A. Lindqvist, and the top St. Thomas manufacturers of finished bay rum were H. Michelson, A. Riise, The St. Thomas Bay Rum Company, Ltd. (J. Paiewonsky, who later bought out Riise), David Bornn, A. Vance and V. Muller.

Picking was done one to three times a year—not exactly steady employment. However, St. John residents in the early 1900s were reportedly heavily involved in bay leaf picking, and they were paid 8 cents per 60 lb. minimum bag, if the leaves came from an estate owned by the bay oil distiller, or 2 cents per pound if the leaves were from another property. There were several bay oil stills on island, most notably at Carolina, Lameshur and Cinnamon Bay, and unprocessed leaves were also shipped in large numbers to St. Thomas. Children were often employed as leaf-

pickers, since they could climb higher without breaking branches. The Bordeaux community was probably the most thoroughly engaged in the cultivation and picking, but all quarters of St. John except East End had a financial stake in the industry, albeit not that lucrative a stake.

We find oddly contradictory reports about bay rum importance from the time: Zabriskie also noted in 1917 that the market was slack and bay leaf prices down by 25%, but the special U.S. Census of the islands in 1917 reported that the industry was suffering for lack of bay oil, since the 1916 hurricane had entirely destroyed the bay trees of St. John. It's probable that Zabriskie's figures were a couple of years old, since the infamous 1916 storm certainly would have at least defoliated many of the St. John trees.

The trees rebounded very nicely a few years later—as did the business, perhaps partly due to Prohibition. The U.S. government outlawed the sale of alcoholic beverages in 1920, and apparently realized quickly that bay rum, although labeled "For External Use Only" was mainly very high-proof white rum or cane alcohol—and even fairly tasty in a cocktail.

Federal agents swooped down on grocers and drug stores around the nation. Meanwhile, the V.I. was still producing rum—and bay rum—that was mainly going to South American markets. In 1921, Prohibition was extended to the islands, but bay rum exports were allowed to resume to the United States provided the product was "denatured" by adding substances that were supposed to nullify the effects of alcohol, make it poisonous—or at least make it taste horrible. It appears that these measures may have been ineffective, or perhaps barbershops just replaced bars as places for men to congregate. In any event, bay rum exports from the V.I. rose to an average of 100,000 gallons per year from 1921 to the end of Prohibition in 1933.

The Depression, the increasing popularity of the disposable blade safety razor for home use, and then World War II, effectively ended bay rum's importance for the V.I. The few producers after 1945 were all using bay oil from other islands such as Dominica, although up to the 1970s some books kept reporting bay leaf cultivation as St. John's major industry. The van Beverhoudt family of St. John and St. Thomas did continue to make "Hurricane Hole" bay rum, that actually contained a percentage of St. John bay oil, until the 1980s—this was traditional in another respect: it was packaged in re-used beer bottles, as the earliest exports of V.I. bay rum had been, a century before.

The mystique lived on: In a 1950s New Yorker magazine I found this ad for the brand *St. Johns Bay Rum*: "Pirates prized St. Johns Bay Rum for the same reasons *you* will!" Their "tough, sea-going beards" were apparently so hard to shave that manly faces were only soothed by the application of bay rum from "aromatic bay leaves, native only to the island of St. Johns." Wrong century? False information? No problem for Madison Avenue!

The brand "St. Johns" still survives today, in handsome bottles covered in woven palm-leaf, a pattern inspired by the woven tyre palm fishpots of long ago, but if you're here on St. John, you can simply rub a few leaves on your skin and breath deeply, reflecting on the many years when that heady aroma was bottled and shipped around the globe.

October, 2009

References:

Department of Commerce, Bureau of the Census, *Census of the Virgin Islands of the United States*, Washington, Government Printing Office, 1917

Dookhan, Isaac, *A History of the Virgin islands of the United States*, Caribbean Universities Press, 1974

The New York Times, *Liquor Signs have Last Day of Grace...Bay Rum gets Grocers into Trouble*, New York, February 15, 1920

Oldendorp, C.G.A., *History of the Mission of the Evangelical Brethren of the Caribbean Islands of St. Thomas, St. Croix and St. John*, 1770, Translation by Arnold Highfield and Vladamir Barac, Karoma Publishers, 1987

Taylor, Charles E, *Leaflets from the Danish West Indies*, William Dawson and Sons, London, 1888

Zabriskie, Luther K, *The Virgin Islands of the United States of America*, G. Putnam's Sons, New York and London, 1918

At Work an' Rest

St. John Place Names in the Cruz Bay Quarter

Presention by Mr. Elroy Sprauve; Summarized by Vicki Bell

Beginning at the mouth of Cruz Bay Harbor, on the south side, is a reef. When Mr. Sprauve was a child, it was simply known as "De Reef." Being rich in marine life, this was the place to set fish traps (or "pots") and to fish from the shoreline. Mr. Elroy also notes that a "ripple" of waves across "De Reef" during hurricane season gave warning of an approaching storm.

Mr. Elroy told of how vessels attempting to enter Cruz Bay harbor sometimes found themselves on De Reef. To facilitate marine traffic coming safely into Cruz Bay Harbor, a kerosene lamp was lit each night on the hillside at Enighed, where our Library is today. By using this beacon, mariners were able to steer clear of danger.

Drawing a straight line north across Cruz Bay from De Reef, takes you to a place that was known as "Ballast." This is the area where a seaplane ramp used to be.

The area from where the Customs House is today, to the National Park Service Headquarters, was, and still is, known as the Creek pronounced the "Crick." In days past, oysters were prevalent there, along the mangrove-lined shore.

Back on the shore south of De Reef, the area known today as Gallows Point was called "Found Out." Fishing was good off the rocks from Found Out and the large rock at the water's edge was known as "First Rock." Thus, people would say they were going to fish at First Rock. The Found Out land was given to the VI Government by one Mrs. White, for use as a cemetery. The government sold a portion of the land to Richard "Duke" Ellington, who perpetuated the name Gallows Point. So far as Mr. Elroy knows, no one was ever hanged at Gallows Point.

Going south toward Moravian Point one comes to Frank Bay, which is still known by that name today. The fishing area below Moravian Point was known as "Snou." St. Johnians would go down to the shore in the evening to bait the waters around the shore with small fish and soldier crabs in order to make a good catch the next morning.

In Cruz Bay Town, the area near the Post Office, going toward Miss Meada's house was known as "The Yard."

Mr. Elroy grew up where Wharfside Village stands today. Cruz Bay Town ended where the Julius Sprauve School is today, and only about 8 to 10 families lived in Cruz Bay Town. Mary Harvey lived where Lemon Tree Mall and the Lime Inn Restaurant are located today, and two ladies (unnamed by Mr. Elroy) lived where First Bank now stands.

Cruz Bay waterfront and park area, c1950

(photo by Dr. George H.H. Knight)

There was "Up-Street," which meant the road from the Catholic Church to the Bank, and "Down-Street," which meant from the Church to Wharfside.

Mr. Elroy attended the Bethany School, with about fifty other students. School began at 9 a.m. and the children walked from Cruz Bay. Going up Centerline Road, past the Seventh Day Adventist Church one would come to an area known as "Grapetree." A short distance along the road from Grapetree was "Pineta Parry," and near where the cement bridge is today was a big, flat rock which has since been blasted away for road improvement. This was simply called "Flat Rock." People would congregate there—it was a good "meeting spot."

Continuing up Centerline Road one came to "Bellagate," most likely so-called for a lady named Bella who lived in the area. The curve where Pastory Gardens Mini Golf is today was known as "Hungry Hill." Going from Hungry Hill in a northerly direction was "Ray Hill," which leads to Caneel Hill. Caneel Bay was known as "K-C Bay," and Honeymoon Beach was called "Plantation." The area on North Shore Road, just before Maho Bay, near Mr. Penn's house, was called "My Land," and the flat, straight-away was used for horse and donkey races.

The intersection of Centerline and Gift Hill Roads, where Public Works is today, was called "Danish Church Hill." Outside Cruz Bay Town, what is called Gifft Hill today was then known as "Sessman Hill." Mr. Elroy recalls the world of St. John was so small, that he was twelve years old before he ever traveled to Sessman Hill. His visit there was part of the school program to assist an elderly lady who lived there. The children were led by their teacher to visit the lady, clean up her yard and bring her small gifts.

More people lived in the Pastory area than lived in Cruz Bay Town, and a number of families lived on Lovango Cay. Only about twenty people lived in Bordeaux when he was a child.

St. John has many natural streams, or guts, that run to the ocean when rainfall is prevalent. These guts contain pools that are very important for wild life, and in days past, were very important for watering livestock. The gut running down through Mongoose Junction was known as "Bufrom Gut." Guinea Gut, above the Westin Resort, and Bass Gut, were used by residents of that area for watering livestock. Banana Gut runs from Centerline Road (below Pocket Money Hill, near Samuel's Cottages) down to where the laundries are today.

Along the South Shore Road, past the Westin going to Chocolate Hole one finds "Roman Hill," still so called today. The salt pond below there was called "Sweet Pond" and when it was dried up, the pond bed was used as a ball field. Traveling on along the South Shore Road brings you to "Randahoo," which is known today as Rendezvous.

Off-Island: When St. Johnians said they were going to "Town" they meant St. Thomas. Making the passage along the south shore to St. Thomas, two rocks protrude from the water's surface; they were and still are known as "Cow and Calf." Crossing Pillsbury Sound going toward Red Hook, mariners were warned to beware the "Bull's Hold," which is a passage between Thatch and Grass Cays.

Mr. Elroy first visited St. Thomas when he was six years old. He found it to be "so large a world." When Mr. Elroy entered the ninth grade he went to board on St. Thomas and attended school at the "Barracks," where the Legislature is today. It was not until the late 1960s/early 1970s that school children began to travel daily to school in St. Thomas.

November, 2005

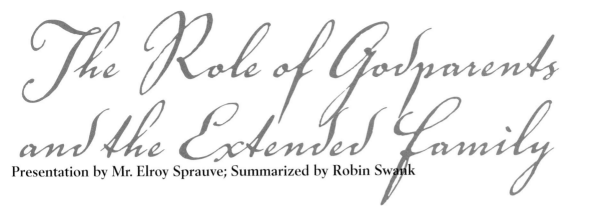

The Role of Godparents and the Extended Family

Presentation by Mr. Elroy Sprauve; Summarized by Robin Swank

Mr. Elroy Sprauve spoke from experience and as an observant historian about the role of godparents in the 1920s through the 1950s. Technically, godparenting was primarily a religious event, with a commitment to guide a child to becoming a good Christian; however, it went much further than that, he told us. A baby's baptism began an outreach system that pulled the community together, creating an extended family.

Not only was baptism a rite of passage for the baby, but also a major honor for the godparent, who would then be involved with that child and the child's family for life. Only people who were highly thought of, people considered stable, mature and with character were sought out. (Mr. Sprauve admits, modestly, that he has about 30 godchildren!). In the early to mid 1900s baptism and godparenting were taken seriously; there was a large probability that a godparent would at some point intervene in a child's life, or the child in the godparent's later life. In the 1920s to the 1950s there was not only an absence of welfare services for children (or seniors) for one to rely on, there was also an absence of ready cash, a way to store or preserve meat or vegetable provisions, and a need to feed your animals and care for the garden, all necessitating on-going daily support for chores.

Many children were raised by godparents, Mr. Elroy states. If a parent passed, or had too many (young) children to cope, or fell on hard times, the mother might ask her 'compay' (her child's godfather) to take full responsibility for the child; there was no legal process or court interference, as godparents were considered 'guardians' by the community. St. Johnians sent children reaching high school age to St. Thomas to live with relatives or godparents to continue their education. More often a godparent stepped into

Speaker and Board Member Elroy Sprauve with the Funeral Booklet of Miss Myrah Keating-Smith, Board Member Andromeada Child's mother. Andro's mother, Miss Myrah, was Mr. Elroy's godmother; that makes them godsister and godbrother. The Funeral Booklet recounts that Miss Myrah was godmother, or Nennie Myrah, to over 500 people.

(Photo by Robin Swank)

the child's life alongside the parents, extending their guiding role to schoolwork and discipline. The community respected their authority—to sign permission slips, to reprimand, and to discipline without parental interference.

Such social ties helped keep children in line. Mr. Elroy related that one day he and his brother observed a man who had had too much to drink in Cruz Bay. They decided it would be great fun to pelt him with wet sand. When his mother was told, they were punished not only because they had been rude, but also because they had been disrespectful of her "compadu;" she was godmother to one of the sand-man's children.

In listening to Mr. Elroy, it becomes clear that in a world where godparenting attaches you to all the children of that child's family, the network of bonds becomes a large part of a small town quite quickly. Andro Childs' mother was Mr. Elroy's godmother; Mr. Elroy and Andro are godbrother and godsister; therefore, Mr. Elroy addressed all the women in Andro's parents' generation as "Nennie;" and all the men in her parents' generation as "Pepe." A child's godfather is referred to as his or her "compay." The network

of these endearment terms associated with godparenting created behavioral expectations and made the entire "village" responsible for all the children. It must have been difficult for a child, (or an adult, for that matter) to get away with anything!

Children were expected to keep in contact with, check in on, and help their godparents; a child might be sent to look in on or to live with a godparent as the elder grew unable to complete daily chores. "My last godfather passed away last week at the age of 96," Mr. Elroy told us, "and until one week before his death, I had weekly contact with him." This was the godfather with whom he stayed in St. Thomas while attending high school.

What eventually diluted and then undermined this support system in the 1960s? A torrent of money and a decade of modern consumerism downloaded to the islands in about two years increased the independence of many people from the network of relationships. Mr. Elroy believes the social network still exists in the countryside on a few West Indian islands. But it is easy to see how the predominance of cash

Godparenting In The 1800s To Early 1900s

Robin Swank

Godparenting has a long history in the Caribbean. Karen Fog Olwig writes about the role of godparents in the 1800s and early 1900s in *Cultural Adaptation & Resistance on St. John - Three Centuries of Afro-Caribbean Life.* Childcare, she says, like provisions or cooked food and favors, was passed freely among relatives living in different households in the 1800s. This practice continued post-emancipation, and she cites many examples of godparents and grandparents being relied upon to care for young children.

"In the 1901 (census) thirty five St. Johnian children fifteen years old and under lived on St. Thomas without their parents. Of those, fifteen were living with relatives or godparents, twenty (as servants) with strangers." (p.116) The census also shows an additional ten children living with a guardian, godparent, or adoptive parent on St. John. Of the 371 St. Johnian children up to 15 years of age, only 64% resided with their parents. (p.133*)

Her book documents how the exchange of children intensified the relationship between wages, the ability for everyone of all ages to travel farther and have modern conveniences, access to off-island provisions, and the "convenience" of government services that pay lip service to the form and function, but not the heart, of caring for children, have weakened the godparenting role. Today's children might sense that they don't feel grounded, or that they are missing "something." They may be missing a time when many caring eyes and guiding words supported them. It is a common refrain that it takes a village to raise a child; today's children don't know what they have missed.

Some Additional Notes: *What a Pistarckle-A Dictionary of Virgin Islands English Creole,* published in 1981 by Lito Valls, a native of St. Croix, provides these definitions of words from the godparenting network:

COMPAY: A male salutation used among close friends. Spanish, Compadre. Also said, Compadu or cumpado.

NANA: (1) Nursemaid. From Twi, nana = grandmother or grandfather. (2) Foster mother. In some African tribes nana is (sic) name given to the chiefs, which means not one who rules, but one whose duty is to take care of others.

NEN: (2) Godmother. Also used as a title of respect or affection of any older female. Also pronounced NeNe or NeNee.

PEPE: Godfather. Used alone or with a person's Christian name. Thus, it is "Pepe Jule," never Pepe Sprauve, for Julius Sprauve. In addition, Pepe is used as a title of respect and affection by younger people to non-related elders. Also said Peps.

May, 2008

specific households. In the chapter, The Network of Exchanges, Olwig describes how some laborers asked estate owners to be godparents for their children, an act that may have encouraged patriarchal generosity. Post-emancipation, the institutions of shared family land, clubs (common shared work efforts with implied reciprocity), and the lending of children, were built on exchange relationships among real or fictive kinsmen. These exchange relationships—of family/common access to land resources, mutual help in farming, and temporary placement of children in the homes of relatives or godparents, she asserts, provided the means for survival and the preservation of this unique way of life. (p.158*)

*Olwig, Karen Fog. *Cultural Adaptation and Resistance on St. John—Three Centuries of Afro American Life*. University of Florida Press, 1985.

May 2008

English Creole: The Spoken Word on St. John

Presentation by Mr. Elroy Sprauve; Summarized by Robin Swank

" 'Creole' is a language patterned from two or more languages by people who live and work together," Mr. Sprauve began. With wit and charm, he gave lively examples of how English and African, along with Dutch and probably some Spanish and French donations coalesced into the modern patois heard on St. John.

Danish was generally not taught or used, so our local patois doesn't include that influence, Mr. Sprauve reminded us. Dutch Creole was, in its time, spoken by estate managers. The Moravians and Lutheran missionaries also generally spoke it, but it has since died out. English was widely spoken, facilitated by its printed use for school texts and church hymnals. It has remained the "lingua franca," and like English in London or New York, neighborhood "dialects" were evident even on this small island during Mr. Sprauve's childhood. "You could tell by a word or accent whether a person lived in Bethany or Gifft Hill" he recalled.

"Those you hear speaking English Creole also speak Standard English," he reminded us. Mr. Sprauve recalled that the linguistic insecurity imposed on the islands' children at not speaking Standard English was common during his youth, a tactic damaging to a child's psyche. This has eased in recent times. Adults, however, may still feel insecure about speaking out at a public hearing in Creole. "Although," he smiled, "you can certainly hear their opinions afterwards."

"Creole is not a wordy language," and understanding some common patterns, he told us, will educate our ear. Here are 8 of the grammatical or verbiage 'patterns' he presented:

1—**Forget 'To Be or Not to Be'**—English Creole generally doesn't use the verb 'to be' (And by the end of his presentation, we were convinced it's an irrelevant verb.) 'Where John?,' 'She my sister,' 'My wife no for good,' and 'I sick' are grammatically correct Creole sentences.

Tonality is used to sort out, for example, the meaning in the phrase 'He problem' between 'he IS a problem' and 'his problem.' Similarly, 'He home' or 'Mother ill' can be statements or questions.

2—**English Creole avoids the letter/sound S**.

S's indicating plural are avoided by using 'dem' after single nouns, as in 'De boy dem' or 'de goat dem.' Of course there is an exception; whelks is always plural—I guess because you can't eat just one.

Possessives, instead of being indicated by an apostrophe and a final s are indicated by sentence placement, as in, 'I play Mary piano.' The 3rd person present tense also ignores the letter S, as in 'He speak French.'

3—**Common to African languages, English Creole future and past tenses are not indicated by verb form changes**. 'We play ball next week,' or 'She come last week' are made perfectly understandable with one form of the verb.

4—**As with most languages spoken over time, Creole fuses words.** For example, 'Where John?' might be answered by 'He'en heah.' 'You goin'?' might be answered by 'No, me'en goan.'

With fusion and pace, Mr. Sprauve pointed out, great privacy can be created; he and several other VI college students successfully created private conversations at school in Pennsylvania surrounded by standard English speakers. And it's done just as successfully today on the streets of St. John!

5—English Creole uses cultural 'substitutions' and 'borrows' from other languages.

There are noun substitutions, such as 'tea' meaning a full breakfast, or 'family' meaning all one's relatives.

The verbs 'make', 'have', and 'do' can be switched around, as they are in other languages—as in, 'I make 50 (years) yesterday.'

French and Spanish based words such as compadu (godparent), nan or nani (godmother), tanti (aunt) used before a person's name, soire (as meant in French, a good party with lots of food and dancing), bagashe (baggage) and a fused version of the Spanish todo el mundo, 'tul mundo,' enrich the English Creole vocabulary.

6—Some sounds are glossed over.

TH is not pronounced; Three is t'ree and authority is at'ority. Nor are final d's and t's accentuated. R's also seem to be up for grabs; someone using standard English will pronounce lots more final R's.

7—Pronouns as objects of prepositions do not change form; a St. Johnian speaking proper English Creole would say 'Give it to she' or 'It is for we.'

AND **8—English Creole is continually evolving.**

There are 'old' words that remain, words like—porah (disrespectful), swai (wander), and macron (achy or in pain)—macrons were slaves too old to work sugar but not cotton, There are also old forms of word usage that still linger. When addressing older respected people fondly by first name, respect requires they be fronted with Friend, Nani, Nan, Miss or Mr.

Some usages are waning. Responding to the question 'How you doin'?' with 'Great! Wonderful! Never Better!' is now more common on the street than 'so so', 'not so bad', 'movin' along,' and other more humble approaches to life. "These people are not hypochondriacs," Mr Sprauve laughed, "they are respectful that tomorrow belongs to God."

New words continue to enter the Creole vocabulary, through hip-hop, reggae and the Rastafarian influence. "English Creole is a healthy language," asserts Mr. Sprauve. "It is one which needn't be taught in the classroom, however, because children bring the latest version of it with them to school."

Mr. Sprauve also noted in his presentation that intense emotions are often expressed in Creole rather than Standard English in the home, in Church and sometimes even in the V.I. Legislature. T'anks, Mr. Elroy. Yo' presentation preserve English Creole as part of St. John multilingual heritage.

March, 2007

Jumbies and Werewolves

Robin Swank, with the assistance of several other ghoulish Board Members

Silk-cotton tree in bloom

(Image from W.K. Brooks, "Aspects of Nature in the West Indies" [Harpers Magazine, Vol. XIXV, no. 9])

Halloween wasn't observed in these islands until the U.S. influence began to strengthen in the 1960s, but there has never been a lack of spirits or hauntings here, with traditions of fright that go back to both Africa and Europe.

Will you see jumbies on St. John, come All Hallow's Eve?

If you have lots of trees, you're especially likely to spot a spirit. Seeing jumbies at the foot of trees is common. In *Remarkable Big Trees of the US Virgin Islands*, Robert Nicholls reports a conversation between two friends: "Any tree a jumbie tree come ah night time." The silk cotton or kapok tree, however, which appears as a spirit tree or kinship shrine in West African stories, merits special mention as a jumbie tree. Cutting down a silk cotton releases spirits that live in the tree, and these homeless spirits will haunt you for years before they settle down again. Also, bats congregate around silk cottons

in bloom. And we all know about bats—Count Dracula's friends? If you're near a kapok tree during Halloween night, perhaps you'll see it pelted with eggs and chickens in order to "catch" a stolen shadow and put its owner at rest. Jumbies are also likely to persist near burial grounds. If a person is not put to rest properly (Perhaps he had no Nine Night funeral wake? Or his toes are not tied together to keep him from walking?), then that person's burial plot is a "hot spot" for meeting a jumbie.

Certain places on St. John, such as Denis Bay and Jumbie Bay, were notorious for an abundance of spirits. By the mid 20th century, the "enlightenment" of modern thought began to erode traditional beliefs on St. John, but jumbie stories were still widely used to frighten children into better behavior.

What about werewolves?

In an excerpt from his book, recaptured in *St. John Backtime*, Desmond Holdridge describes his St. John arrival so: "In the weighing of a strange white man, the first day or two goes by in trying to please him......Should the stranger decide to stay, it is decided that he is a detective, a millionaire or a werewolf." According to additional authoritative texts consulted, werewolves were always European; many local anti-werewolf remedies, such as garlic hung over doors and windows, came straight from Europe as well.

You can easily identify a werewolf by his physical characteristics.....or perhaps by the furniture in his house. Heed this description from J. Antonio Jarvis' *The Virgin Islands and Their People*: "The werewolf is described as a large-headed heavy quadruped about the size of a sheep, very fleet and nimble, since it can climb house roofs, vault over fences and scamper faster than the average dog. It is supposed to be a Dane or a German who has divested his humanity in a Jekyll-Hyde transformation by using drugs, incantations and a number of backward somersaults over a four legged stool."

Hamilton Cochran's *These Are the Virgin Islands* relates: "From St. John comes a curious tale about a were-wolf, the truth of which cannot be gainsaid." He identifies the supposed werewolf as Henry Jordon, a "gaunt" engraver or "etcher" who lived a secluded life in a cottage near Trunk Bay. Reticent, quietly tending his bees, liking walks in the moonlight, he was suspected of being a werewolf. While walking home one night a huge commotion on the path ahead made him pause. A small donkey, that could indeed sound and seem like a 4-footed werewolf in the dark, had been attacked in his stead. The "real" Henry Jordon was most likely Wilbur Davis, who, Rafe Boulon and his cousin Erva Denham report, was an engraver who lived in a 1929 cabin near the beach, at the base of the hill going up to Trunk Bay house. If we are to believe Mr. Cochran, this house was burned to the ground to rid the area of that pesky werewolf; Rafe maintains it was termites.

So if you are in search of jumbies and werewolves on Hallow E'en, you now know what to look for! If you'd rather *avoid* jumbies and werewolves, then lock your dog and donkey up tight, hang bapoos (jumbies in a bottle) in your trees, put an obeah lamp (or jack o' lantern) under your bed; throw 99 gains of corn or barley on your doorstep (the werewolf will search interminably for the 100th), play Michael Jackson's *Thriller* very loud, chalk "Only Goblins under ten years old welcome" on your door, and either wear a hat or stay inside until dawn breaks.

October, 2007

THE GHOST OF RENDEZVOUS BAY

If you've ever walked the Ditleff Point trail to Rendezvous Bay, you might have noticed the crumbling ruins of a mid-twentieth-century structure hidden away in the dense vegetation behind the beach. For over half a century, tales of haunting and the mysterious disappearance of its owner have circulated throughout the island. Now thanks to a probate document identified by SJHS Member Margie Labrenz, the facts behind the abandonment of the old house on Rendezvous Bay have come to light.

"In the matter of the Estate of Clide Eugene Osborn:

That Clide Eugene Osborn, a resident of St. John, VI., fell or jumped overboard from his boat 'Shadow I', in Rendezvous Bay, St. John, on July 1, 1948, at or about 4:00 pm; that the bay was reputed to be infested with sharks; that his body was not recovered and that he was never seen again, according to the Coroner's Inquest held at the courthouse in Cruz Bay, St. John, VI. On July 8, 1948; the court, therefore, find that Clide Eugene Osborn met his death on July 1, 1948 at Rendezvous Bay; that Clide Eugene Osborn died intestate leaving a widow, Agnes Aileen Finton Osborn, and three children, Clide Eugene Osborn II, Carolyn Joan Osborn, both adults, and Judith Ann Osborn, a minor. That he left the following property, namely: 15A Estate Rendezvous and Ditleff, Cruz Bay Quarter, situated in St. John, VI., valued at $14,850.00; a motorboat named the 'Shadow I', and personal property; that the motorboat was sold for $900.00 and the personal property for $418.75, the total Assets being $16,168.75."

October 2003

Maybe there really was a "good ol' days" after all.

David W. Knight

Stamped postal envelope addressed to Mr. Fritz A. Francis in Haiti, 1902

(Courtesy D. Knight Collection)

For many years now I have been collecting stamps, tokens, coins, and paper money from the Danish West Indies. So, recently when I had an opportunity to purchase a postal cover with two rare 1902 St. John postmarks, I jumped at the chance.

This envelope, however, turned out to be even more interesting than I had hoped. Along with two nice St. John cancels over one-, three-, and four-cent Danish West Indies stamps, there were also three postmarks on the reverse of the envelope, which tell a startling story of the letter's journey nearly one hundred years ago.

According to the postmarks, the letter, which was addressed to Mr. Fritz A. Francis in Gonaives, Haiti, was mailed on St. John, February 4, 1902. It arrived at St. Thomas the same day, where it was postmarked and quickly forwarded. Amazingly, the letter reached Cape Haitian on the north coast of Haiti a mere three days later. After being post marked once again, the letter was sent on to Gonaives, where it arrived on February 13th.

For a grand total of eight cents, Mr. Francis' letter had traveled from St. John, all the way to Gonaives Haiti in only nine days—less time than it presently takes most mail from the U.S.A. to reach the Virgin Islands!!

You know, when you think about it, maybe there really was a "good ol' days" after all.

March 2000

Hey driver, how many Francs for a lift to Cruz Bay;
and, by the way, do you have change for a Piece-of-Eight?

David W. Knight & Lolly Prime

A "Five Francs" Danish West Indies banknote, 1905

(Courtesy D. Knight Collection)

"Spanish Silver" 8-Reals, or "piece-of-eight"

(D. Knight Collection)

(Front and back) Danish West Indies 2-Cents/10-Bits and 10-Cents/50-Bits coins, 1905

(D. Knight Collection)

Although the Danish West Indies colony was well established by the close of the 17th century, it was not until 1740 that the first official coinage was minted for general use throughout the islands—a I Skilling and a II Skilling, made from copper, and a XII Skilling, struck in silver.

The standard unit of Danish currency in those days was the Rigsdaler, which was equivalent to 96 Skillings—hence the 12 Skilling unit. Aside from the issuance of additional denominations of coinage, the Rigsdaler and Skilling system remained little changed for some one hundred and sixty-five years.

But, in 1904 a monetary system comprised of Francs, Bits, Cents, and Dalers was instituted, and new coins and bank

A "Ten Dollar" Danish West Indies banknote, 1849

(Courtesy D. Knight Collection)

notes were issued (5 Bits to a Cent; 20 Cents to a Franc; 100 Cents to a Daler). This baffling currency was still in place when the Danish West Indies colony was sold to the United States in 1917. And, as agreed to in the treaty of secession, Francs and Bits were to remain the official units of currency in the islands up until 1934. However, that's not the end of our story.

No one ever held much faith in Danish West Indies currency. Not only could it not be exchanged at face value anywhere outside of the Danish colony, the coins also had a bad reputation for poor and inconsistent quality. As a result, silver Spanish Reales, and especially the large and coveted Pieces-of-Eight, had long been adopted as the true "coins of the realm" throughout the Danish West Indies. Widely accepted, and prized for their precise weight and purity of content, Spanish silver coins were still legal tender in the U.S. Virgin Islands (as they were throughout the United States) up until the passage of the Coinage Act in 1965.

So, long after the transfer of the Danish West Indies to the United States, Spanish silver Pieces-of-Eight (or Pesos) still rivaled the good ol' Yankee Dollar as a preferred method of payment. If you needed change, however, you probably just ended up with a pocket full of Francs and Bits.

January 2000

At Work an' Rest

Chapter 6:
THE NATURE OF THINGS

The Forest Island

Eleanor Gibney

Lignum vitae, *Guaiacum officinale*

(Photo courtesy of Doug White)

When the first Europeans landed on St. John, did they see a dramatically different landscape and vegetation from what we observe now? In the absence of detailed reports from that time, we have to make a lot of educated guesses. The early accounts that do exist are often misleading, perhaps due to the same kind of confusion of plant names that still exists today.

Although the forests and dry shrub-lands of the island have certainly been altered by the human activities of the past 300 years, there has been no large-scale extirpation (eradication) of native plants. How do we know? There are at least 646 species of indigenous plants on St. John, and this diversity compares very favorably with the least historically disturbed dry forests of the Caribbean.

Climate has always limited potential forest cover on the island to an extent; droughts and hurricanes of devastating degree recur several times a century. Before plantation agriculture, the soil on slopes would have been deeper and thus retained more of the rainfall—but there is no evidence that actual rainfall was higher over any significant period in the past.

Almost certainly, the moister sections of St. John (guts, coastal plains etc.) had massive trees, taller than almost anything we see now. Many of these trees were desirable timbers (red locust, mastic, satinwood, gre-gre, bulletwood etc.). The drier forest of the south and east probably contained quantities of short but stocky lignum vitae, one of the most valuable woods of Tropical America, now threatened throughout its original range, including St. John. All of these are hardwoods that take centuries to attain optimum size; some became rare and are now slowly reappearing. In the absence of annual growth rings, we can only estimate the ages of trees from modern observations and records.

The driest land was certainly always dry, and some of this habitat is probably virtually untouched by events of the past 500 years, as we find numerous rare plants here, including many found only in the VI, and at least one found only on St. John. The hardwood trees of these areas grow very slowly indeed, and larger specimens probably have been here since the Tainos occupied the island.

We know that the British from Tortola had been lumbering St. John up to the time the Danes officially settled in 1718. What happened after Danish arrival is open to conjecture, but most scholars of the island's past agree that the plantation era caused considerable clearing of original forest, but no more than 50% of the cover was removed at any one time. Thus, when land was abandoned, as it frequently was with the tides of time and fortune, there were always native trees nearby to provide seeds to re-colonize the clearings.

Although traditional accounts of the island's history implied that agriculture never fully recovered from the 1733 rebellion, we now know that the heyday of sugar production here wasn't until the late 18th and early 19th centuries. Surprisingly, we find many references to the forests of St. John right through this period. Starting with Peter Lotharios Oxholm, who produced the invaluable map that shows the cleared and forested areas of the island at the end of the 18th century, we find writer after writer extolling the wildness, and usually the beauty, of the wooded hills. Oxholm himself wrote in 1780: "...large trees and mountains eliminate all possibilities for passage..." In 1807, Danish Naval Officer Hans Birch Duhreup said: "...St. John is undeniably the most picturesque of our islands and the most beautiful scenery I have ever beheld... The return trip at midnight through dense woods the most beautiful I have ever ridden."

In the 1830s the Danish naturalist A.S. Orsted visited the three Danish West Indies and was captivated by the natural beauty of St. John. He writes at great length about the vegetation in "Islands of Beauty and Bounty," the text that accompanied six plates in "Danmark," a sort of coffee-table book of the time on Denmark and its colonies. The St. John text contains this interesting observation: "It is not only the more untamed, romantic mountain terrain that makes St. John so different from the other islands, but since by far the major part—11/13—remains uncultivated, its mountains and valleys are overgrown with forests and brush so that we have an opportunity here to acquaint ourselves with the vegetation in its original form, while on the other islands it is mostly imported plants that meet the eye everywhere." This was written over 150 years ago, at about the time of emancipation. The island's population in 1846 was 2450, by 1900 it was 925 and it didn't rise above that level again until the 1960s.

The post-sugar era on St. John saw the emergence of four land-based economic activities: cattle ranching, charcoal burning, bay rum oil extraction and basket making. Interestingly, 3 of the 4 activities were reliant on indigenous forests: mostly native hardwoods for the charcoal; the indigenous bay rum tree (St. John trees were famous for their fine scent); and hoopvine and wist for basketry. Many of the former sugar estates converted to cattle operations: at Caneel Bay, Cinnamon, Carolina, Lameshur, Susannaberg, Mary Point... the 1932 St. John cattle census lists 1243 head on the island. Probably at least as much land was kept clear by cattle as by sugar production formerly, and most of these areas still contain highly disturbed vegetation today. Charcoal production in contrast was a surprisingly benign activity for the forest—most trees re-sprouted vigorously from their stumps, and we find many older trees that have been coppiced in this fashion. The areas where bay rum was actually

Aerial view of Coral Harbor, c1960. Note extensive grazing areas on surrounding hills and neighboring islands.

(Photo courtesy of Eleanor Gibney)

cultivated are also still evident: on Bordeaux, at Cinnamon Bay and sections of Mollendahl and Hawksnest.

Some of the island's moistest areas that remained in use into the 20th century, like Cinnamon Bay and the lower Reef Bay valley, have returned to forest relatively quickly, although this is where we tend to find many of the weedy plants from elsewhere dominating the scene, such as the South American genip and the East Indian sweet lime. The genip is believed to be a Taino import that became commoner in the plantation era as a sturdy source of fruit and shade. Unfortunately it tends to seed in thickly and prevent the growth of other plants, perhaps through chemicals produced by the root system. Genip dominates many of the formerly cultivated guts, especially on the North shore. Larger genip trees, including many in Cruz Bay, are all well over 150 years old.

The dry lands of St. John tended to have less historic disturbance, since even cotton requires some depth of soil and protection from the prevailing easterly wind. Grazing, particularly of goats, has been the major altering force. Over time, the animals consume all of the young plants that are not poisonous or thorny, creating a vegetation cover of the most noxious species, both native and introduced. This is very evident in sections of the south shore, where maran and casha prevail. This semi-desert will recover very slowly from disturbance, even if goats are no longer present.

Somewhere along the line an aggressive "pioneer" plant was introduced from the mainland of Central America: the wild tamarind or tan-tan. The transfer may have been intentional (it is still promoted as a fuel and forage plant for the third world) but the plant soon did what it has done all over the tropics: occupied any land that had been disturbed or cleared. Eventually this sun-loving plant gets shaded out by taller-growing trees, but hurricanes and grazing animals can help keep it around for at least a century. Most of St. John's former cattle lands are still heavily covered by this pioneer. From Bellevue looking across the upper Fish Bay watershed, one can pick out a solid patch of wild tamarind on a knoll, marking Seiben Estate, the cattle operation of Julius Sprauve Sr., sold to the nascent National Park in 1954.

St. John is unique among all the islands of the Caribbean today in having retained a large percentage of indigenous dry forest that is protected. Many of the fine hardwoods, such as satinwood and lignum vitae, are gradually regenerating. Every section of the vegetation can reveal clues to the land use and activities of the past: like so many aspects of the island, an astonishingly large and rich source of knowledge and enjoyment.

January, 2005

$\mathcal{F}ever$

Eleanor Gibney

As I write this on a very wet and cool October night, another drenching tropical wave is passing over us. After 23 inches of rain in the past two months, this begins to seem normal. I can again hear the gut roaring in the distance, and I can anticipate another major outbreak of mosquitoes in about a week. Mosquitoes have been a serious annoyance this year, but not a life-threatening annoyance. For centuries, inhabitants of these islands suffered agonies of severe and recurring fevers that were spread by mosquito bites, and they never had an inkling that was what was happening; they blamed the climate, or the bad air of swampy areas, for the disease that became known as "bad air"—*mal aria* in Italian, direct from the Latin.

While smallpox and cholera produced the deadliest epidemics in island history, three mosquito-borne diseases were constantly prevalent in the islands: yellow fever, the deadliest but the rarest locally; malaria, notoriously persistent, recurrent for years and often fatal; and dengue, severe but usually limited in duration and fatality. Although yellow fever was soon recognized as a separate disease, producing a characteristic yellow jaundice that was hard to mistake, the several varieties of malaria and dengue were not usually differentiated in the early days. Most settlers were soon stricken with one or another—or several—fevers. The Danes were apparently extremely susceptible to these illnesses; the Dutch, who had been here for generations, had perhaps better immunity to begin with, they certainly lived longer. The Africans would also have arrived with immunities to some strains of malaria and yellow fever, which occurred on both sides of the Atlantic. Of the numerous species of mosquitoes present in the islands, only two are of real health concern, one is the potential yellow fever and/or dengue carrier, the other the malaria vector.

From the earliest writers onward, every chronicle of life in the Danish West Indies devotes considerable space to fevers, and all of them sound remarkably similar.

Leaves and distinctive flower of the Princewood Tree, an evergreen, 10-25 feet tall and up to 4 inches in trunk diameter.

(Common Trees of Puerto Rico and the Virgin Islands [Little and Wadsworth])

Here is J. L. Carstens writing of St. Thomas in about 1730: "Because the air and soil are unwholesome, several illnesses prevail… among which the following are so common that everyone must suffer and survive them… he catches a fever, which is persistent among the people there to greater and lesser degrees… it strikes some more seriously than others."

And Reimert Haagensen on St. Croix in mid 1700s: "I have neither knowledge of nor a good reason for the pronounced unhealthy conditions of the island… there are examples showing that hardly anyone escapes without suffering and sickness just after having arrived there…"

At the turn of the eighteenth century, Hans West, also on St. Croix, said: "The vapors of this rainy season and the resulting cold air are what cause the many fevers that prevail toward the end of the year. Traveling through the island after sunset or before sunrise is therefore risky to one's health, especially in a damp year… until the sun appears and dissolves or attenuates the heavy vapors."

As I mentioned last year in an article on rainfall, the residents of earlier centuries recognized a

The Nature of Things

connection between fever and rainy weather, wetlands, swamps, light clothing and going out in the evenings and early mornings but they never made the real connection: to mosquitoes. One creative theory put forth asserted that the extreme heat of the summertime actually opened the pores of the skin to a large degree, then the cool rains of fall produced unwholesome vapors that entered these enlarged pores that hadn't had time to revert to their protective closed state. It was best to cover the body in wool garments to guard that vulnerable skin. They were actually on to something there… woolen underwear would certainly guard pretty well against mosquito bites.

Quinine, extracted mainly from a South American tree in the coffee family, *Cinchona officinalis*, came into world-wide use as an effective malaria remedy by the late 18th century. The bark of a closely related tree, *Exostema caribaea*, princewood, a common native tree in the VI, was also used locally, and apparently worked well. Elsewhere in the region it is still called fever tree and Jesuit bark. Hans West sent a sample of princewood bark to Denmark for testing in 1790; the Regimental Surgeon "found the effect to be reliable."

In spite of available malaria treatments, fevers continued to take a large toll on the local population up through the nineteenth century. The St. Thomas sanitary report for the 4th Quarter of 1887, for instance, lists 436 cases of "intermittent and remittent fever" reported by doctors in those 3 months, and 24 people died of those fevers, a figure matched only by "consumption"—tuberculosis. This was in an island population of about 15,000.

By the time the mosquito/disease connection was figured out, in the years before transfer, the Danes weren't especially interested in devoting resources to disease eradication. Periodic outbreaks continued to take lives into the early 1930s. Then, U.S. President Herbert Hoover removed the USVI from the naval rule that had been in effect since transfer, and gave control to the Department of the Interior, installing the first US civilian Governor, Paul M. Pearson. Medical facilities, such as they were, on St. Thomas and St. John were directed by the brilliant Danish doctor Knud Knud-Hansen. When the Navy medical officers all had left the islands, a desperate Dr. Knud-Hansen dragged his former colleague Dr. Viggio Christensen out of happy retirement in the St. Thomas countryside to assist him.

In 1932, a terrible epidemic of malaria hit St. Thomas and St. John. With the support of Governor Pearson, Dr. Knud-Hansen put every case in St. Thomas in the hospital, and Dr. Christensen came over to St. John, walking and riding to all the far-flung little settlements of the island to find every single resident, test everyone's blood and put all the infected cases under treatment.

Governor Pearson obtained "magnificent" federal appropriations to drain and fill wetlands on St. Thomas, including the huge Mosquito Bay swamp west of town. The large flat area of land that was created there was quickly converted to an airfield, known then as Bourne Field, and the bay was officially renamed Lindberg Bay. (Charles Lindberg had landed the" Spirit of St. Louis" in St. Thomas in 1929, but it may have been on the other side of town, in the then empty expanse of Sugar Estate.)

Dr. Knud-Hansen and Dr. Christensen were wildly successful. Malaria has not been known to occur as a locally generated disease in the Virgin Islands since that fateful outbreak of 1932. A vaccine eliminated yellow fever, but dengue is still very much with us. On the bright side, we no longer feel compelled to cover our bodies in several layers of thick woolen cloth to repel the noxious—and potentially fatal—vapors of the evening… Although the clouds of mosquitoes may seem just as insidious.

October, 2008

Lignum vitae

Beauty, Strength, and the Fallibility of Medicine

Eleanor Gibney

Most people who have spent any real amount of time in the West Indies are at least vaguely acquainted with the small tree known as lignum vitae—a Latin name meaning "wood of life," but oddly enough, NOT the tree's scientific name: that would be *Guaiacum officinale*—from the Taino name guayacan, and "*officinale*" meaning official, or prescribed in pharmacy. Early settlers in these islands called it buckwood, pockwood and sometimes frenchwood (for reasons we'll later reveal), and Virgin Islanders have often pronounced the Latin with a certain softening: "lingy whitey."

Apparently lignum vitae was a major species in the original dry forest of the Virgin Islands. The Buck islands, off both St. Croix and St. Thomas, the island now called Le Duc off Coral Bay (once Bocken Island), and the area known as Pockwood Pond on the south shore of Tortola were all named from the former abundance of this tree.

Real St. John lignum vitae is a south shore species, still found in the wild from Chocolate Hole to Round Bay. There are probably more lignum vitaes in island gardens now than are left in the wild, although St. John has far more wild trees remaining than any of the other Virgins. These islands are pretty much smack in the middle of the tree's natural range, from the Bahamas to Venezuela. Over-harvesting certainly led to the species becoming rare or extinct throughout its range. The great beauty of the tree, with masses of sky-blue flowers during the dry days of early spring, followed by masses of orange seed-pods in the fall—and a beautifully mottled "camouflage" patterned bark at all times—has certainly been the main point that has kept it in public awareness. Other valuable and now rare native hardwoods, such as satinwood and mastic, are not now well-known. We can see the

Guaiacum officinale.

Botanical illustration of Lignum vitae from *Woodvilles Medical Botany*, 1790

(Eleanor Gibney Collection)

distinctive cross-hatched grain of lignum vitae timbers in historic buildings ranging from the lofty Susannaberg windmill to the numerous small homestead sites of the far East End.

Lignum vitae wood is among the hardest and heaviest of all commercial woods, with a specific gravity of 1.3. Specific gravity is a measurement based on the density of water, with 1.0 being the same density as water… so, any wood over 1.0 will sink, as lignum vitae will, readily. (A surprisingly large number of other native woods do the same). What makes lignum vitae wood so valuable is not the density alone, but the combination with the oily resin that permeates the wood, lubricating and making it almost indestructible. "The self-lubricating resinous wood is so valuable that it is sold by weight…It is famed for its special use in bearings and bushing blocks for the propeller shafts of steamships. It serves also for pulley sheaves, deadeyes, and as a replacement for metal bearings in roller mills. Other uses include bandsaw guides, awning rollers, furniture casters, mallets, bowling balls and turned novelties" [Little and Wadsworth, *Common Trees of Puerto Rico and the Virgin Islands*].

So… back to those names. There is still debate about the origin of syphilis, a disease known as the "great mimic." Was it originally European or American? Was it present in Europe in a different form before Columbus's crew came back from the West Indies? Did that crew infect the un-resistant Tainos of this region, causing the disease to mutate, and hastening the Taino's tragic end? What is sure is that a new form of Syphillis appeared in Europe at the end of the 15th century, spreading rapidly along the trade routes of the continent. At almost the same time, Spanish sailors in the Caribbean were apparently given guaiacum wood by helpful Tainos, and shown how to prepare it as a remedy for the "bubbles" affecting their skin.

The widely accepted date for the introduction of the wood to Europe is 1508. It quickly became the treatment of choice for syphilis—"pox" of course was the plural of pock, as in pockwood (and pockmark), and syphilis was already known as the French disease, hence the frenchwood. The anti-syphilitic properties of lignum vitae were heavily promoted by the Italian physician Francisco Delicado, who credited it with curing his 23-year case of the disease (it was probably spontaneous remission), and published a treatise in the 1520s entitled *Del Modo del Adoperare e Legno de India Occidentale, Salutefero Rimedio a Ogni Piaga et Mal Incurabile* ("On How to Employ the Wood From the West Indies, a Beneficial Remedy for any Ulcer and Incurable Disease").

The process of treatment with lignum vitae appears to have been a true case of the cure being possibly worse than the disease. Before

Preparing *Lignum vitae* in the sick room, engraving by Galle, based on a drawing by Giovanni Stradano, c1550

(Eleanor Gibney Collection)

The Nature of Things

the treatment began, it was necessary to purge the patient thoroughly. He was then put on an extreme restricted diet and kept in a dark hot room for 40 days, drinking decoctions of lignum vitae wood three times a day, but allowed no light, fresh air, meat or wine. Sweating, starving, and frequent lignum vitae tea enemas should help effect the cure.

Although it is probable that most of the cures attributed to this harsh regime were temporary remissions due to the length of the treatment, lignum vitae soon became very popular as a cure for a wide variety of other ailments, from sciatica to epilepsy. When it was discovered that it was not actually poisonous when mixed with wine, as had been earlier supposed, a decoction in wine became the favored form of administration.

The use of guaiacum for syphilis waned over the next century, gradually replaced by mercury as the drug of choice. Despite the imaginably dire side effects, mercury remained common in syphilis treatment until the 20th century, while lignum vitae gradually sank into obscurity in the pharmacopoeia, although still employed in combination with other woods and roots as late as 1855.

The Italian scholar Rodolfo Taiani, in *Pharmacy through the Ages*, considers that one of the main factors in lignum vitae's popularity was the "....Brilliant sales campaign, prompted by the Fuggers, a powerful German family of traders, entrepreneurs and bankers, financers of the Emperor Charles V (1500-1558) and of princes and prelates. This family had the monopoly of this drug, which became extremely valuable and was sold at very high prices."

J. L. Carstens, writing of St. Thomas in the 1740s, says "...There are many different rich families that live well under the Danish flag as the result of their trade, especially in sugar and cotton planting, but also from tobacco, coffee, and cacao....rice, ox-hides and various dye-woods, including ebony wood or bock-wood." (The black lignum vitae heartwood was often confused with the East Indian ebony.)

Riement Haagensen, describing St. Croix in the same period, said: "One finds on St. Croix two other kinds of trees, fustick (the source of khaki dye, either extinct on St. John or never here) and pockwood, which has brought many a man some thousands and thousands of rixdalers....In the forest, such trees are considered practically as good as money in the bank."

A few years later, in 1767, the wonderfully thorough recorder of all he found in these islands, the Moravian missionary C.G.A. Oldendorp, goes on at length: "Pockwood is indeed difficult to work with, both on account of its hardness and its crooked growth. However, it takes precedence over all other varieties of building timber in terms of its sturdiness and durability... Iron will rust away before timbers of this wood begin to rot. The trunk of this tree grows to a width of three to five feet in diameter. (!!!) The wood of this tree is as expensive as fustick, and is, like the latter, exported to Europe in considerable quantities."

With such fortunes being made, it is a wonder that any native lignum vitae survives on St. John, but it is further testimony to how wild the island remained in the colonial period, compared to many others in the region. Oldendorp's reference to three to five foot diameter trees should give us pause, though. At Caneel Bay's main ruins, you can see a large number of small lignum vitaes, grown from seed planted over 50 years ago by the irrepressible Ivan Jadan. Even under Caneel's luxurious conditions, they've got quite a few centuries to go before they're full grown.

Lignum vitae is one of very few woody plants protected under CITES, the Convention on International Trade in Endangered Species... almost all other plants with those protections are orchids, cacti and succulents that are still collected from their natural habitats in vast quantities for the illegal horticultural market.

March, 2008

Guavaberry

Eleanor Gibney

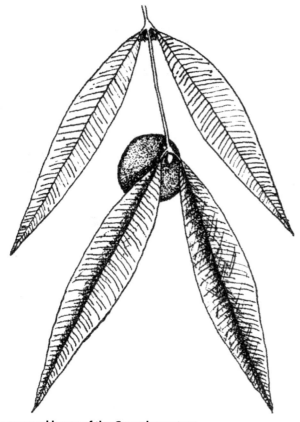

The leaves and berry of the Guavaberry tree

(Common Trees of Puerto Rico and the Virgin Islands [Little and Wadsworth])

The guavaberry tree (*Myrciaria floribunda*) is a widespread species in Tropical American forests; found in the West Indies from Cuba down to Martinique, and on the mainland from the south of Mexico to Brazil. It is fitting, however, that the species was first officially described from a collection on St. Croix by Hans West in the year 1800, for nowhere in its wide range is this small tree more beloved than here in the Virgin Islands.

Guavaberry is a member of the myrtle family, with many edible and medicinal relatives, from the bayrum, guava and allspice of tropical America to the cloves and eucalyptus of Asia and Australia. St. John has 20 native species of the myrtle family, and several of them have edible fruit, none nearly so well used as the guavaberry.

The "guava" of guavaberry probably comes from the great similarity of the tree's beautiful smooth bark to that of its frequently cultivated cousin, the guava, but the similarity ends there. Like many Caribbean trees, the guavaberry is programmed to bloom in the spring after the first heavy rains following the dry season. If the rainfall remains adequate through the summer, the small berries will ripen in late September. There are two varieties, one with yellow-orange berries, the other a deep purple, and apparently the two forms remain true when grown from seed. Both varieties have a unique and very strongly aromatic flavor, but, while blind tests have not proved any difference in taste, it is widely accepted that the purple berries are better. They are undeniably better looking, especially in tarts and in the color they give to guavaberry rum. Both varieties are notably tedious to harvest from the trees… hand picking takes forever, and the remarkable sturdiness of the trees makes it a challenge for the strongest men to shake hard enough to bring down even the ripest berries.

Once a sufficient quantity of fruit has been gathered, they may be used for an excellent jam or a fabulous tart filling; a very palatable wine has been made with the fermented fruits, but the berries macerated and soaked in rum produce a festive beverage with a taste that seems to evoke centuries of island history in its marriage of flavors. The classic preparation was simply rum, guavaberries and sugar to taste, placed in the beautiful big green glass demijohns that were common in the islands until the

1970s (cheap red table wine from France was sold in demijohns by all the larger St. Thomas merchants); the demijohns were put away in a dark corner to age at least until Christmas of that year—or, with discipline and self-control, until December of the following year.

The preparation of guavaberry rum as a Christmas drink is not quite unique to the Virgin Islands; Dutch St. Maarten and Saba also have a long tradition, and today a variety of guavaberry products are marketed from a large gift shop in Phillipsburg. The idea probably began with European traditions of fruit liquors popular at the holiday time, and the beautiful color and aroma of rum infused with guavaberries was already popular in these islands by the mid-1700s. Oldendorp's exhaustive account of daily life in that era includes: "I must also make mention of another small tree which I have not at all seen, but whose berries—they are called guavaberries—I have eaten, like cherries, they are very round, black or yellow. They have one or two small kernels, a pleasant, spicy taste, and are quite healthful. They are eaten in the morning on an empty stomach. When prepared in rum, they take on a strong, sweet taste."

Guavaberry rum is the best-known festive beverage of the islands, but several other local libations were once common and are now rare. The drink known as "Miss Blyden" was a favorite in dry areas like East End—similar to guavaberry, it was made from the fruit of native prickly pear cactus (*Opuntia dillenii*), steeped in rum and sweetened with sugar. Bottles of Miss Blyden were often buried for proper aging—and perhaps to stifle temptation to sample out of season—to be unearthed with proper ceremony at Christmas time. The cactus fruit imparted a gorgeous crimson color. Children were served a non-alcoholic version made with raspberry essence and red coloring. "Sorrel," a red drink made from the sorrel hibiscus (*Hibiscus sabdariffa*), was another appropriately-colored soft beverage.

Caroling was very much a part of St. John at Christmas time, with groups going from house to house in their communities, beginning at dawn on Christmas morning. With libations flowing, the progress slowed as the day went on, but a sturdy group of carolers and their instruments could still be serenading well into the late afternoon, with increasing cheer and decreasing balance. By the 1960s a large group of men from Cruz Bay would pack themselves

Demijohn
(Photo courtesy Eleanor Gibney)

in a small ramshackle jeep and carol all the way to Coral Bay—and back along the north shore—stopping at every house along the way to spread joy and fortify themselves to continue with guavaberry and sweet breads and cakes. The instruments may have been homemade, but the tunes were jubilant and the participants had certainly caroled together for many decades, infusing the occasion with hilarity and a pure Christmas spirit of comfort and brotherhood. With practically no other traffic on the road, the assigned driver—often Herman Sprauve—could return to Cruz Bay very slowly in the middle of the road, with a cargo of friends who were perhaps less tuneful than when they had started, but filled with love and peace—and the need to sleep.

December, 2007

Soldier Crab Saga

Rafe Boulon

Soldier Crab in Whelk shell

(Photo by Rafe Boulon, 2009)

I was born and live on St. John, USVI, and have been living with Soldier (land hermit) crabs all my life. They are part of my every day life - in my pond getting a drink, around my bird cages, on my deck, in my dog's food, on the paths we walk (carefully so as not to step on them), and in general, everywhere!! As a kid I used them for bait to fish, now I prefer to let them go on their own way, wherever that is.

During the late summer and early fall, their way is usually down to the sea to shed their eggs in the ocean. They seem to use a traditional beach where the population of crabs from that watershed aggregate over a week or so period of time before actually going to the sea and shedding their eggs. I live on one such beach. In fact, in 1985, during one of several aggregations I have seen during my lifetime, I estimated approximately 40,000 crabs in the

total aggregation. This aggregation covered an area about 50 feet by 100 feet and they were piled up over a foot deep around the base of trees. I estimated numbers by using a one-square meter quadrant and randomly placing it ten times within the area occupied by the crabs. By estimating the number of crabs per square meter and multiplying that by the number of square meters occupied by crabs, I came up with approximately 40,000 crabs. This number of crabs makes an incredible sound as shells click and clank against each other. It's a wonder many are not broken. Another amazing thing is that approximately 90% of the shells were Whelk shells, with the rest being mostly Green Star shells and a few other species. To digress, at Hawksnest I once saw a crab living in an empty guava jelly jar!! This crab was around for a couple of years until presumably the jar broke.

Once these crabs have aggregated for about a week and all the stragglers have arrived (remember they have to come from the tops of the hills), one morning, just at dawn, they make a rush for the sea. I have no idea what the cue is but they all do it together. They go down to where the waves are just washing the beach and they pump the water in and out of their shells to flush out the eggs. The sea will actually turn pink at this time, and fish and seabirds will move in for a feeding frenzy. But because so many eggs are released at one time (probably several thousand per crab), enough survive to come back as soldier crabs in the future. (The eggs hatch and the larvae drift with ocean currents until near shore where they change into little crabs, crawl up on a beach and find tiny shells to live in.) After shedding their eggs and maybe finding a new shell, if the old one is worn, broken or too small, they head back to the hills. By nightfall that day, you only see the

Rafe Boulon's son Devon (and friend) inspect the Soldier Crabs gathered to spawn on their beach, Windswept.

(Photo by Rafe Boulon, 1985)

usual number of crabs where earlier there were thousands. One of the wonders of nature!

While our Soldier crabs seem to be doing fine, I do have concerns for their long-term future. I have heard of resorts being built in traditional reproductive migration pathways and rather than design the resort to incorporate this natural phenomenon into one of their attractions, the resort management elected to exterminate the crabs. This resulted in a watershed on St. Croix with no soldier crabs. Being that these crabs have a great dependence on the availability of shells (mostly whelk) in a variety of sizes to enable growth, the over harvest of whelk in particular may be having a serious affect on this species. You rarely see large whelk anymore and this must limit the size to which our crabs can grow. The larger the crab, the more eggs they can produce so this could have long-term effects on the overall populations of Soldier crabs on St. John and throughout the Caribbean. While few people still use them for fish bait, I'm sure the collection of crabs for this purpose had an impact on the populations in the past, from which they seem to have recovered. Roads have also had an impact where crabs have to cross them to reach an aggregation site and then

return. So next time you see a Soldier crab, reflect for a moment on what these little guys have to go through to survive. It's amazing to think that once a year or so, some of them make the trip from Bordeaux Mountain to the ocean and back!

November, 2005

November Rain

Eleanor Gibney

The Weather 25th February 1844
"Our island was visited on the 25 by an unusual outbreak of wind and rain. At 11am the wind was blowing from the SW suddenly shifted to the west, then NW bringing a deluge of rain that continued for 5 hours with little intermission…"

(Henry Morton Sketchbook & Diary 1843-44)

Until very recently, the most critical factor for human existence on St. John was water: How to collect it, how to save it, how to move it to where you needed it…

These days, all that's required is a cistern, and a few hundred dollars, and you can truck in hundreds of gallons of desalinated seawater to almost any location on the island. Although anyone concerned about their "carbon footprint" (or their wallet), certainly needs to still be a water conservationist here, the rental-villa business relies enormously on the local Water and Power Authority (WAPA), and the printed requests to conserve water disappeared from Caneel Bay's bathrooms about 25 years ago.

Throughout island history, water has equated to rainfall, and our rainfall is strongly variable. Although there are persistent rumors that the Virgin Islands climate was wetter at some vaguely defined time in the past, this seems

very unlikely, though certainly there were always periods, some as long as a decade or so, of higher rainfall—we are in one now, with the past 5 years in a row all above average. Just as surely, there have always been severe droughts, and these can be more destructive to plant and animal life than hurricanes.

It is likely that the original forests of the island caught and held the rainwater much more efficiently than is the case today. A ground layer of organic debris that has been undisturbed for millennia can't help but be absorbent. Because of this, it's probable that most of the larger guts flowed almost all the time…not rushing, but trickling and clear. We can still get a sense of this when there's enough rain to recharge the high central aquifer between Margaret Hill and Mammey Peak; the guts of the north shore may run for months - or even years, as occurred in the late 1960s.

The first task undertaken by the group who came from St. Thomas to Coral Bay in 1718 was to dig a well, in the flat of Carolina Valley; but even in the early 18th century, local groundwater may have been less than ideal. J. L. Carstens, a Creole native of St. Thomas, writing of that time period, said: "During prolonged droughts, these guts may dry up and disappear. On these occasions the local inhabitants resort to wells, locally called 'pytter' which are located by their houses; there are many others, as well as some along the bays. These wells have been dug out of the earth, and are made of brick. The water in them is brackish because they have been fed by the sea."

Carstens also wrote of the importation of water from Vieques to St. Thomas (which had its modern parallel during the years before reverse osmosis plants in the Virgin Islands: Cruz Bay

The Nature of Things

dock in the 1960s and 70s was dwarfed every few weeks by the enormous water barge from Puerto Rico that seemed destined to crush every boat in the harbor, as well as the dock itself). Carstens described water shipped in casks from Vieques. During the drought of 1737, it sold for 12 Danish skillings per bucketful on St. Thomas; elsewhere he equates the value of a quart of water during that drought to the value of a quart of beer or wine.

By the 19th century we get a lot of real weather data being recorded in the islands, and see patterns identical to those we're familiar with today. Pastor John Knox of the Dutch Reformed Church included a whole chapter on climate in his *Historical Account of St. Thomas, W.I.* published in 1852. To the modern eye, it seems odd that almost half of the chapter is devoted to invalids, disease and burial, but it was still decades before the official connection was made between mosquitoes and malaria, yellow fever, and dengue, all of which were endemic in the islands. Without knowledge of that connection, it was no wonder that rain, moisture, and exposure to night air, were considered risky to life itself.

At the beginning of the 20th century, the shift from plantation crops to cattle ranching on St. John probably re-activated many old wells that had been too brackish for human or plant use, since cattle have a tolerance for salt greater than many other species of land life.

Government dollars built hillside catchments and community cisterns on all three islands… often a long hard walk with heavy buckets from people's houses, but immensely helpful for the many small dwellings that relied on barrels for water storage.

In the 1950s, Caneel Bay began experimenting with primitive desalinization by evaporation, an activity overseen by Gus Stark, one of the island's early American residents, who worked at Caneel from the pre-Rockefeller days up into the 1960s. Laurance Rockefeller later gave financial backing to Israeli scientists working with new reverse osmosis techniques—the challenges of running Caneel and Little Dix with inconsistent water supplies must have been immense.

Rainfall records have been kept on St. John for varying lengths of time for various locations,

Weather log from Cruz Bay for November, 1867. Note intense notations beginning on November 18, the day of the Earthquake and Tsunami

(Rigsarkivet, Denmark)

longest at Cruz Bay, where records apparently began in the mid-1800s.

Dr. Bernie Kemp, while doing research in Copenhagen a dozen years ago, found beautifully written weather records from the Battery in Cruz Bay in the 1860s. Rainfall was noted in mysterious increments of 1/8 of an "English inch," but once converted, the monthly totals look very predictable from our modern averages.

Caneel Bay kept continual records from 1955 to 1998, and those 43 years give us a great snapshot of St. John patterns. On average, at 48.56 inches, Caneel appears to get an inch or two more than Cruz Bay each year, although we're all familiar with how localized rain can be, with one bay's roadsides filled with rushing torrents while the next bakes in the afternoon sun. During those 43 years, February and March were tied for the position of driest month of the year at Caneel, with a total of under a tenth of one inch possible in either month, and just over two inches as the average (March wins by having more days in which rain *could* have fallen). Sometime in late April or May, in many years, the drought would break with a major rain, pushing April's average to 3.36 inches, and May's all the way to 5.11 inches. May was the month with the greatest variability, with under two inches in nine of those years, and over six inches in another nine—and over twelve inches five times! June would then be drier, back down to a 3.5 inch average, but then it would get steadily wetter up to November, with its whopping 6.11 inch average… Although there were still 5 years out of 43 with under 2 inches for the month, there were 16 Novembers with over 6 inches. December could stay rather damp, with a 4.28 inch average; and January might be muddy, even with its low 2.76 inch average, especially with the weaker winter sun and the autumn's accumulation in the soil. St. John's wettest and driest years of the 20th century occurred during those 43 years.

The memorable year 1979 holds the record for rain at Caneel: 75.11 inches! Over 14 inches fell in May that year, and then the passage of Hurricanes David and Fredrick to the south of the island in September added more than 16 inches, and then there was an 11.55 inch November…

In contrast, 1994, apparently the driest year of the century, was approximately a third of that amount, at 26.11 inches. The drought continued until a month or so before Hurricane Marilyn, in the summer of 1995, and there was widespread devastation, including the deaths of the famous silk cotton tree at Cinnamon Bay, and many mangroves in land-locked pond areas around the island. The salt in the soil concentrated as the soil dried, and pulled moisture out of the roots of the trees.

The greatest single-day event record was the memorable flood of April 17-18 1983, when some parts of the island got over 18 inches between 9 at night and 10:30 the next morning. The most intense rain on record was the 3.4 inches per hour that fell toward the middle of that night. Caneel's official total for the flood was 17.05 inches, but the relief weather recorder who took the measurement confessed that his hand had been shaking while pouring the "overflow" outer rain-gauge contents repeatedly into the inner 3-inch measure. Damage in St. Thomas/ St. John was estimated at $12.5 million, and one person died in St. Thomas.

As concerns have grown over the effects of silt and mud from hillside construction on the coral reefs of the region, the joyful thrill many residents had when the guts filled and rushed to the sea has been dimmed by knowledge of the damage being caused. To help counter this somewhat, recent research has shown that the high seawater temperatures that cause coral bleaching in the summer are dramatically lowered by our autumn rains. The bigger the rain the quicker and greater the decrease in water temperatures, hastening the potential recovery of the coral.

The only certainties are that we will have devastating droughts again, and also seriously damaging rainfall—perhaps even one right after the other—and, with luck, we'll get a few more stretches like these last five years, with the happy just-a-little-more-than-medium.

November, 2007

The Tektite Program...

Cutting Edge Science on St. John

Bruce Schoonover

"... Tomorrow, in a $2.5-million project called Tektite, four marine scientists in scuba gear are scheduled to enter a dumbbell-shaped metal 'habitat' 50 feet below the surface of Beehive Cove in Lameshur Bay off St. John, Virgin Islands.

They plan to live there for 60 days—twice as long as earlier aquanauts—and to swim out of their underwater home each day to perform oceanographic studies..."

NY Times February 14, 1969.

What is today the Virgin Islands Environmental Resource Station (VIERS) at Lameshur Bay, St. John, was established by the Navy Seabees and served as base camp for an incredibly complex and important series of missions in 1969 and 1970. Not only would these missions extend our Nation's knowledge of the sea, but would also provide important insights into our ability to endure both isolation and confinement— conditions that would soon be realized within the space program.

Tektite was probably an obscure word at the time. But this mission to link oceanic and space exploration was aptly named after the space-borne matter that falls into the sea.

The 1960s was a stressful time for our nation largely as a result of the ongoing cold war with the Soviet Union and the early successes of its space program. However, this fear would help bring together industry, educators and the government in an effort to overcome our deficiencies, and as a result, the 1960s would see huge strides forward in science and technology. The Tektite Program was largely a product of this era.

Naval Floating Dry Dock (LSD), the U.S.S. Hermitage, carrying the 'Habitat' and other support materials and elements, arrives in Lameshur Bay, January 1969

(Image courtesy Gary Davis, NPS)

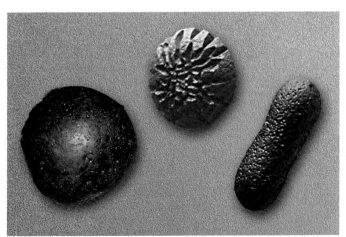

Tektites are a kind of meteoric brownish 'glass' which comes in many shapes, formed by the entry into earths atmosphere. There are two on display at the Tektite Museum at VIERS.

(Image courtesy of Bruce Schoonover)

Aquanaut Ed Clifton shown leaving the living quarters, *The Habitat*, located 49 feet below the surface of Lameshur Bay

(Image courtesy Gary Davis, NPS)

Pictured are aquanauts Rick Waller, Conrad Mahnken, Ed Clifton and John van Derwalker.

(Courtesy of Conrad Mahnken)

The connection to space exploration. In November of 1966, the National Air and Space Agency (NASA) and the Office of Naval Research met to discuss the similarities between space travel and undersea isolation. Living in a confined place in comradeship, while conducting productive scientific research, needed study. Beneath the sea seemed to be the place. Grumman, Inc. and GE's Missile and Space Division proposed an undersea dwelling to simulate the isolation and confinement of living in space, but GE's proposal was more consistent with NASA's objectives. Ultimately, the U.S. Navy (the lead agency), NASA and the Department of the Interior jointly proposed a program which would include a 49 ft. underwater living and working structure, with a mission to last 60 days to mimic a contemplated orbiting Skylab mission duration.

Extending man's knowledge of undersea exploration. At the same time, it was recognized that for thousands of years man's efforts to explore and exploit the oceans of the world had largely been hindered by an inability to remain submerged for long periods of time without getting, at best, 'rapture of the deep,' or at worst getting the 'bends' and dying. The Tektite program provided not only the arena for figuring out whether people could live confined in close proximity for 60 days without committing mayhem on each other, but also a venue for researching saturation diving limits and decompression requirements.

When one descends to the depths of the ocean, pressure increases and the nitrogen contained in the breathing mixture begins to be absorbed by the body's tissues. Once a threshold time and depth is reached, one must go through decompression—the gradual reduction of pressure, that allows the nitrogen to be passed through the blood stream and from there to the lungs where it is exhaled. A failure to observe this requirement is what results in decompression sickness or the "bends."

However, in the 1950s, experiments had begun which theorized that if one stayed submerged for an extended period his tissues would ultimately reach their capacity in terms of nitrogen absorption (a condition known as saturation- thus the term 'saturation diving'), in which case the amount of time required for decompression would no longer increase. The significance of this was that if true, for the first time in the history of man, it would permit extended stays underwater, thus increasing man's ability to work and study the undersea environment.

Preceding the Tektite program were other projects that were conducting saturation diving research, among them Edwin Links' 'Man in the Sea', Jacque Cousteau's 'Conshelf' and the US Navy's 'Sealab' program.

Tektite's effort had three unique goals. One was to increase safe submersion time significantly… doubling the previously set record of 30 days. The second was to calibrate the use of nitrogen rather than helium (which was commonly used but more expensive and more difficult to obtain) as part of the breathing mixture. The third was to test man's ability to conduct bona fide scientific research under these conditions, rather than to collect physiological or biomedical data on professional divers. Scientists were selected primarily on the basis of their research proposals and only secondly on their health and diving skills.

Rick Waller was selected Crew Chief. He took a 60 day hiatus from his 3 pack a day cigarette habit to breathe 92% Nitrogen while conducting fisheries research. Ed Clifton was to study marine geology; Conrad Mahnken was to study ecology, plankton, and cleaner shrimp; and John van Derwalker, a fisheries biologist was to study, among other things, the life cycle of lobsters. R.L. Phillips from the US Geological Survey, Gary Davis from the National Park, and Ian Koblich from the College of the Virgin Islands were chosen as alternates.

Great Lameshur was selected as Tektite's site. Its isolation, the warm, clear, and protected waters, and its undisturbed marine diversity, which gave the scientists something to study, were ideal qualities. GE's Missile and Space Division was very familiar with the VI, since it had conducted undersea weightless studies off Buck Island south of St. Thomas in the 1966-67 timeframe. No doubt also weighing in on the choice of Great Lameshur Bay was the Interior Department's familiarity with the Virgin Islands National Park waters as a result of the early and extensive marine research undertaken by Jack Randall under contract with the National Park Service.

Components of the program. First, a *Causeway Pier* was brought in by the U.S. Navy in three 90 ft. sections. Building materials could then

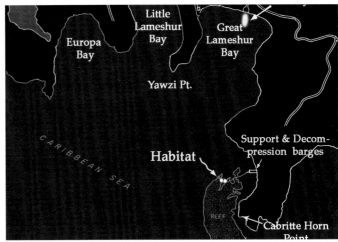

The Causeway Pier, Base Camp, Support Barge, Decompression Barge and Tektite Habitat were five essential building blocks of the project.

(Image courtesy of Bruce Schoonover)

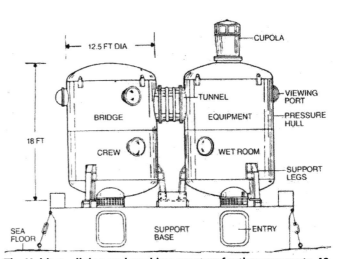

The Habitat—living and working quarters for the aquanauts, 49 feet below the surface of Beehive Cove in Great Lameshur Bay.

(Image from Naval Service Report, DR 153)

Habitat being readied to be submerged.

(Image courtesy Gary Davis, NPS)

aesthetic and scientific visual entrée to the sea. The *Wet Room* was the Habitat entrance and its submerged stairway was always open to the sea; the wet lab, the scuba gear and a hot shower resided here. Above the Wet Room was the *Equipment Room*. This area housed the electrical panels, breakers and switches as well as all of the air treatment equipment, plus the toilets, and frozen food lockers. Also, food was lowered to them daily from above via Transfer Pots made out of commercial paint tanks. In the other silo, the lower level *Living Quarters* housed four bunks, an emergency exit, small galley (space-travel testing those GE appliances, of course!) a table/desk and storage lockers for personal gear, and a radio and a television set that received local channels. Above it, the *Bridge* housed the Control Center, with all the communications and personnel monitoring gear, and the Dry Lab. Umbilicals ran from the Support Barge to the Habitat, bringing fresh water, high pressure air for the scuba tanks, the Habitat's breathing mixture and all the communications cables.

Talk about living in a fish bowl! Not only were the aquanauts monitored for their physical health, but they were monitored at least 18 hours a day visually and by sound—to make sure there was no behavioral mayhem! Over 400,000 'observations' were taken on their state of being during the 60 day submersion.

In addition to the five major components of Tektite's program, there were five 2-person 'way stations,' bubble-domed cages with phones and extra scuba tanks, placed as refuges from the sharks which, thankfully, never materialized and as geographical outposts for use during scientific excursions. During the submersion period, aquanauts spent about 7.2 hours per day outside the Habitat in marine research.

On April 15, 1969 the Personnel Transfer Capsule (PTC) descended to pick up the four aquanauts. Although they volunteered to stay down longer (the food was excellent!), their handlers were firm. They entered the decompression chamber for 19 hours and 22 minutes, returning their blood Oxygen/Nitrogen to safe levels prior to being reunited with their families and then entering a 2 day debriefing period. The team set a world record for time underwater, previously held by Scott Carpenter in SeaLab II. Were there lingering after-effects? None, concluded Dr. Edward Beckman. Other than a few ear problems, all men resurfaced mentally and physically

be brought in and offloaded onto the pier. *Base Camp* was set up by an amphibious crew of the Seabees; it consisted of thirteen living units with generators, cook tent, sanitary systems and two 10,000 gallon fresh water tanks with pipes leading to the Pier. A *Support Barge* provided scuba gear charging units, the Habitat air supply and monitoring equipment, the EEG equipment, and fresh water. The support barge was moored about 400 ft. from the Habitat and was the communications link (data, visual, sound) between the aquanauts and 'Earth.' The *Decompression Barge* housed and managed the raising and lowering of a Personnel Transfer Capsule (PTC) and linking it to the decompression chamber. The fifth element, the *Habitat* itself, was built by the GE Missile and Space Division in Valley Forge, Pennsylvania and then shipped from the Philadelphia Navy Yard. It was floated off its transport on airbags and then loaded with steel shot to help it submerge. Once it was winched to its rectangular base on the sea floor at 49 ft. below sea level in Beehive Cove, the pressure was set to 2.5 atmospheres and the breathing mixture set to 92% Nitrogen and 8% Oxygen. This is the equivalent of a 78% Nitrogen and 21% Oxygen environment at sea level.

The Living quarters known as the "habitat." The two Habitat 'silos,' 18 ft. tall and 12 ½ ft. in diameter, were connected by a flexible tunnel. Inside this comfortable apartment/laboratory, large hemispherical portholes provided healthy. And importantly, they proved valid the most obvious advantages of saturation diving from the Habitat—a huge increase in the time available for productive research and the research advantages of 24 hour observation.

Tektite II followed. Coordinated by the Department of the Interior, Tektite II used the same physical facilities but in many ways was quite different than the U.S. Navy's Tektite I program. While Tektite I had emphasized the Navy's & NASA's interest in saturation diving, man's ability to stay submerged for long periods and the effect of long term isolation and confinement, Tektite II would capitalize on this knowledge and shift its focus more to marine science.

There were 11 separate missions of from 13-20 days duration involving 53 scientists. A fifth aquanaut, an engineer, was added to each team to manage the equipment. And an additional 7 missions were to be dedicated to 100 ft deep exploration in a new structure known as the "Minitat," in order to determine man's aquatic competence and Nitrogen saturation tolerance at continental shelf depth. Eleven government agencies, 40 academic institutions, and 15 additional groups jumped aboard for Tektite II, providing projects and nominating aquanauts for missions. All in all, about 500 off-island and warmly welcomed St. John residents chose to belong to Tektite II.

One disappointment was the Minitat. Teams spent five months trying to properly deploy the top-heavy Minitat. Once it broke loose in a tropical storm and was retrieved by a BVI fisherman and taken to Roadtown Harbor, Tortola—causing some embarrassment and the need to negotiate its release. Eventually they had to scrub its missions.

There were many successes. By the end of Tektite II all diver decompression tables were recalibrated, increasing the amount of Oxygen and the decompression time advised for safe diving. Rebreather units proved their worth. Invented by C.J. Lambertsen in 1942, the redeveloped GE Mark 10 rebreathers proved invaluable to biologists attempting to observe seafloor life unobtrusively. With their internal Baralyme air 'scrubber,' they enabled divers to stay submerged for 12 hours without noisy bubbles and the up and down movement caused by inhaling and exhaling. Forty-eight divers used the Rebreathers on tasks for 1-6

Members of the Tektite II all-women mission, review the fundamentals of the BE 'Mark-10' rebreather unit which greatly extended dive time.

(Image courtesy Dr. James Miller)

hours in length, producing more accurate behavioral observations with their less obtrusive marine research. The units proved, however, 'unforgiving' when human error was made; they were "classified" by the Navy, depriving the aquanauts of their use during Tektite I, but all but one of the 11 missions of Tektite II took advantage of this technology.

Mission 6-50, the all-women's mission, received a lot of publicity; they also accrued more in-water research time than their male counterparts.

The Tektite I program and its aquanaut participants received much national attention, including a ceremony at which VP Spiro Agnew recognized Tektite's *"…historic contribution to man's quest for knowledge…"* and presented the Navy's Distinguished Public Service Award to Rick Waller and Meritorious Public Service Award to the others; and also presented the Dept. of Interior's Distinguished Service Award gold medal to all *"…for outstanding contribution to science and the skill and ability in performance of duty…"* (And, all four even made an appearance on the popular Ed Sullivan TV show.)

To the dismay of the majority of aquanauts and others involved in Tektite II, their accomplishments went largely unnoticed by official Washington. However, Dr. James Miller, Deputy Project Director of Tektite I and the Director of Tektite II—who has been involved in scientific marine missions virtually all of his life—recently concluded:

> *Regardless of those in Washington,*
>
> *"the findings of Tektite I—that humans could safely survive for 60 days breathing nitrogen enriched air—opened the door for future seafloor programs…"; and*
>
> *"As a result of the success of Tektite I, over 500 people choose to be involved in Tektite II—in a myriad of ways… and they and the Country benefited ;*
>
> *"In addition to the marine, scientific, medical, behavioral and other technical information obtained, Tektite I & II opened the eyes of scientists and sport divers around the world…"*

And to think, all of this took place at the still remote location on St. John known as Lameshur Bay.

May, 2009

Chapter 7:
DONKEY YEARS TO MODERN DAY

A Narrative of the Life of M. C. Knevels

St. John Historical Society members Marillyn and Denise Newville have graciously allowed the publication of this wonderful family document. The narrative chronicles the life of Marillyn's third great-grandmother, Margaretha Cathrine Vriehuis Knevels, affectionately known as a child as "Miss. Peggy." Margaretha's story is far more than a simple tale of eighteenth-century life, it is a rare firsthand account of a family's efforts to endure and provide educational opportunities for their children on colonial-era St. John—a situation that island residents struggle with to the present day. [Text annotated by David W. Knight]

Silhouette of Maria Susanna Tonis Vriehuis mother of Margaretha Cathrine Knevels

(Image courtesy of Marillyn and Denise Newville)

My father's name was D'Juno Vriehuis. He was a Prussian by birth and was educated in one of the German Universities. He made the choice of medicine and surgery for his profession, and after finishing his studies he returned home, but was anxious to obtain a situation and left his paternal home to seek elsewhere a permanent employment. He soon found a situation, having applied to the Danish government and obtained as king's physician a place on board a Danish man of war, which was shortly to sail for St. Thomas as a government vessel.

Some time after my father's arrival in the island, he was introduced to Miss [Maria Susanna] Tonis, daughter of Henry Tonis of Amsterdam.[1] A few years afterwards they were married. They had four children who all died in infancy excepting myself. I was born in St. Thomas on the 19th of January 1779. I was baptized by Domini Brandt, a minister from Holland of the Dutch Reformed Church. My parents were both members of that church. Some years after my birth my father purchased property in the island of St. Johns,[2] a neighboring island belonging to the Danes, where he settled his family, retaining still his place as King's physician; but after some years he gave up his practice it being very laborious. The government then constituted him burgher master of the island, head of the burgher council held every month at his home. Five or six of the principal inhabitants were associated with him to transact business pertaining to the island.

My father having lost all his other children felt very anxious about me, as the climate did not seem to agree with infant life, and he thought a change of climate might strengthen my constitution. He likewise began seriously to consider the disadvantages they labored under, not having good schools to educate their children, they were necessitated to send them either to Europe or America. About this time the United Brethren or Moravian missionaries, who resided in the islands as teachers to show the poor Negroes the way of Salvation and tell them the history of the cross, informed my father that their society at Bethlehem in Pennsylvania, had lately established a school for girls with competent teachers. The information pleased my father, but it pierced his heart and that of my mother and grandmother to part with their only child; to send her far, far away from them over the ocean,—how could they consent. It required strong faith and trust in God, and great anxiety for my future welfare, both here and hereafter. In the good providence of God a way was opened for the accomplishment of this desirable end. Mr. Hook, an intimate friend of my father, owned a vessel of which he was master or captain. He traded between St. Thomas and Philadelphia. His vessel lay at St. Thomas collecting freight; they met together and my father related to him the circumstances which gave him great anxiety with regard to sending me to school. Mr. Hook kindly offered his aid and promised if he would trust me to his care, every attention should be paid me and every comfort afforded while on ship board. Preparations were immediately made for my voyage, and with a faithful and attached black woman, to whom I was much attached from my earliest years;[3] I was entrusted to Mr. Hook as my protector under God. My father procured from the missionaries (a letter of introduction) to a gentleman in Philadelphia (Mr. Haha) whom my father wished to become my guardian while at School. Our voyage was short and pleasant. I do not speak from memory as I was only eight years old at that eventful period, which separated me for eight years from them. During that period I never saw them. On our arrival in Delaware Bay, Mr. Hook kindly conveyed myself and attendant to my guardian's house, where I was received and most kindly treated both by himself and wife. They did everything to make me feel at home. At this distant period I still recollect their tender attention and kindness toward me. I stayed some days at my guardian's to recover from the effects of the voyage. I was

then conveyed to Bethlehem, my future home, the distance from Philadelphia being sixty miles. My faithful attendant accompanied me and stayed some weeks with me; for I was quite incapable of helping myself as there had been no necessity having someone always at hand to minister to my wants; but I soon learned to do.

There were but a few scholars when I entered the school, but the school increased rapidly and gave universal satisfaction to the parents and friends of the scholars. But to return to the faithful attendant [Mintje]; she went back to Philadelphia and my guardian procured a berth in a vessel for St. Thomas. She arrived in safety and related to her master and mistress all the various adventures she had gone through, and how she left me happy among my playmates. She faithfully fulfilled her duty.

Among the many blessings and mercies which had hitherto followed me, I must mention one of particular interest to, and its bearing upon, my future character. Among the teachers was a lady, Miss Languard, who took particular interest in me. She became a second mother; to her kind attention and tender care I owe much. With gratitude and love, I dwell at this distance of the time upon her amiable character. It was under her tuition I learned to excel and to cultivate the talents and improve the time that was given me to the best purpose. What a blessing it was to me to have a person of her character to watch over me, instructing me and correcting all my faults with tenderness, and directing my views both in temporal and spiritual concerns. I have reason to bless her memory. But I must resume my narrative, and relate how in the course of time I was brought back in safety to my delighted and thankful parents. I spent eight years among these kind people, and bless God for his kind providence in placing me among them at so early an age. Then I learned that Jesus died for me; gently he drew me with cords of love, and—greatly do I admire His goodness and adore that love that caused Him to be the guide of my youth; and I live to record with praise and gratitude, the support of my age. Oh leave me not now when my strength faileth, Oh God of my salvation, for in Thee do I put my trust.

In the spring of the years 1796, in the month of May, we left the Delaware bay and sailed for St. Cruze [St. Croix], but my kind father had sent on my faithful servant a month before the time arrived for my return that she might be with me during the voyage. We had beautiful weather, but on account of long calms the voyage was a long one—full three weeks. We had a very kind, fatherly and gentlemanly captain, a fine vessel with good accommodations. Myself and servant were the only passengers. The captain began to feel uneasy as we approached the island, as the seas were infested at the period, (during the French Revolution), with French privateers. He had for some days been applying his spy glass to his eye on the watch for their appearance. Three days before we made land, we were startled by an exclamation from the captain—"There is a privateer in sight." In a moment every eye was turned toward the spot and all hands were employed in trimming the sails to try to out sail her; but the captain soon perceived she was a fast sailor and would soon overtake us. However, we sailed away and gave little heed to their firing, for they began to fire at us as soon as they spied us. Our vessel was a fine brig—a merchantman—carrying American colors; a neutral vessel. Having no weapons or hands sufficient to engage them, the captain, to save his vessel and papers, gave up the chase. They were so near their shots fell close alongside of our vessel. In a few moments they were lying alongside of our vessel; their men jumped on board dragging their grappling irons with them, and soon secured us by fastening the two vessels together. They then took our captain on board and placed him under arrest. The captain and mate with an interpreter entered the cabin where they found two defenseless women, the only passengers on board. There we were without any human protector, but God was a very present help; not a hair of our heads did they dare touch, neither had they the power to make us afraid. They were perfectly civil and treated me with respect. The captain restrained his men and would not let them search my trunks or baggage. And now at this distant time, when I reflect on the dangerous situation in which I was placed, and recollect with what courage and self possession I passed through this exciting scene, I must exclaim; truly God was a very present help. After having searched everything in the cabin and the other parts of the vessel, they found they could find no plea for detaining captain or vessel. They let us go, and happy were we to escape from so eminent a danger; but they met their doom. Three months after my arrival home the very identical vessel was captured by a British Man of War, and carried into Tortola, a small English island lying near St. Johns. They were condemned and the vessel sunk.

"In each event of life, how clear,
Thy ruling hand I see."

MINTJE'S ROOM

(Excerpt from: Elizabeth Lehman Myers, *A Century of Moravian Sisters; A Record of Christian Community Life* [Fleming H. Revell Company, New York, Chicago, Toronto, London & Edinburgh, ND])

"…The Moravian schools were known in many lands and wealthy planters of the South and of the West Indies sent their daughters to the seminaries.

Little Miss Peggy Vriehuis, of St. John's W.I. aged eight years, was sent to the Bethlehem school in charge of a faithful negress who remained for months until the little lady was accustomed to the new residence beyond all danger of homesickness. "Nurse Mintje" was given her own room in the building, and here seated on a high backed chair, she spent most of her time, her fingers busily occupied with strange new materials, in the making of woolen garments for Miss Peggy; garments that must have been hard to fashion for fingers accustomed to fine cambric and linen.

This room was known for a long time as "Mintje's room" although the negress was here only four months. She made a great impression with her broad, black face under the gay turban of printed cotton, its tropical suggestions such a contrast to the austere chastity of the snow white cap the sisters wore."

Three days after this dangerous encounter we anchored as Bass End St. Cruze [Christiansted, St. Croix], the port to which we had been bound. There I was met by a gentleman, (Mr. Rogers), a kind and intimate friend of my father, who conducted me to his house and introduced me to his amiable family. There I stayed until my father received the welcome news of my safe arrival, when he procured a government vessel to convey me to St. Johns. A few hours' sail brought me to the desired haven. The vessel anchored at Cruze [Cruz] Bay, the principal harbor, where the fort is located and the government officers reside. I found that my expected arrival had created quite an excitement. The beach was lined with spectators, both white and black. There among the crowd stood my father and mother, who through the goodness of God had been permitted once more to embrace their long absent daughter. There were no convenient wharves to accommodate and make the landing of passengers easy and safe, as the vessel lay at some distance from shore. The long boat was lowered, the passengers were soon seated and we rowed to the shore; but here we encountered another difficulty. The waves washed the beach a yard or so beyond the boat; boards had to be placed in a temporary bridge to prevent the disagreeable necessity of getting wet. A gentleman advanced and offering his hand, assisted my landing and led me to my mother. Oh, what a moment. Words cannot convey the feeling that took possession of our hearts. Suffice it to say that everybody [participated] in the joy and happiness of my dear parents. My father was a most estimable man and beloved by all who knew him. Oh, often I bless his dear memory, as an instrument of good to me under the guidance of God.

The gentleman who led me to my mother was a stranger to me at that time, but a few months later became my husband. I had yet another beloved parent, (my grandmother [Margaretha Zytsema Tonis]), who remained at home [Estate L'Esperance] awaiting my arrival. The next day we rode to her house, where I had the satisfaction of finding her in health and anxiously awaiting my arrival, and thankful that she had been spared to embrace her almost idolized grandchild.

Some time after I had been home I united with the Dutch Reformed church and have been a member ever since, ever happy to unite with the people of God wherever I met [them]. Not unto me, not unto me, oh God, but unto Thy great name.

On the 23rd of February, 1798, I was united in the bands of wedlock to Mr. I. A. Knevels, a native of St. Johns.[4] His father was from Holland, educated for the ministry, and came to St. Thomas. From there he went to St. Johns, having received a call from the church in that island, where he settled and preached twenty-five years. He married a Miss Borm, a rich heiress, with whom he had eight sons. All died in infancy except my husband and an elder brother, who died a few years after leaving college, at the early age of twenty-nine years. Their father's last request was that his two surviving sons should be sent to America for their education. Accordingly after his death, (Mr. Knevels being about twelve or thirteen years), they were sent to New York under the guardianship of Mr. John De Wint, who was going to settle in America; and being merchant he chose New York, and the two lads went to college there. My husband chose medicine as his profession, and had returned home only two years before my arrival there. After my marriage, my grandmother desired me to make her house [Estate L'Esperance] my home, as she could not bear to be again separated from me. My husband and myself complied with her request, and we resided with her two years, when Mr. Knevel's brother sickened and died. We then removed to the estate occupied by his mother [Estate Susannaberg], with whom we lived until we came to this country, and very happily. But experience taught us that, "This life's a dream, an empty show," and days of darkness and sorrow were gathering around our horizon. Death entered our windows. One of our darling babies was taken away from the evils to come. Next my grandmother and my dear beloved father. I had the sad, and melancholy satisfaction of being with them through their illness; of closing their eyes. My father's last words conveyed unspeakable comfort. "Father into Thy hands I commend my spirit.

In the course of time some of our older boys were advancing in years and of an age to go to school. There were no schools in the islands and parents were mostly obliged to send their children abroad for their education. We found after considering the subject, that we must conclude what course to adopt. We were not the only parents who labored under the difficulty. Our neighbors and friends were in the same predicament. On broaching the subject to each

Detail from a painting of Estate Susannaberg rendered by Frederik von Scholten in 1838. Von Scholten was a childhood friend and schoolmate of the estate owner, Henry Tonis Knevels.

(Image from SJHS Archives)

other we found that five or six families had sons and daughters whom they greatly desired to send abroad, but found it difficult to find proper persons to whose care they might commit them. Finally we concluded to go with our three eldest sons,[5] leaving one, (the youngest), as a hostage for our return with our parents, both being alive at that time. Shortly after we had come to this conclusion, we had applications from our friends on behalf of children they wished to place under our care. We could not refuse their entreaties and complied with fears and trembling. We found when counting the numbers that there were five girls and five boys of different ages, among whom were the governor's two sons who were to be placed at school with two of our sons at Nazareth, Pennsylvania, ten miles from Bethlehem.[6] The girls all remained at Philadelphia except one. She went to Bethlehem, the same lovely spot where I spent so many happy years. At this distant time, how many sweet associations and pleasant recollections cluster around Thy name. We spent the summer there; the following

winter we spent in New York and in the spring returned to our home, leaving our three boys at school, the governor's sons returning to their parents in St. Thomas. My father had suffered very much from an attack of gout a little before our arrival, and I was sorry to find him very feeble in body and mind. He never recovered fully from the effects but lived only a few years after my arrival home.

I had a friend in New York, a young lady, (West Indian by birth), who for some time had been threatened with consumption, and was in very delicate health all winter. The doctor recommended change of climate as the only remedy that might prove salutary. We, (my husband and myself), had some difficulty in persuading her to consent to our request of taking a voyage with us and spending some time in the island as our guest. We had lived in great intimacy and overcame all scruples, and she consented to go with us. The change proved very beneficial to her. She had not been many days out at sea before she perceived a change. She stayed a year with us and the following spring she returned to her friends in New York, and was very thankful that she had accepted our offer; She lived many years after and I had the pleasure of renewing our friendship after settling at Fishkill, where she resided with her aunt, Mrs. De Wint, the same lady who brought my husband to New York, when a boy, for his education. She died only two years ago last May,—two months before my beloved and lamented son John.

"Midst Changing scenes and dying friends, Be thou my all in all."

But to return to my story. We returned to the West Indies leaving our three oldest boys at Nazareth, another Moravian settlement about ten miles from Bethlehem, where there was an academy for boys. We remained several years in the island, saw a great many changes, met many losses by hurricanes and droughts destroying the crops. My father's health declined day by day and finally he sank peacefully to rest, committing himself and family into his faithful redeemer's hands. About this time Mr. Knevel's health began to fail, the climate of late years not agreeing with his constitution. He thought a change would be beneficial; however, he could not immediately put his desire into operation, and delayed some two or three years before he determined what steps to take. Our three sons were still at Nazareth, and time approaching for their removal. This circumstance at once determined him and we once more left the island and sailed for Philadelphia, with a little boy seven years old and an infant about two years. Our passage proved safe and pleasant until we reached the Gulf Stream; there we were overtaken by a tremendous storm; thunder and lightning, high winds and waves running high, waves dashing the decks; dead lights were put in and in a moment the vessel lay on her [beams] end. What so grand and awful as a storm at sea. I had witnessed hurricanes and storms on land, but this beggared description. Through kind providence of God, we had an excellent captain and mate who exerted themselves to the utmost and succeeded in righting the vessel. Oh, what an escape. Here again I acknowledge the goodness of God.

"Oh, that men would praise the lord, for his goodness and his wonderful works to the children of Men." "He maketh the storm a calm, so that the waves thereof are still."

A few days after we arrived safely in Delaware Bay. After a few hours rest Mr. Knevels traveled on to Nazareth in the public stage, and the next day had the pleasure of meeting his boys, who were delighted to meet their father after

A Description of Estate L'Esperance
SJHS Newsletter Staff

The ruins encountered today on Estate L'Esperance represent the residential and industrial compound of a working sugar plantation developed by Doctor D'Juno Vriehuis at the peak of the great West Indies sugar boom at the close of the eighteenth century. Vriehuis acquired L'Esperance in 1790 after having lived on the estate for 15 years. Previous to this date the property had been owned by the Tonis family, of which Vriehuis's wife, Marie Susanne Tonis, was a primary heir. An ancestor of Mrs. Vriehuis had been the recipient of the first land grant on the property issued by the Danish West India and Guinea Company in 1721. Early records show that one Claus Tonis of Amsterdam had initially shared ownership of the property with Eric Bredal, the Danish West Indies governor who led the settlement of St. John in the face of British and Spanish threats of military action to dislodge them. The Tonis family was of Dutch origin, as were the majority of original colonists on St. John—the balance being composed of a mix of persons of Danish, English, French and West Indies heritage, as well as a few disenfranchised individuals of no determinable national background.

L'Esperance is exceptional for its compact layout and adaptation of its design to fit the rugged terrain of the site. As on all sugar plantations of this period, the structures on the property included an animal-driven sugar mill, a boiling house, a worm cistern, a rum still, a warehouse, and animal pens, all commonly referred to in the period as a "works." Additionally the planter's residence, with its associated cook house, bake-oven, and servants quarters were located a short distance up grade overlooking the works. A cemetery, a bridge, stone fencing and a village of the enslaved laborers completes the primary elements of the compound. The architecture of the plantation's primary residence is notable for the use of volcanic sandstone as a building material. This sandstone is not native to St. John and was most likely brought here on ships as ballast. The ground floor walls still stand to their full height and once supported a wooden superstructure. The walls are rubble masonry with cut and dressed stone and coral around openings and at corners. The cemetery on the site is significant as it is the location of one of the oldest marked graves of a plantation owner on St. John. The inscription reads:

Hendrick Tonis

Born on S. Thomas

the 15 January 1733

Delivered on S. Jan

the 23 September 1765

a separation of nearly six years. As soon as accounts could be settled and baggage arranged and stowed away in the public stage, my husband and sons returned to Philadelphia, and from there to New York, where I had the pleasure of meeting and embracing many dear friends. From there we traveled on [to] Morristown in New Jersey, and placed our sons in a private school under Mr. McCulluch, to prepare for college. Here we remained two years. But I must curtail this long narrative. Suffice to say that the following year Mr. Knevels, (through the persuasion of Mr. De Wint who resided at Fishkill), bought a farm and settled his family very pleasantly near Mr. De Wint. At this time we had five sons, and a son and daughter were afterward born. Here we remained stationary for some years, and became acquainted with many valuable and able friends. Many are still living, but many have been called to rest with Jesus; among them my husband, some of my children, and many near and dear to my heart. Many have been my days of mourning, but I trust the Lord has not forsaken me. I still hope, I still trust in that "Friend who sticketh closer than a brother." While living at Fishkill we met with many losses. The islands were visited with violent hurricanes which destroyed the crops and buildings on the estates. Our house at Fishkill was burned to the ground and we were brought low. Mr. Knevels sold the property that he owned in Fishkill, and bought a small farm in Sullivan County near White Lake. There I moved in the spring of 1832 with my family. My three oldest sons had been married. Two returned to the West Indies.[7] One continued to reside in Fishkill.

January, 2010

Footnotes

[1] The Tonis family were among the earliest settlers on St. John having received an original land grant from the Danish West Indies & Guinea Company in 1721 (see accompanying account: "A Brief Description of Estate L'Esperance").

[2] D'Juno Vriehuis purchased L'Esperance on Oct. 31, 1789. The property had been in the hands of his wife's family since the early 1700s, but had become mired in debt and was put up for sale after the death of Maria Susanna's stepfather, Ditlif Petersen. On Feb. 2, 1792, Vriehuis also purchased Estate Parforce, which had formerly belonged to the family of his mother-in-law, Anna Margaretha Zytsema Tonis.

[3] The "faithful and attached black woman" referred to here was an enslaved "nurse" owned by D'Juno Vriehuis named Mintje (See accompanying sidebar, "Mintje's Room").

[4] Isaac Adrian Knevels was the son of Reverend Johannes Wernerus Knevels and Maria Susanna Borm, who was the sole heir to Estate Susannaberg (Maria Susanna Borm's grandmother was Susanna vanBeverhoudt Runnels, for whom Estate Susannaberg was named).

[5] The three oldest sons that Isaac and Margarethe Knevels accompanied to Pennsylvania were, D'Juno Vriehuis Knevels, John Wernerus Knevels, and Henry Tonis Knevels.

[6] The sons of the governor referred to here were Frederik and William von Scholten, children of Governor and Commandant of St. Thomas & St. John, Casimir Willhelm von Scholten. Another son of Casimir von Scholten, Peter, later became Governor-General of the Danish West Indies. Two other boys from St. John traveled to school with the Knevels, Christian H. von Cronenberg and Samuel H. Walloe.

[7] D'Juno and Henry Knevels returned to the Danish West Indies to uphold their cumulative family legacy on St. John. D'Juno died soon after his return to the island, but his brother, Henry Tonis Knevels, settled into life on the family's Estate Susannaberg & Denis Bay. He became a prominent member of the community and served for many years as the island's Stadhouptsmann (sheriff). During his lifetime Henry reacquired the L'Esperance property, and went on to purchase estates Beverhoudtsberg, Belview, Grunwald and Fish Bay, as well as leasing estates Adrian & Trunk Bay and Catherineberg & Jochumsdal from the Danish Crown. He married Mary Catherine Docke Groebe c1831, and, although the couple produced no children, Henry left a number of mixed-race children. He died on April 13, 1846, and was buried on Estate Susannaberg. His wife, Mary Catherine Knevels, died on her sister's property, Estate Sieban, on November 11, 1870.

Account of a Visit to St. John, c1830

ESTATE HERMITAGE ON THE EAST END

Excerpt from the book, TORTOLA: or, The Native Missionary [Reminiscences of the West India Islands, Second Series, vol. V, Edited by Daniel P. Kidder, Published by Lane & Scott for the Sunday School Union of the Methodist Episcopal Church, 1852], a collection of stories of the Methodist Missionaries in the West Indies.

CHAPTER VI

The Methodist Society, in Tortola, was at this time in a very flourishing condition. Large accessions had been made to it during the preceding year. The lady of the governor-general of Tortola and the Virgin Islands was a member; and the governor himself, the Honorable George R. Porter, was very friendly, attending regularly, when his health would admit, and rendering every facility in his power to the missionaries to prosecute their labors. He was a man, too, who feared God, and led a strictly moral life, though he made no open profession of religion until his last and fatal illness.

There was, at this time, connected with the Methodists in Tortola, a very remarkable colored woman, named Fanny Waters, who was one of the excellent of the earth. She had been a class-leader for many years, as among the Wesleyans female leaders always are appointed to female classes. Such was the estimation in which Fanny was held, that a large majority of the female converts would select her class in preference to others, to which they would join themselves…

…Fanny Waters had been a slave—a slave from her birth. Her mistress was a poor widow woman, who could not afford to emancipate her. As Fanny grew into notice, and became so useful a member in the Methodist Society, and a class-leader, the question became agitated— ought she to continue in bondage? Some two or three gentlemen, who were merchants in Road Town, took the thing in hand, ascertained what sum her mistress would take for her, and then started a subscription, in order to raise the amount. It was soon done. Planters, merchants, every one having anything to bestow on a benevolent enterprise, regarded it as a privilege to give in this case. The sum was made up; and the year preceding the appointment of Messrs. Whitehouse, Burton, and Seaton to Tortola, Fanny Waters had been made a free woman, through the generosity of those lovers of our holy religion. Often has Fanny adverted to these facts, in conversation with the writer of this little book, while the tears of gratitude to God and his people rolled down her cheeks.

As soon as the missionaries were a little settled, their kind friend, Mr. Moore, of St. Johns, insisted on a visit. Mr. and Mrs. Whitehouse could not join the party, but the Burtons and the Seaton family, in Moore's fine large boat, were soon rowed over, and spent a pleasant day at Mr. Moore's beautiful country seat [*Estate Hermitage*]. This spot was most romantically located. Like the mission premises at West End of Tortola, it was also situated on a narrow part of the island of St. Johns, with this exception, that the buildings were not on the most elevated part of the premises, but on the brow of the hill facing the south. A good path led from the beach, on the north or Tortola side, up the hill, and then down on the other side, to the residence of the family. The buildings were

CATCHING TURTLE WITH A SCOOP-NET.

comparatively new; the old house in which Mrs. Bryan had resided having been destroyed in the hurricane of 1819.

To the south side, one of the most beautiful little coves that the strangers had ever seen lay at the foot of the hill. It was so completely shut in from the wind, as to be almost always calm and smooth, though the water would be gently lifted up and down by the rising and falling of the tide. Here Moore had constructed an ingenious turtle-kraal, which afforded him, at all times, a plentiful supply of that delicious kind of shell-fish.

The West Indians are very fond of turtle. The waters of the Caribbean Sea, the coves and bays around their islands, abound in the green-back as well as the hawk's-bill species. The former is preferred, both for the delicacy of its meat, as well as the superiority of its shell.

Mr. Moore's pen, or kraal, as it is there called, was built in the following manner. A wall was made on the beach, running out into the water, describing three sides of a rectangle, the beach itself being the other side, with a wooden gate. This wall was high enough to be above the high-water mark; and loop-holes were left, in its construction, to admit the constant ingress and egress of the water.

Mr. Moore owned slaves, and one or two of his men were very expert at catching turtle, by means of a net adapted to the purpose. The turtle, when caught in the net, were put in this pen or kraal, and then fed with the entrails of poultry, and other kinds of flesh or fish, and

some kinds of vegetable matter, such as a variety of the cactus, the prickly-pear, so common in these islands. In these pens turtle grow fast, and become very fat; and at any time Mr. Moore would have a very fine dinner, by causing one of his men to stand on the wall, and, with a kind of scoop-net attached to a pole, with a hook at its end, catch any one selected from the rest, as they come up to gather around the food thrown in for them.

The day was most pleasantly spent by these Christian friends. A Mr. Richardson, a native of St. Croix, with an amiable wife and family, who lived near Mr. Moore's added not a little to the social intercourse. He, too, had been the subject of God's saving grace, and was now a member of the Methodist Society, and one of Moore's class. Mr. Seaton had known him in St. Croix, when both were out of the ark of safety, and it was a source of mutual pleasure to them to talk over the great things which God had done for them.

CHAPTER VII

As the gentlemen were walking around the premises, enjoying the scenery, and engaging in conversation, Mr. Moore remarked to Seaton, "Have you heard that our friend Richardson here came very near losing, at least, a thousand dollars lately?"

"No, I did not. By what means was it?"

"Why, two of Mr. Coakley's valuable slaves stole his boat, and were making their way rapidly to Tortola; but, most fortunately, Richardson heard of it in time to pursue them, and just overtook and captured them before they landed."

"Why, cannot a fugitive slave be arrested in Tortola?"

"No. So soon as they arrive on British territory, and report themselves to the authorities, they claim the protection of British subjects; and a man of our community, or any other Danish island, may as well give them up at once as attempt to recover them. Do you not think it hard in the British government to hold slaves themselves, and yet make free the slaves of other nations?"

"To look at the subject in that light, it would seem so. But I suppose this is the true idea. They have long ago abolished the African slave trade; and their armed vessels capture slaves, bring these slaves to British ports, and set them free. No individual, then, of any nation or complexion, coming into a place where the English flag flies, can be regarded as a slave."

"But why not, then, set all their own slaves free?"

"No doubt that will be done before many years have elapsed," answered Mr. Burton. "Things are looking that way very much in England. Wilberforce is at work, and that with certain effect."

"Still, I think," said Mr. Richardson, "that they should give up our people who abscond from us, and go to their islands, if we can prove our property."

"Do many of them run away from St. Johns," asked Seaton.

"Instances occur very often. Hence the law about boats. Every man having a boat is subject to a heavy penalty, if that boat is not every night hauled up above high-water mark, chained to a strong post well planted in the ground, and secured by a good lock and key. In addition to which, the boat must be scuttled, and the scuttle carried away, and locked up by the owner."

"How did they come to get your boat, if you took all this precaution?"

"Why, I must confess that it was through absolute carelessness on my part. I will tell you how it was. I had been at Tortola all day, on business. I had many little purchases to make; for it is so much nearer than St. Thomas, that many of us Danish subjects prefer to trade with the English merchants in Road Town. We were very late on our return home. We had a very heavy row, for the wind and tide were against us, until we came round the point, nearly opposite your West End establishment. On arriving at my landing-place, I said to the boys, 'Never mind locking the boat; scuttle her, and carry home the scuttle: that will do. It is so late that nobody perceives us, and we can send down early in the morning, and chain and lock her fast to the post.' But, behold, in the morning the first news I learned was that the boat was gone!"

"Why how in the world could the fellows make any head-way in a boat with the scuttle out? I wonder she had not filled the moment they launched her!

"O, they took care of that! They had no means of making a regular square scuttle of wood, to fit tightly in the place left open for it, but made a kind of wad, or stopper, of old cloth, dried plantain flagging, and other materials, and so plugged up the hole. But it was so imperfectly done, and they in such a hurry, that the boat leaked very much. There were but two of them. I know the fellows very well; and I suppose, as one had to bail out the boat almost continually; and the other, with one oar, and that a very poor one, for my boys brought up our oars, could make very little progress in his voyage; and, owing to this, I was enabled to overtake them"

"Did they make any resistance at all?"

"None whatever. Harry, the principal fellow, as soon as I drew near to them, and ordered them to stop and surrender, cried out, "Ah, Massa William, you caught me! But a little longer, and I would have been out of the clutches of old Coakley, I tell you. I'll go back. You shan't have any trouble with me; but I'll not be so easily taken next time, I assure you."

"What did Mr. Coakley say?"

"The old gentleman was very much excited, and censured me a good deal for neglecting to secure the boat. But we are relations, and of course he would not complain of me to the authorities. If the men had made good their landing on English soil, however, I should have been compelled to pay Mr. Coakley for them, at an appraisement made by three gentlemen— one chosen by him, another by myself, and the third by those two. These would have fixed the price of the slaves; and I should have also been fined, for not securing the boat, and, what is very likely, have lost my boat also; for they are very apt, when they abscond in such a manner, to send the boat adrift, and the tide carries her out to sea."

"Has brother Moore, or yourself, ever lost any of your people in this way?" inquired Mr. Burton.

"Not one," answered Moore. "I can trust my men to go in my boat to Tortola, any day in the year. They land, walk about, go where they please, and I have only to say what hour I want them to be ready to start, and when I go to the boat, there they are, punctually and faithfully."

"It is the same with my people," said Richardson. "I know they would not leave me; for they have had numerous opportunities of doing so."

"Well, now, to what do you ascribe this faithfulness?" inquired the missionaries, almost simultaneously.

"To the influence of our holy religion," said Moore. "Some of our people are Christians, and would not leave us, because they think it would be wrong. Again, they are treated kindly by us. We do this for conscience' sake. All their wants are supplied; and they do no kind of work, nor any amount of work, but what they can reasonably perform. In this condition, they doubt whether they would be benefited by running away from us; and then without friends, money, or home, being thrown on their own resources."

April, 2008

George Francis: The Man from Annaberg

Excerpt from the book: "Over Viden Strand" with text and illustrations by A. Riis Carstensen, published in Denmark, 1897

Translated from Danish by Camilla Jensen

Illustration of Maho Bay, St. John, from the book: "Over Viden Strand" by A. Riis Carstensen

(D. Knight Collection)

The following story is a extraordinary account of an encounter between a touring Danish author and illustrator, A. Riis Carstensen, and one of St. John's most notable figures, George Francis. Although Carstensen does not give an exact date of his visit to St. John, references in the text suggest that he traveled through the Danish West Indies in the late 1860s or early 1870s—George Francis died on St. John in 1875. As our story unfolds, Mr. Carstensen is sitting amidst the ruins of a sugar plantation working on a painting of Maho Bay, when he hears a "Good day, Sir!" from behind:

As I turned around I saw a rider, who, as he raised his hat apologized for interrupting. He had been riding along the road and noticing that I was a stranger, wished to greet me. But was I not thirsty? He would send for some wine; but if I would come up to his house perhaps I would find even more beautiful scenes and more space. Having shown me where he lived, he invited me to visit next time I found myself in the area and thereupon removed himself.

Illustration of Maho Bay, St. John, from the book: "Over Viden Strand" by A. Riis Carstensen

(D. Knight Collection)

This man was obviously a rare black specimen. He was well built, had healthy African features and a glistening skin color like the ace of spades. In addition, his behavior was very affable. Upon visiting him I was surprised to find so much coziness inside and so much activity outside. I asked if his property, like the others on St. Jan, had not been damaged by the hurricanes. He answered that it had certainly suffered some damage, but he had quickly repaired most of it and was now able to continue work. During the course of the conversation I learned how it came to be that he had acquired the property that he now possessed. As a slave, he had belonged to the Governor on St. Thomas. As he had distinguished himself over the other slaves, the Governor suggested that he take the position as overseer; but the thought had frightened him as he feared about his ability to assert himself in front of his co-workers. The Governor's persuasion helped and it was proved that the people worked just as well under him than had he been a white man.

Although he seldom participated in Negro disturbances, upon emancipation, he did join in the excesses prompted by the sudden transition from enslaved to free condition. He kept his position until the Governor persuaded him to take over the plantation on his own account and risk against a yearly installment. At first he objected, and reminded the Governor that he was without any education, but to that the Governor answered that practical skills, a sound mind and will power were worth more in his position than any education in the world. His children had been sent to the Moravian school, and by going over their homework he had taught himself to read. Thereafter, he had worked hard for some time practicing his writing and when he had acquired sufficient skills he had sent his former master a letter. He dwelt upon pleasant memories about the various circumstances surrounding this letter. The Governor's surprise (as he had not thought it possible for his former slave to have ambition, time and the opportunity to acquire literary proficiency), and also his visit to St. Jan to hear from George Francis himself how the incredible had happened, belonged to Francis' happiest memories, and one can understand his pride. Long ago the property had been paid off in full and was the most profitable one on the island. He was engaged in agriculture, cattle breeding and boat building. Francis was well liked, judging by the neighbors' praises for his helpfulness, resourcefulness and other virtues, and the most esteemed of all the whites and blacks on St. John.

January, 2010

Donkey Years to Modern Day

A Week On St. John

Notes from Denmark's most beautiful island

Translation of an article by Olaf Linck [1874-1958] published in "Gads Danske Maqasin," March 1914.

Translated from Danish by Leif C. Larsen

During my second journey to the West Indies in the winter of 1912-13, I had sufficient time to accept an invitation to visit the smallest of the Danish West Indian Islands, the most beautiful and neglected of them all: The stepchild of St. John.

"You will probably return tomorrow," some prosaic gentlemen of St. Thomas exclaimed, wishing me a pleasant journey with skeptical smiles. But I remained there for a week, and it was so difficult tearing myself away from the adventure implied in the name of St. John that I wished I could have stayed longer.

Though the island is situated close to St. Thomas, its bigger brother, the journey over there is still a bit of an expedition. Incidentally, these two islands share the same Colonial Council, while St. Croix has its own Council. The man I was to visit sent his boat to St. Thomas to pick me up. It was manned by three, young, strong Negroes, of whom the "captain" came to the hotel to hand me a letter, in which my host advised me to bring along provisions, as we would not arrive at our destination until late in the day.

The morning sun was just rising over the mountains as our boat drifted out through the spacious harbor. There was no wind to catch at all. The captain stood whistling on the thwart. It was an odd, melancholy hissing between his teeth that his helpers repeated like an echo. He looked so serious and ceremonious that I asked: "Why do you whistle?" "We call the wind," he quietly answered. "Does it come, then?" "Usually," the black man replied with the same serious tone.

Indeed, a little later we actually perceived a breeze, the dead calm water rippled, and having rounded the lighthouse the sails caught all the

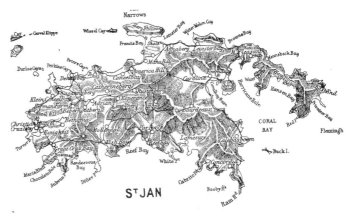

Map of St. John, 1907

(Image from Kay Larsen, Dansk Vestinden 1666-1917)

wind that could fill them. Unfortunately, the wind was against us, so we had to beat against it. Each time the boat went about I had to lie down in the bottom to keep my head out of the boom's way. Finally, I just stayed down, trying to tell myself that it was not worth the trouble to change position every minute. However, as a cup of tea and two rather soft eggs had been swimming around in my interior long enough, I had to get up. It was an embarrassing situation. No, I would prefer a storm in the Atlantic Ocean! How supercilious you are when you are on a steady deck. I suddenly realized that nemesis had revenge on me here in the strait between St. Thomas and St. John. After beating uneventfully against the wind among small rocks and islands for three long hours, we reached Cruz Bay on St. John. Here my host awaited me with horses, but before making for his home on the opposite end of the island, we naturally had to visit the island's only Danish white man, Dr. Winkel, St. John's physician and police superintendent.

There are only 2 white men among approximately 950 inhabitants on the island

Hauling "fish pots" off East End, St. John, c1900

(Postcard by Johannes Lightbourn [D. Knight Collection])

the West Indies according to countless recipes. There are men here whose fame rests entirely on their ability to mix a heady cocktail!

Eventually we mount our horses and commence our ride across the island. At first the road is so broad that carriages could pass, if such means of transport still existed on St. John. But, they belong to a golden past. After some hundred meters the road narrows into a footpath. Thereafter, we ride continuously through the forest, at first a low thicket, then tall trees, a magic wood where the vegetation alternates with an imaginative vigor. Frequently we pass sugar factory ruins, the remnants of slave days. The walls still stand, but palms have grown up between them and it seems as is if the plants have pushed off the roofs. White and blue flowers strike our cheeks. Yellow guava fruits delight the eye. We seldom see a negro hut as we ride up and down steep mountain paths. The horse, which knows the way and the rocks, does not once stumble as it crosses murmuring creeks in the valleys and wades through meter-high grass.

and the other white man lives in Emmaus, the church town and the capital. He is a young Englishman and Moravian minister. The two young men are, by the way, both married to white women from their homelands, and in their homes small white children run about the rooms. Little, half-wild white children with big, amazed eyes.

Doctor Winkel lives in the picturesque, timeworn Administration building, which, situated on a palm-covered spit of land, is reflected in the crystal clear water. You can sit on its gallery and watch the sharks glide in and out of the bay like dark, furtive shadows. The little bathing pool below the house is carefully fenced in.

The doctor's family welcomed us with transports of joy, which soared because we had brought along some ice. A while later the house echoed with the sounds of cocktail mixing. This delicious but treacherous drink is prepared in

On the mountain tops we pause to enjoy the impressive views. Around and below us we see a green carpet of wood, and in the distance are indented bays with chalk white beaches that almost strike sparks from the sun. About the island we see green, rocky islets, where humans neither live, nor have ever been. Finally, there is the infinite sea, on which you can just make out the misty outlines of St. Croix. It is a treat to see steamer smoke rising in the distance.

"Carib Inscriptions at Rif Bay," c1900

(Postcard by Johannes Lightbourn [D. Knight Collection])

It is almost sunset when we reach our destination beneath Bordeaux Mountain, the "Lamesure" plantation whose owner is Chamberlain H. Grevenkop-Castenskjold, the Danish Ambassador to London. The plantation is managed by Mr. White, a native St. Johnian, who takes pride in having cleared and planted 100 acres for the owner, who visits the island only at intervals of several years. Practically the whole of St. John is overgrown with bush, where only a few generations ago there were sugarcane and cotton fields.

Donkey Years to Modern Day

Chamberlain Grevenkop-Castenskjold is one of the few in our time who has bought land on St. John in order to cultivate it. Here on "Lamesure" it has been the practice to clear the bush and plant bay trees and lime trees. The bay tree, which is the most important planting, requires some comment. It is a slim tree, usually 7-8 meters high, with many coriaceous leaves that are stripped off and then pressed. After the bay oil has been manufactured by pressing, it is diluted with alcohol to produce the famous bay rum. In the heat the refreshing qualities of bay rum are highly prized, while a bath infused with it is like a rejuvenation treatment. However, the claim that the Negroes drink the bay rum is incorrect. Bay rum has become a major export article, in particular to the United States and Central America. It is the article first offered to steamers calling at St. Thomas, and signs of competing bay rum merchants are the first thing you see entering the harbor. On St. John the bay tree grows wild in the forest, but on "Lamesure" it is cultivated and is said to be a good business. It is a fact that the best bay rum in the West Indies comes from St. John.

Although bay trees and lime trees are the most important plantings on St. John, it should be mentioned that coconuts, bananas, oranges and sweet potatoes are also cultivated, and a little coffee and cocoa have been tried out. On the entire island only about three or four plantations are being systematically operated. One of these is "America Hill," owned by a Danish Company that is going into cattle breeding. For some years they have experimented with cross-breeding native cattle with Danish or English breeds, and the issue seems to thrive. Cattle breeding on St. John should prosper, for when St. Thomas becomes a port of international importance it will need large amounts of fresh meat, which St. John and St. Croix are capable of producing. The planters of this little island are quite rightly concerned with current and planned harbor improvements on St. Thomas.

On St. John I spent the days riding from sunrise to sunset. Mr. White was tireless in taking me all over the island. We rode to the church service at Emmaus, where almost all the island's residents gather on Sundays. We also visited the famous Carib inscriptions that are the only visible relics of the aboriginal inhabitants. Neither wind nor water has been able to obliterate these mysterious signs and figures that the Indians hewed out of the rocks on the mountain now called Dublin Hill. A negro cleared a path for the horses through the wilderness surrounding the rock, which goes unfrequented for years. There is a temple-like atmosphere about it; the only thing breaking the silence is the noise made by the wings of a humming bird, as it, insect like, drinks from a flower on the rock. On Saturdays, when work on land is suspended, most of the island's able men sail out to fish, and usually return with their boats full of fish all colors of the rainbow. When these fish are salted, there is food in the hut for most of the week.

The day is too short. The incomparable bath on the deserted beach occupies one hour each morning and evening, and the incursions into the wood cannot go far enough. There is always something new to see: a new flower, a new berry, a new tree, a new songbird; half-wild cattle and half-broken, small, hairy horses. Gorgeous peacocks, imported by Chamberlain Grevenkop-Castenskjold some years ago, have multiplied so much that you can meet them wild in the woods, where their shrill screams echo through the mountains.

The most widely distributed animal of St. John is the mongoose, a snappish, little carnivore that was introduced in the past to exterminate the rats. However, this objective failed, presumably because the mongoose found it much easier to hunt wildfowl and chickens, the latter of which are a fair way to disappearing from St. John.

The short evening could appear to be long. The sun sets about six o'clock year round and darkness falls quickly. Then you sit down with your host and hostess on a veranda that is surrounded by many green plants on whose leaves the beautiful lizards sit immovable as if they were cast iron, seemingly listening to the human conversation. Just ahead we know is the dark sea, and behind us are the mountains. If it happens during the evening that a navigation light glides past in the darkness, it is felt like a gleam from another world.

The night - well, the night was indeed overwhelming and long. We bade good-night at 8 o'clock and took to bed behind the mosquito net in order to rest saddle sore limbs. You lie on the bed, not in it. At the very utmost you are covered by a sheet. Because the night is sultry all windows are open and the sweet, intoxicating fragrance of jasmine sweeps through them. The star jasmine grows vigorously in the tangle near the house that hides the old "Lamesure" cemetery. Each plantation on the Island has its own burial ground. The dead are the only souls on St. John not conveyed by horse. When someone dies they are, preferably on the same day, buried in the ground outside their home. The fragrance of Jasmine mingles inseparably with the eternal jingle of cicadas. The whole mountain sings and you fall asleep with the feeling that nature has embraced you. What infinite peace! And, when you awake in the darkness, because you are not used to such a long night, the feeble song of the cicadas lingers on and ceases only when sunrise puts night dreams to flight.

Yes, the island of St. John is a dreamland. But how long will the dream continue? When will it learn from the nearby English island of Tortola, which is like one great flowering garden, in whose soil (which is not more endowed by nature than St. John) is cultivated coffee, cotton, limes, oranges, bananas and many other kinds of fruit. Several years ago Doctor Fishlock, an agronomist, established an experimental station on Tortola with government support. It was similar to the one established on St. Croix and managed by Doctor Longfield Smith. However, while the latter has not been entirely successful in establishing contact with the planters, that on Tortola has become the island's cornerstone. The Negroes learn to cultivate their land, and, more importantly, the agricultural products are sold for them by the station, which only exacts a minor charge for the station's maintenance.

Governor Helwig-Larsen has long been aware of the possibilities of St. John. Previously, during a stay in Denmark while Government Secretary, he tried to interest the Danish nobility and landowners in St. John, arguing that it would be a worthwhile task for these men to acquire and cultivate land on the island. So he invited them to a meeting on Zealand where the idea could be discussed; but those he had counted on did not attend, so the matter was shelved.

Since then several projects have been considered. One plan was to send out about twenty Danish farmers, but how to guarantee that those to be sent were of the right stamp. Life on St. John, with its enchanting remoteness from the outside world, is quite different from that of Denmark, where neighbors can always be called upon. Another plan was to tax the uncultivated land of St. John, while reducing taxes on cultivated land. It was argued that this would encourage the many absentee owners on St. Thomas to sell off their properties. But, other forces came into play that proved stronger than the proponents of this excellent scheme. The Colonial Council, at least, doesn't feel the time is right for such experiments.

It is strange to imagine that a pearl like St. John, so gifted by nature and blessed with a mild, refreshing climate, might soon be "discovered," not by Danes, but by far-sighted Americans. A luxury hotel on top of the island would have every prospect of transforming it from a Sleeping Beauty into a flourishing Caribbean tourist Mecca. In the last decade the southward flow of wealthy American tourists has progressed by leaps and bounds. The Danes must take good care of St. John while it still rests with them to control its destiny.

A notice in the newspaper encouraged me to write these lines. It is reported that Lady Daisy Grevenkop-Castenskjold, a daughter of Count Mogens Friis, had gone to St. John to spend the winter at her husband's estate "Lamesure." The ambassador's young wife is so enchanted with St. John's nature that she has decided she would like to live there forever. Thus, the little, densely wooded island in the sea bewitches every new visitor, making another lifetime friend.

Why not go out there yourself instead of your usual trip to the everlasting Riviera. Adventure awaits you on St. John.

December, 2007

Cruz Bay Christmas Recollections

of the 1930s and 40s

As told by Andro Childs

"I remember how we prepared for and celebrated the holidays," Mrs. Childs began. "Cruz Bay was so small then, probably not more than eight or ten families. There were two little grocery stores that sold the basics," she recalled. "For oil, you took a pint bottle to be filled; for butter or lard, you got it in a tin or a piece of paper for three or four cents; or you could get a quarter pound of sugar or three cent matches."

"Thanksgiving signaled the beginning of preparations for Christmas. Special liqueurs had to be prepared, not only bottles of the traditional guavaberry, but also guava and seagrape liqueur. My Mama was a master at blending and creating these drinks from native berries and rum.

My Aunt Meada was in charge of baking breads and cakes in the family outdoor stone oven. For Christmas, Sweet Bread was always high on everyone's list. On Christmas Eve the serenaders would come," Andro said. "For weeks before, you'd hear people crooning, tuning up, and getting ready for serenading. The serenaders went from house to house Christmas Eve and during the night singing Christmas carols and we served them guavaberry drinks, ham, sweet bread, etc."

"Christmas presents were important to children as they are today. I remember receiving a little red wagon, a tea set and other special toys. The tea set was played with for a few hours and then put away. On Sunday afternoons and other quiet times it would be brought out for play. These were times of caring and sharing, an everyday occurrence on St. John that was magnified by the joyful season."

During the weekday afternoons, we would hear the church choirs practicing Christmas carols and children practicing Christmas recitations.

Myra Keating-Smith and daughter Andromeada Childs

(Photo courtesy Andro Childs)

They were preparing to perform for family and friends who would walk or ride on donkeys and horses from all over the island; Coral Bay, Monte, Gift Hill, Pastory and Good Hope. Almost all of the people were either Moravian or Lutheran. They celebrated the season together and greeted each other with "COMPLIMENTS OF THE SEASON!"

"The most precious memory was walking home from Bethany in the moonlight, singing Christmas carols and eating candies from small Christmas gift boxes given to us children at the program."

December, 2004

Estate Sieben & Mollendahl Memories

Related by Mr. Elroy Sprauve

Elroy and Vernon Sprauve before the Sieben Estate hike, 2008

(Photo courtesy of Jeff Spear)

My brother, Vernon, and I were born at Estate Sieben; that meant that somebody had to get on a horse and go to Cruz Bay and get Miss Myrah, for whom the Clinic is named, and then she had to get on her horse and come all the way down to Sieben to make the delivery.

I wish you could have seen the Estate when it was cleared. The bush is all grown up now, so you really can't get a feeling for what it was like then, but it is a beautiful Estate when cleared, because the topography is so varied. There was a very large beautiful flat area, deep, deep valleys, and rolling hills. There were a lot, a lot, of fruit trees. There was no shortage of water because there is a gut, part of Fish Bay Gut really, which passes through Estate Sieben. And in that part of the gut, there were large pools, so large that we could swim in them. They were filled, filled, filled with lots of fish and lots of freshwater shrimp. So there was lots of water for the families who lived here and for the animals.

There were two types of mango that were grown only from this part of the island—one was a tiny very sweet mango called 'centbread', I guess because it was named after the small breads that were sold for just one penny, and then there was another larger one called a peach mango. There was a gobi, or calabash, tree which might still be there, as calabash trees live a very long time, and the calabashes used to grow THIS large.

Our maternal grandmother is buried at Estate Sieben. She died in January of 1935. It was sad and yet happy at the same time, as my brother Julius Sprauve, who would have been her first grandchild, was born in the next room one hour after she died. We had life and death at the same time. You can imagine how it was out there, with no neighbors around, with this happening. The gravestone may still be standing.

I think one thing I should bring to your memory—some years ago I was a member of the VI Humanities Council, and there was a Dr. Rashford who applied for a grant to study baobab trees, trees that are considered sacred in many parts of Africa. Dr. Rashford said he discovered that the largest concentration of baobab outside of Africa was in the U.S. Virgin Islands. In his presentation to the Council, he said there were several on St. Croix, a few on St. Thomas and none on St. John. And I said, "Dr. Rashford, I think I can recall on Estate Sieben, there is a tree that fits your description." Dr. Rashford said that in that case, he would have to completely go over his proposal and asked if there were any way he could come to St. John. So he came to St. John, and we hiked down there—Noble Samuel, Dr. Rashford and I think Jim Provost. When we got down to Estate Sieben, I was completely disoriented. My memory of Estate Sieben was when it was cleared, but it was all overgrown.

And then I began to have all these doubts; was the tree a figment of my imagination? Did I bring Dr. Rashford all the way here and there's no tree? So we decided to try; we began to look around, and then someone said 'Look Up' and there was the baobab tree. I don't know about now, but for many years it was the only known baobab tree on St. John; it was about 100 years old then.

As I said, the Estate was beautiful when it was cleared. There are lots of old ruins on the Estate. There is an old cemetery with several families buried there, as it was a very active Estate.

So I was born there, but when I made a month, my mother took me to Cruz Bay to be baptized and we remained there. We came back and forth, though, at least once a week; we picked fruit and kept animals here, and we had people living there and working on the Estate. During the summers, especially when the mangoes were ripe we came very, very often. We kept primarily goats—many, many goats—and sheep, and one or two cows. My father had a rapport with animals; he would just clap his hands and they would come out of the hillside to him.

Our closest neighbor was a lady we called Sarah Rasmus. For all her years, she never left this home; I don't believe she ever saw electricity. And she told us we would know when she passed, as we would see the blue flies. Close to her would have been a gentleman named Batiste. They would have been maybe 2 miles away.

In those days, the Sieben Road was a little more traveled. People from John's Folly/Mollendahl (there are 2 Mollendahls on St. John; this refers to the one now usually called Mandahl) would have used this road. There was no one at L'Esperance. There were people at Reef Bay and Little Reef Bay; however it was still very dark at night. I remember a story told me by Miss Myrah—she was returning from making a delivery of a baby in John's Folly and she became caught in a rainstorm; it became so dark, all she could do was hold on to the horse. When she saw lamplight at my mother's house, she managed to go there and spent the night.

People used to walk everywhere; it wasn't unusual for my father to ask us to walk to Sieben/Mollendahl from Cruz Bay 2 or 3 times a week, and you met everyone walking to and from Coral Bay or Cruz Bay. Of course it wasn't on the existing road that people walked; there were more direct paths. And Centerline Road wasn't paved until the early 1960s.

There is a chilling story of a murder here at Reef Bay in 1937; a man killed Anna Marsh. Rumor has it that he passed by Sieben and wanted to do harm to my father also. My father was not at home and a woman who lived by Mollendahl was spending the night with my mother. Someone called and knocked on the door, but they refused to open it. And then the next day they heard about Anna Marsh's murder.

People going to Sieben also came to the Estate from the sea. I remember my grandmother saying that when she came to see my mother, they sailed into Fish Bay, put her into a rocking chair and carried her up the steep hills to the Estate. My father, an early businessman who acquired pieces of land as they were sold off and owners moved away (land wasn't that expensive then), cut fuel to stoke the ovens for the Bakery on St. Thomas; they would cut the wood and carry it down to Fish Bay for transport. The last person my father hired to work here was Mr. Christian, the grandfather of Alvis Christian. He (Julius Sprauve, Sr.) sold the Sieben Estate to the National Park in the 1950s.

January, 2008

Report from Paradise... The Virgin Islands

Its Faults, Flaws and Satisfactions, Reported by one who lives there.

Nancy Gibney

Jane Boulon, Anna Knight & Nancy Gibney at Trunk Bay, c1956, with (l to r) David W. Knight, Rafe Boulon, Ed & John Gibney.

(photo by Dr. George H. H. Knight)

Nancy Gibney was the mother of Historical Society member Eleanor Gibney. The following account is from an article published in Vogue Magazine, *October 1, 1948 (used by permission of Condé Nast Publications).*

Since my husband and I arrived in the Virgin Islands a couple of years ago, we have seen a great many magazine and newspaper articles equating the place to Paradise. Paradise it may be, but if it is, there must be some petty sore saints. It takes a lot of muscle or money to live at all well here. It takes a lot of patience and *folie de grandeur* to think that life here is an eternal reward.

Despite the big new tourist boom, this is still far from a professional resort. Of course, the American Virgin Islands are free ports, and you can smoke and drink yourself to death with great speed and small expense, if that is your idea of a good time. But there isn't a golf course, or a good restaurant, or a casino in the islands, and you get your tennis workout trying to find a tennis court… St. John has a boarding house

with a National Geographic strand, and a few miles away—a small colony of furnished beach cottages where you can live a hard, inelegant life, for six or seven hundred dollars a month. But wherever you stay on St. Thomas you have to take a long automobile ride to swim.

Almost any one of the French or British West Indies has more to offer in the way of atmosphere, sport and entertainment. And still the tourists crowd the incoming boats and planes—the honeymooners and the divorcees arriving together; the people that wail that Taos, Mallorca, Acapulco are ruined, are arriving with the people who ruined them. And a surprising number of tourists outstay their round-trip time to buy land and build houses.

I suppose our own case is a typical one. When we left New York in 1946, we had no thought of skipping the country forever. My husband had contracted to write a book and he thought it would be nice to write it underwater—under well lighted tropical water. We went first to Haiti, hoping to rent a house for the winter there. We were enchanted with Haiti—the loom of the jungle mountains, the drums playing like juke boxes, the people moving like cats, and speaking better French than the French ever felt they had to. But Haiti had sharks and malaria; no one dreamed of swimming in the sea or living at sea level. And Haiti had the authority and complexity of a continent; we wanted something simple and island size. We came to the Virgin Islands.

St. John was the place for us, everyone told us. St. John was only four miles from St. Thomas, hot dog! St. John had the best beaches in the world.

We came to look at St. John, and we saw it with the heart—a steep wilderness without roads, without towns, with dazzling, empty beaches, and great ruins fallen under great trees. We have lived on St. John, or on a cay just off it, ever since. When we came, we didn't know how tenaciously all the handsomest beaches and trees were owned; and we couldn't have guessed at the company we'd keep. Only seven hundred negroes and half dozen whites live year-round on this island, but a lot of transients have turned up here in the past two years—among them, Henry Morgenthau and John Gunther. Last Christmas the St. John boarding house housed four New York psychiatrists and an FBI man; we certainly haven't escaped.

St. John is by far the hardest of the three American Virgin Islands to live on, and we have done everything the hardest way. The hard way has always been so satisfying that we've never gone back to the easy. We could live on canned food and crackers, drink Klim and routine coffee from the states; but we try to grow fruits and vegetables; we bake our own bread, pasteurize milk, buy coffee in the bean from Puerto Rico and roast and grind it ourselves. A native butcher sells us excellent pork and lamb for thirty-five cents per pound; and for a carefree while, we were able to buy fish from a couple of native boys. They soon started feuding and so terrorized each other that they both went out of business—now we catch our own fish, when we can first catch the bait. We dive for conch and langousta, gather whelks. Once every week we go to St. Thomas for liquor and staples; this is an all day excursion that often involves drowning on the way and fainting in the streets by noon.

We wish the process of living didn't take so much of our lives, and we envy our friends on St. Thomas and St. Croix who have better trained servants, cars to take them to market, the mechanics to fix the cars when they break down. But we wouldn't change places with them. As my father felt about Roosevelt, we feel about the development of St. John. The face turns purple; and teeth grind. Right now, the natives seem happy and dignified as members of a sporting leisure class; we can't believe that they'll be better off as bellhops. Right now we find this such a perfect place for working; for seeing the people we love, and for dodging the ones we don't. And any small comforts we manage in the wilderness seem such great luxuries by contrast.

Twice in two years we've been back to the states: the first spring, we went to Florida, were felled by the heat and oppressed by the landscape that seemed to have all foreground and no perspective. (Here we have perspective to burn—the problem is finding foreground to break the brutal expanse of view.) Last June, we spent a little time in New York and on Long Island. New York seemed a splendid place for doing business, but we couldn't think of a single thing to do for pleasure. We came away not caring if we never see the town again. Of course we want to see our New York friends again—but we know where the light is brighter and more becoming.

When we got back here, it was summer, and summer is the most becoming of local seasons. In the summer, a winter resort belongs to itself again, and to the people who truly belong to it. In the summer the gaunt Flamboyant trees recall their name, and the guavas and avocado ripen. The Spanish mackerel and kingfish get careless and get caught; and at night the big sea turtles stump up on the beaches to lay their celluloid eggs. In the summer, the Sea Blast is tempered to a breeze, and the boat stops being a perilous means of transportation and becomes a positive joy.

In the summer we sometimes sail to the British Virgin Islands, a few miles east of St. John. They are the quietest backwaters of Empire; the tourist sun has yet to rise on them. The capital of the group; Road Town on Tortola, is a sad village with privies rimming the harbor and a fancy pink Government House in such disrepair that the Governor moved out of it long ago to rent a neat cottage outside of town. But we have our reasons for liking Tortola. In the summer we can buy grafted Julie mangoes there, and they are surely fruit from Eden. And once in Road Town we went to see some friends who were replacing their termite- eaten louvers with screens of woven coconut fronds. This seemed to my husband a God-given chance to say, "Just fronds, louvers no more." At least for him, at least for a moment, these islands have been Paradise enow.

November, 2006

To Market, To Market

Erva Boulon

Trunk Bay Estate Guesthouse kitchen. From left to right: Eve Boulon, Rafe Boulon, Ms Eulalie Christopher and Ms Dalia, c1956.

(Photo by Jane Boulon)

Erva Boulon was the grandmother of SJHS member Rafe Boulon. Erva and her husband, Paul Boulon, came to St. John in 1927. They owned Trunk Bay, raised four children there, and ran a guest house. This is an excerpt from an article which was originally published in the February, 1948, edition of "Villager Magazine," Bronxville, New York).

The one question that is always asked by newcomers is how do you get your provisions? Here is one answer.

The trip started with a toothache I had been trying vainly to ignore. We were vacationing in St. John, stores were getting low, tooth was not getting better and a trip to St. Thomas was indicated. That entailed catching the bi-weekly mail sloop, which meant staying in St. Thomas overnight or longer if some return sloop could not be found the next day. According to yachtsmen, these native sloops are unusual. They are built without drawn plans, and each one is as much of an individual as its owner. They average a bit over twenty feet in length, and use some odd little ideas of their own in the rigging, so that you never see a regular Marconi or gaff rig.

I had a long list of groceries and dry stores and many errands of importance to the girl and the boys, and Friday morning they all saw me off.

Feeling stiff in my city clothes (shorts and shirt had to be discarded for the time) my overnight bag in hand, I stepped into the row boat on our beach. The three boys pushed us off and in a flurry of waving hands the first lap of the trip began.

I was the idle passenger. My cook's two brothers rowed the boat. One was dark, huge and pleasant, the other black and dour. I relaxed and enjoyed the cool morning air and the scenery. Trunk Bay with its gleaming white beach fringed with sea grapes and coconut palms slipped behind us. The Fishing Club at Denis Bay slept. The water and the birds made the only sounds except the regular stroking of the oars. Hogsnest, (pronounced Hawksnest and meaning just that) usually a rowdy stretch of water, was smooth in this early morning calm. The various small beaches at Caneel Bay, then its historic ruins, fell astern. We were now at the point just before turning into Cruz Bay. There is always that thrill of fear before rounding the point, that we might be late. No, there lay the sloop at the small cement pier. We had been about an hour and a half going some three and a half miles, and the sun was high above the hills, reminding us that it would be a hot day.

The sloop was being loaded, a terrified bleating goat, several small squealing pigs and a box of fish being among the cargo. At nine the sails were spread to the early breeze, which we hoped would last, and we were off!

It was a fair trip, as such trips go. We were stepping ashore at one o'clock on Tortola wharf in St. Thomas, somewhat warm, a bit weary from sitting so long, otherwise none the worse for wear. The distance traveled was some eight miles, and I had been on my way from Trunk Bay for more than six hours.

No marketing could be done until I knew just how and when I could return to St. John. As I went about my other errands, and that inevitable visit to the dentist's chair, word got to me that a launch would be leaving Saturday noon for Tortola. This was luck, and meant that I could be landed with all my packages at Trunk Bay without having to transfer everything to our own row boat at Cruz Bay.

All island markets are at their best in the early morning, so I finished my other shopping on Friday. I had been told that marketing in St. Thomas was at best a futile gesture so I was

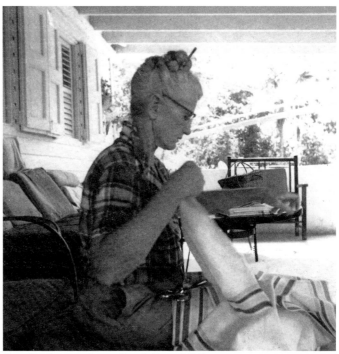

Erva Boulon sewing at Trunk Bay, c1954

(Photo by Jane Boulon)

somewhat dubious of results but determined to do my best.

The market place itself is an open air affair. There is a stout roof under which there are two rows of cement tables, each queened over by a dusky lady who is conscious of her power over

Local sloops at the Dock in Cruz Bay, c1949

(Photo by George H. H. Knight)

Donkey Years to Modern Day

us who have to be fed. At one table I found plantains, ripe and yellow, okra so tender that there was no need to test it by bending the ends, cucumbers and tomatoes (they were a real prize) tanias, called dasheens in Florida, and bananas (called figs locally). Plantains are outsize bananas and must be cooked to be edible. The only way I could really indicate the difference between plantains and bananas would be to take you down into the grove where we now produce our own and show you the bunches of fruit growing on the trees.

My marketing was completed, but to my dismay there were no bags, no paper, no twine, for making up parcels. There was much good-natured laughter at the ignorant woman who did not know that one should market properly, with a basket. Some scurrying around brought forth a big carton which a kind brown woman donated to the cause. It was more than adequate but remarkably clumsy to carry, as I am not able to balance my marketing on my head even now after years of living in the islands. One has to be born to it!

I can tell you a bit of gossip I overheard, but I can not give you the conclusion of it, because I never found it out myself. While I was packing my box of vegetables quite a commotion arose behind me. I tried to appear indifferent, but my ears were fairly wagging in my effort to understand the lively controversy.

It seems there was to be a wedding. The niece and nephew of the two opponents were to be married, the larger and more aggressive woman being the nephew's aunt and much in favor of the marriage—"dat de t'ing to do, it very much in style now," The niece's aunt did not want to see the girl married to any such as the nephew. I could not resist turning my head to see how things were coming. The two women were shaking their faces at one another in a very disagreeable way. I fear if there was a wedding it was an unpleasant one.

I was returning in a motor launch at noon. After the usual delays of loading gasoline, picking up a forgotten package, collecting a tardy passenger, etc., we left St. Thomas about half past one. Two hours later I stepped onto the beach at Trunk Bay in St. John. The whole camp turned out to bid me welcome. I have a sneaking suspicion that the packages had something to do with it!

March, 2006

A Remembrance of St. John

Anna W. Knight; edited and condensed by David W. Knight

Anna Welner Knight (affectionately known to most folks on St. John as "Billy") was the Mother of SJHS member David W. Knight. She was born in New York in 1911, the first child of recently-arrived German immigrants. At the age of 18 she married Dr. George H. H. Knight and settled into life as the socialite-wife of a prominent Westchester dentist. Dr. Knight, however, loved to wander. While on an extended sojourn through the West Indies Knight was invited by the Danish Counsel on St. Thomas to accompany him on a trip to St. John for a dinner aboard the Danish training ship "Danmark," which was anchored off Caneel Bay. Before leaving St. John Dr. Knight was told of plans to build rental cottages for tourists at Caneel Bay. Impressed by the tranquil beauty of the island, Knight pledged that as soon as a cottage was built he would return to St. John. And indeed, in 1936, accompanied by his 25-year-old wife, Billy, the Knights were among the first guests at Caneel Bay Resort. Billy's remembrances, along with photographs taken by both her and husband George, portray a time of discovery, innocence and wonder, still shared by new visitors to St. John to the present day; St. John is not new to capturing romantic hearts.

Anna (Billy) Welner Knight at Estate Carolina in Coral Bay, 1936

(Photo courtesy David W. Knight)

Caneel Bay Ruins, 1936

(Photo courtesy David W. Knight)

We awake under our mosquito nets to the sound of a cock crowing somewhere behind the ruins of the horse mill and sugar house at Caneel Bay. Above us, upside down on the ceiling, a gecko lizard dashes out after an unsuspecting insect. It is dawn and soon Darcus will come over the hill riding her donkey, work shoes tied around her neck by the laces. She will go to the backyard cook house to do the laundry, and while it drip dries on bushes and wire fencing she will sit on the back steps smoking her corn-cob pipe. Then, piece by piece, she will do the ironing with a charcoal "goose."

Setting out to Coral Bay on horseback, 1936.

(Photo courtesy David W. Knight)

We sip our morning coffee on the gallery overlooking the sea grape fringed beach and a harbor of turquoise water. Little black and yellow sugar birds, bananaquits, fly in and help themselves to the contents of our sugar bowl. Trade winds rustle the banana leaves blending with the sound of the ebb and flow of waves on the shore. Later, young men in small boats come from Frenchtown on St. Thomas to cast their nets in the harbor and we buy colorful fish with strange names for Iantha to prepare for lunch.

In the afternoon, ground doves scatter at the sound of our horse's hooves as we ride over the hill to Cruz Bay; a great blue heron flies up, legs dangling, from the mangroves that line the Cruz Bay waterfront. Had it been blown off course on its long flight from a summer in Maine to Trinidad? We visit the country store with its large wheels of cheese and barrels of lard and salted codfish. Or perhaps we visit the commissioner and his wife who live at the old Danish fort known as the Battery.

This was 1936 on the island of St. John, U.S. Virgin Islands. In those days the commissioners of the island were required to be doctors as well as heads of local government. Dr. Hughes was a friendly, pink-cheeked, white-haired gentleman, who wore a white pith helmet while making his rounds of the island astride a white horse. I remember that he rode up Centerline Road to a wedding in the Moravian Church at Bethany, while Mrs. Hughes walked with us. I also remember that I wore a lavender afternoon dress, a flowered hat with a veil and saddle shoes.

St. John, an island of approximately five hundred indigenous folk and perhaps nine continentals in 1936, was considered an escapists' utopia. On this island of five by nine miles of overgrown bridle paths, deserted pristine beaches and few visitors, a mail boat arrived once a week. There were no roads, in fact no wheels, and a choice for exploring was a horse, a donkey, or on foot. Little thought was given by a visitor to the crumbling ruins of ancient great houses hidden behind a tangle of bush, strangler figs, thorn acacia and catch-and-keep, or to the appalling events that had taken place there during the uprising of slaves in 1733-1734.

For those of us who rode the trails the rewards were spectacular views and deserted beaches. We learned to make ice cream with the soursop, to flip the seeds of the sugar apple, to eat mangos and guava, and to cook the green papayas for lunch and eat the ripe ones for breakfast. We used bananas in every way we could think of and we ate cassava bread and the jelly of green coconuts with a spoon. There were reef fish in startling hues—parrotfish, angel fish, butterfly fish and the flat-bottomed hard-shelled trunk fish that could be cooked over a charcoal pot—caught in fish pots woven from palm fronds. There were no telephones, and the only electricity at Caneel Bay was supplied by their own generator.

We had Christmas dinner that year as guests of Mr. Thrigo, the Caneel Bay plantation manager and his wife and daughter Elsa. Though the United States had purchased the Virgin Islands from Denmark in 1917, and the name of St. John had been changed from St. Jan, the cultural influence throughout the Virgin Islands remained charmingly Danish.

The world as we knew it had been left behind and we especially felt this to be true on a trip

Donkey Years to Modern Day

Dr. George H. H. Knight stands in the cockpit of Capt. Billy's sloop, becalmed off of Lind Point, 1936

(Photo courtesy David W. Knight)

to Tortola, British Virgin Islands. Capt. Billy owned a small island sloop which he used to transport goats and charcoal, and whatever else he needed to carry. We "chartered" Capt. Billy and his boat for a trip to Tortola. Becalmed off Mary's Point I tried to sleep stretched out on a dirty old sail where I overheard a discussion between our house boy and a member of the crew about live ghosts, werewolves and jumbies.

A visitor to St. John was Professor Robert Woodworth, on sabbatical from Bennington College to study plants and animals and marine life. We went on a field trip with him and I found myself very much involved with the study of tide pools and reefs. This was before scuba diving and we wore water goggles and a diving bell that rested on our shoulders. A whole new world was opened to me and became a life-long interest. Sometimes we would row out to Carvel Rock to fish for yellow tail or just sit and watch for migratory whales.

A trip from Cruz Bay to Coral Bay over the paved Centerline Road takes about twenty minutes today, but in 1936 the round trip was more comfortably made in two days. We

would ride the narrow overgrown trail until it reached the Bordeaux overlook, where we would dismount and walk our horses down the steep and rocky trail to Coral Bay. A quiet little settlement, Coral Bay's one claim to fame was a primitive little still where leaves of the bay trees that grew on Bordeaux Mountain were processed for oil. Mixed with alcohol it became Bay Rum.

On a wall of the Elaine Sprauve Cruz Bay library today a picture hangs of two women and a man on horse back, riding the Centerline trail—I am one of the women. It pleases me that I am able to prove that I was once young enough to ride a horse!

Today Caneel Bay is known as an exclusive playground for the rich and often very famous. It grew into this only after World War II, but even before the war, in response to Desmond Holdridge's book "Escape to the Tropics," some well known folks were already discovering our island paradise. As the West India Company expanded on their Caneel Bay Plantation by adding cottages on the [northern] point, we moved with them. In 1936 we had been the

Caneel Bay, Cottage No. 1, 1936

(Photo courtesy David W. Knight)

first tenants in the first cottage which was placed on a knoll overlooking the beach. The newer cottages on the point had wrap-around galleries and two bedrooms, but still had a cook house out back where one had to keep the door closed against the resident raider, the mongoose.

We found ourselves the following winter with interesting neighbors. Robert Ripley (Believe it or Not) and his male secretary were in Cottage #4. Mr. Ripley was regarded by the locals as "not quite right." He would wear a black wool turtleneck sweater and run the hilly trails. Jogging had not been heard of on St. John!

Leon Henderson, Director of President Roosevelt's OPA was in Cottage #5. Leon liked canned shad roe with his scrambled eggs, which I prepared for him before he and George went deep sea fishing for king fish with Rudi and Ernest of Lovango Cay.

There were evenings spent on board the Danish training ship, *Danmark*, with Capt. Hanson, who had found St. John an ideal place to give his young crew shore leave. The stars, without competition, would be unbelievably bright as we sat on deck and studied them.

Today bananaquits still steal your sugar, humming birds visit your hibiscus, and African Tulip trees bloom. African Guinea grass thrives where sugar cane once grew and the hee-haw of donkeys can still be heard in the hills—but now they are homeless and wild, and some wear radio tracking collars, and no one seems to know what to do about them. The Commissioner, who is now called the Administrator, still lives in the old Danish fort, the *Battery*, but he is no longer required to be the island doctor. There are hourly ferries and visitors from all over the world—hikers, campers, day visitors and people who buy condos and stay. The little town of Cruz Bay suffers from progress with restaurants, bars, boutiques, liquor stores and all the services that free enterprise can offer, including a pick up and deliver laundry. All this because on December 1, 1956, Laurance Rockefeller, as a gift to the Federal Government, handed Secretary of the Interior Seaton the deed to approximately two thirds of the island of St. John. Our little island paradise became the first tropical United States National Park. In 1962 Congress added offshore areas to the Park as well.

Now, fish pots are no longer permitted over protected reefs, and life guards stand watch on once-deserted beaches. Sea turtles and their eggs are protected with heavy fines and even jail for offenders. The Audubon Society plans birding trips, the Historical Society plans hikes to plantation ruins and schedules archaeologists as speakers for their meetings, and a yacht club plans regattas. There are telephones, electricity, TVs, taxis, safari buses, boats to charter and jeeps to rent. A letter I have received from Secretary Potter of the National Park Service of Cruz Bay, dated December 7, 1987, informs me that "the annual average number of visitors to the Park in the last five years has been 1,115,920 persons." The little island that had once been enjoyed by so few is now being enjoyed by the many.

April, 2009

Childhood Memories of St. John

Presented by Gaylord Sprauve; Summarized by Jan Frey

Gaylord Sprauve of St. Thomas was warmly welcomed as a speaker at a St. John Historical Society meeting held in the courtyard of the Cruz Bay Battery. His cousin, Mr. Elroy Sprauve, a member of the Society, introduced him. Mr. Sprauve shared his childhood memories of summers on St. John with family and friends in a bygone era.

Mr. Sprauve told the group that he would come to St. John with his family as soon as school was closed for summer vacation. To this young boy, St. John was a place of sand, sun and sea to be enjoyed, unlike St. Thomas where there was only pavement near his home. His mother had no sisters of her own, and she enjoyed the companionship of her other "sisters" on St. John who were relatives of her husband.

At the time, St. John was a small community with no vehicles, so the children roamed freely, days and evenings. Fishing was the most important pastime for them and they first fished from the dock, where Nana—Elroy's Mother, could keep an eye on them. As they grew older, they would fish at the reef at the entrance of Cruz Bay harbor and later they went to small cays and fished all day. Some days they spent so many

> "The (power) boat in the picture is believed to be what was known to us as "the black boat." This boat was assigned to Administrator George Simmonds and was used extensively for his transportation to St. Thomas on official business and also to transport the sick to St. Thomas. There was a second boat that was known to us as the "gray boat" that was also assigned to the administrator's office. It is believed that both boats were surplus US military equipment. Since the only inter-island communication between St. John and St. Thomas was by radio-telephone it was necessary for the administrator's office to relay the need for ambulance service at Red Hook through either the Office of the Government Secretary (now the Lieutenant Governor) or the police department."
> —Gaylord Sprauve, 2009

Melee! Cows being loaded onto a boat at the Cruz Bay Dock, c1950

(Photo by Dr. George H. H. Knight)

hours fishing that the fish they caught early in the morning would be spoiled by the time they returned in the late afternoon. Soldier crabs, which they used as bait, were harvested with kerosene lanterns in hand after dark from around decaying century plants. On one occasion when they were out in a rowboat in "Plantation Bay," they heard a rumbling sound made by thousands of crabs washing themselves in the sea. This scene was only observed once.

The family owned a farm at Adrian with cows, sheep, goats and pigs, where Eastern Caribbean people were the farm hands and lived on the property. Some mornings Gaylord would leave Cruz Bay at 5:30 in the dark, to go to the farm for milk with either one or two carts pulled by mules in which to fetch the awaiting milk for transport back to Cruz Bay to share with other relatives. Vegetables were grown at the farm, which were used by the family and other community members. Charcoal was used in the coal pots for cooking. In the community pigs and goats were cooked on spits over the charcoal fires on special occasions.

There were family trips to the Island's East End, when they would ride from Cruz Bay to King's Hill, down to Carolina and on to the East End. Their stays were short as they returned the same day.

The families hunted wild ducks on the ponds, often on Thatch Island off Tortola. The older boys and their father would go ashore and hunt, while the younger children waited in the boat. Because the ducks would easily spoil, they rented refrigerator boxes on St. Thomas, which were very cold, to store the birds—as well as fish caught by trolling or in fish pots. When the accumulation of fish and ducks was sufficient, a feast was held that included both family members and friends. Some homes had kerosene refrigerators, but daily food shopping was done at small "shops" in Cruz Bay or on St. Thomas. One event that Mr. Sprauve told the group about was when a calf was brought to St. John from St. Thomas on the family boat "Trade Wind." For the young ones, this was a big and exciting event. The trips to St. John were sometimes very long and at other times very short, depending on the weather and the need to return to the home base. The "Eveready" the "Speed" and the "Lillian" were privately owned sailing boats that moved most of the materials, supplies, and livestock to and from St. John. Without motors these sail boats would often

blow near Lovango Cay, where their crews would then use oars to scull to St. John. At the end of Gaylord's presentation, he asked for questions or comments from the audience. To everyone's delight, Gaylord's brother, Gilbert, joined in the sharing of random reminiscences of that time in St. John.

There was a large open area where Wharfside Village is today that was used as a cricket field when it was dry enough. Where the Post Office is located today, there were goat pens. The goats would spend their nights there and be taken to an area just past where Mongoose Junction is to graze during the day. The goat's grazing area was fenced and gated. There was no road past the bottom of the hill to connect to connect Cruz Bay with either Caneel Bay or Trunk Bay. Travel between these points and Cruz Bay was by boat.

They talked about their mules, named John and Jim, as well as horses Lady Armstrong, Pepper and Flash. They also talked about making rope by taking vines off trees and twisting them for use in setting fish pots, and the trips to the commissary at Caneel Bay to buy kerosene in a cranky aluminum boat powered by a one-quarter horsepower outboard motor. Under the direction of their father, local dentist Gilbert Sprauve, they even brought grass sod from along the roadside on St. Thomas to be transplanted at Adrian on St. John.

Naturally, fishing was discussed and the brothers told about using fish pots, which were positioned in various spots. The brothers' father would not mark the spots, but triangulate mentally the spots using various landmarks such as sugar mills, so their fish would not be poached.

They spoke of Julius, Elroy's father, who was St. John's Councilman to the Virgin Islands government, with its headquarters in Charlotte Amalie. Julius would visit with people of St. John to hear about their concerns and even ride over to Coral Bay on a mule to speak with the East End residents. Gaylord told the gathering of the eulogy he gave at his cousin's recent funeral. He ended it by calling St. John "our playground" remembering their childhood summers spent here.

April, 2005

Caneel Bay Estate Before Laurance Rockefeller

Hjalmar Bang

The following is a transcript of a memo dated April 5, 1956 from Mr. Hjalmar Bang to Mr. Laurance S. Rockefeller. In this text, Mr. Bang describes the Caneel Bay Resort's origins on St. John. [Published by permission of Rockefeller Archive Center. Ads are from a VI Tourism magazine produced by the VI government].

"In connection with my contact with the Caneel Bay Estate in St. John, Virgin Islands, I might give you the following data:

I came to St. Thomas, V.I., in the year 1919, two years after the transfer of the Islands from Denmark to the United States, as an employee of the West Indian Company, Ltd., a subsidiary of the East Asiatic Co., Ltd. of Copenhagen, for which concern I was working. The West Indian Company, Ltd., owned harbour facilities and an electric power plant in St. Thomas, and engaged in various kinds of shipping and trading business connected therewith.

In 1934, a small enterprise, by name Maison Danoise, was started in St. Thomas for the purpose of introducing and selling Danish silver, porcelain, and other Scandinavian objects of art to the tourists, who were just then beginning to find their way to St. Thomas in increasing numbers. This little enterprise soon became a considerable success, so much so that it gave rise, directly, to an

Caneel Bay Plantation Resort

BUNGALOWS FOR RENT. Each bungalow is a self-contained unit, two large rooms and a porch. Equipped with all modern comfort: Bathroom and toilet with running water, electricity installed throughout, radio, fully furnished with comfortable furniture, full supply of linen and towels. Separate kitchen with Frigidaire, oil range and complete equipment of kitchen utensils, silver and china.

Each Bungalow has its own swimming beach. Opportunities for a lovely vacation in unspoiled tropical surroundings with all the comforts of today.

Excellent opportunities for horse-back riding, swimming and fishing.

Operated in conjunction with the Grand Hotel, St. Thomas. Interchange of guests between Hotel and bungalows arranged.

WRITE: The Virgin Islands Tourist Company or the Leading Travel Bureaus for further information and reservation.

M-Y FLAMINGO

Advertisement for "Caneel Bay Plantation Resort," 1938

(Virgin Islands Magazine, Vol. II, 1938 [The Art Shop, St. Thomas, VI])

The Virgin Islands Tourist Company

Charlotte Amalie, St. Thomas, V. I.

A Corporation formed for the development of the Tourist Trade of the Virgin Islands

Operating:

THE GRAND HOTEL, Charlotte Amalie: An old hotel in the charming and picturesque city. Completely renovated and modernized without spoiling the old West Indian atmosphere of the place.

CANEEL BAY PLANTATION RESORT, St. John. Here, in the neighboring island of St. Thomas, an old Estate has been converted into a bungalow resort. The island of St. John is still unexploited and offers a restful place for a vacation. (See opposite for detailed description).

M-y "FLAMINGO". Regular inter-island service between St. Thomas and St. John. May also be chartered for fishing trips, excursions, etc.

MAIN OFFICE, INFORMATION & TRAVEL BUREAU at King's Wharf, Charlotte Amalie, St. Thomas. V. I. Cable Address: "Tourist, St. Thomas."

Write us for authentic information on the Virgin Islands, Hotel reservation, Bungalows, etc., etc.

Representatives for leading travel bureaus.

Passenger Office for The West Indian Company Limited, Agents for leading Steamship Lines.

increasing number of calls of tourist ships of the prominent steamship lines.

In 1935, Caneel Bay, St. John, was bought by the Virgin Islands Tourist Company, which was formed by friends of the West Indian Co. to take

Caneel Bay Estate, c1936, with Danish training-ship, *Danmark*, moored offshore.

(photo by Dr. George H.H. Knight)

over the Maison Danoise and the Caneel Bay Estates. The inspiration to this step was given by Mr. Robert Herrick, the writer, a man of high principles and intellect, and former professor at the University of Chicago, who had accepted the appointment of Government Secretary,

Advertisement for "Maison Danoise," 1938

(Virgin Islands Magazine, Vol. II, 1938 [The Art Shop, St. Thomas, VI])

to the Virgin Islands, at the specific request of his former pupil, the then Secretary of Interior Harold Ickes. Mr. Herrick, I should like it to be noted, possessed vision, and a deep affection for the Virgin Islands and its Danish traditions and background, and he was anxious to see at least St. John preserved for the Nation, for its people, and its many remnants of the Colonial period protected against indiscriminate exploitation. No better fate could therefore have befallen Caneel Bay Estate than to be taken into the protective custody of the Rockefeller Foundation.* *(see note below.)*

Caneel Bay, an old deserted sugar estate of about 550 acres, overgrown with tropical vegetation, was in ill repute owing to the prevalence of mosquitoes and sand flies. Work was started immediately, with the profits from the silver shop, to clear some of the brush and to drain the lagoon, the breeding place for the insects. At the same time construction was begun on two substantial cottages, soon afterwards to be increased to six.

The insects were successfully eliminated, and the Caneel Bay resort very quickly became known to the extent that a waiting list existed at the time the United States entered World War II.

During the War years Caneel Bay was used for purposes other than in connection with tourism, and about 1946, two years after the termination of my association with the East Asiatic and West Indian Company, the Caneel Bay Estate was sold, for the first time, at its book value, about $80,000, to a firm in Puerto Rico..."

> *As pointed out by the Executive Director of the Rockefeller Archive Center, Mr. Bang was mistaken about the role of the Rockefeller Foundation. In fact, it was a private act of Laurance S. Rockefeller, who initially turned the property over to Jackson Hole Preserve, Inc., which, in turn, gave a portion to the U.S. government. Ultimately, the remaining Caneel Bay property will be turned over to the Department of the Interior as a result of an agreement signed by Mr. Rockefeller in 1983.*
>
> *December, 2005*

Lost People and Forgotten Places

David W. Knight Jr.

No Trespassing! A donkey skull serves as a foreboding trail marker

(Photograph by David W. Knight Jr.)

David W. Knight Jr. is a third-generation St. John Historical Society member. He wrote the following article for the SJHS newsletter at age 15.

For as long as I can remember I've felt at home in the forgotten places of St. John: crumbling ruins strangled by vines, centuries of abandonment leaving them shadows of what they once were. My father has also spent his lifetime exploring and studying these "secret" places, so that's why it isn't every day that the two of us mount an expedition to a site lost even to us. We almost hesitate to do it sometimes. The number of historic sites that humans haven't touched in perhaps a hundred years or more is growing slimmer by the day. Perhaps it's better to leave some places undisturbed and still mysterious. But on the other hand, the sad fact is that we're losing these sites rapidly. If someone doesn't properly document them soon they will slip unnoticed into the past forever. If there are ruins out there that are unknown and historically significant, the pros of finding them seem to outweigh the cons.

Keeping this in mind we set out to find one such site above Water Bay. With so many huge plantations like Annaberg and Brown's Bay in the area, the remnants of a small, struggling, early-colonial homestead could easily go unnoticed. The Oxholm map shows a small house site on the knoll east of where the Leinster Bay estate house ruins stand. Why is it on this map but no other? Was it a mistake, since the Leinster Bay estate house ruins don't appear on the map? Had Oxholm just mixed up the two knolls? For years this was thought to be the case, until further research revealed that the map predates the Leinster Bay house. Could Oxholm's map show a different site?

But how exactly could we get to this forgotten place. Pausing for a moment on the Johnny Horn trail my father points to an old shady tree in the valley, "let's make for that" he says, "from there we'll head up the hill and check the flat by that rock outcropping." His hand wanders further up to a group of boulders perched on the steep slope. We duck off the trail into the thick dry bush.

The first thing noticeable about this area is that we are certainly not the first people since colonial times to follow the overgrown roads here. Bags, boots, and jeans litter the area in a way that would make you think a nearby department store had been blown apart. Smugglers often use this part of the island as a landing point for their human cargoes of Cubans, Chinese, Haitians, and other illegal immigrants attempting to enter the USA. After boats drop them near the coast they swim to the rocky north shore beaches and tear off through the bush with little-to-no knowledge of the island. When they change, they leave their wet clothes, backpacks and old suitcases strewn about the landscape. Maneuvering through the dense catch-and-keep bushes we finally reach our tree. It isn't quite as big as it looked from up above, but this is definitely the spot. Straight up is our next destination. The following hill is steep, almost vertical, while loose rocks and rotten branches lie waiting for our missteps all the way up. Needless to say we made it.

From the rock out-cropping you can look across and see all around the surrounding hills. A cool blast of wind hits us, a welcome change from the thorny humid valley. In the more dense vegetation to the left I hear my father's excitement at our first clue. There, lying on the ground is a complete bronze horse bridle. "Why would that be on this steep slope?" we both wonder aloud. Clearly no one was riding a horse here; it must have come from higher up. We press on.

At the peak of the hill the vegetation changes drastically. Tall cactus starts to spring up along with those horrible little monsters, the "suckers." For those who have no idea what I'm talking about, suckers, or thimble cactus, are the tiny prickly things that are the most evil plants on the face of the earth. As you walk they seem to leap maniacally onto your clothes slowly inching their way up until they are repetitively stabbing you somehow in your face. If you've ever had a piece of tape stuck to your hands that sticks to the other hand when you try to remove it and then sticks to your leg as you try to wipe it off and so forth, you know the feeling of frustration.

After stopping every few minutes to remove the suckers from our legs with the machete, we find ourselves in the exact spot our mystery site should be, but there is nothing. Not a thing that would indicate early habitation except for a single tiny shard of old black glass. However, everything else on the flat is surprisingly modern. There are modern plates, modern utensils, modern sheets of galvanized roofing. There is a scorched patch of ground where a large tent was burned. There are nine fifty-five gallon drums, rusted and on their sides. There is a pair of binoculars left on a stone as if the place had been abandoned suddenly a decade or so ago. In fact, there is stuff all over the place, just not what we were looking for.

If there had been anything old on the site we were in agreement that it was now long gone. With that conclusion we set off down the hill to the north, noticing more and more modern debris, as well as more discarded clothes and luggage. At the shore we sit for a while and rest, examining our surroundings. This remote beach seems to be the main landing point for countless illegal immigrants. The most abandoned clothing we had seen yet made a path all the way down the long rocky bay. This "human smuggling" is obviously a more common phenomenon then I had ever imagined. Unfortunately we hadn't set out to find dirty jeans and sneakers. If we had, I'm sure we would have stood there in amazement of our newfound fortune.

I guess that hike closed another chapter in our book of "lost sites." Perhaps a house had at one time stood at the top of that hill, but any surface evidence of it is now long gone. Not as much discouraged by not finding anything new as happy to have this mystery solved, we returned home. Our hike opened new questions though. What is the story of the burned encampment we found on the exact spot where we had imagined the old site to be? On what scale is illegal immigration occurring in the territory?

April, 2003

Contributors

Andromeada Childs

Brion Morrisette

Bruce Schoonover

Camilla Jensen

Crystal Fortwangler

Daniel Smothergill

David W. Knight

David W. Knight Jr.

Denise & Marillyn Newville

Don Near

Douglas V. Armstrong

Eleanor Gibney

Elroy Sprauve

Gary T. Horlacher

Gaylord Sprauve

George F. Tyson

Jeff Spear

Jane Bowry

Jan Frey

Lief C. Larsen

Kimberly Boulon

Lolly Prime

Margaret Labrenz

Mark W. Hauser

Mike & Jane Sheen

Per Nielsen

Philip Sturm

Rafe Boulon

Reggie Callwood

Robin Swank

Rudolph "Pimpy" Thomas

Stephan Lenik

Vicki Bell

Traditional St. John Market Basket
(Artwork created for the SJHS by Kimberly Boulon, 2009)

Designed by Cardinale Design, *Ludlow, MA*
Printed in the USA by Hadley Printing, *Holyoke, MA*

"Carrying Baskets to Market, St. Jan, D.W.I." postcard by Johannes Lightbourn, c1900

(Image courtesy of the D. Knight Collection)

"A Bit of Nature in St. Jan, D.W.I." postcard by Johannes Lightbourn, c1900

(Image courtesy of the D. Knight Collection)

To contact the St. John Historical Society or to order
additional copies of this publication, please visit:

http://www.stjohnhistoricalsociety.org